Prints

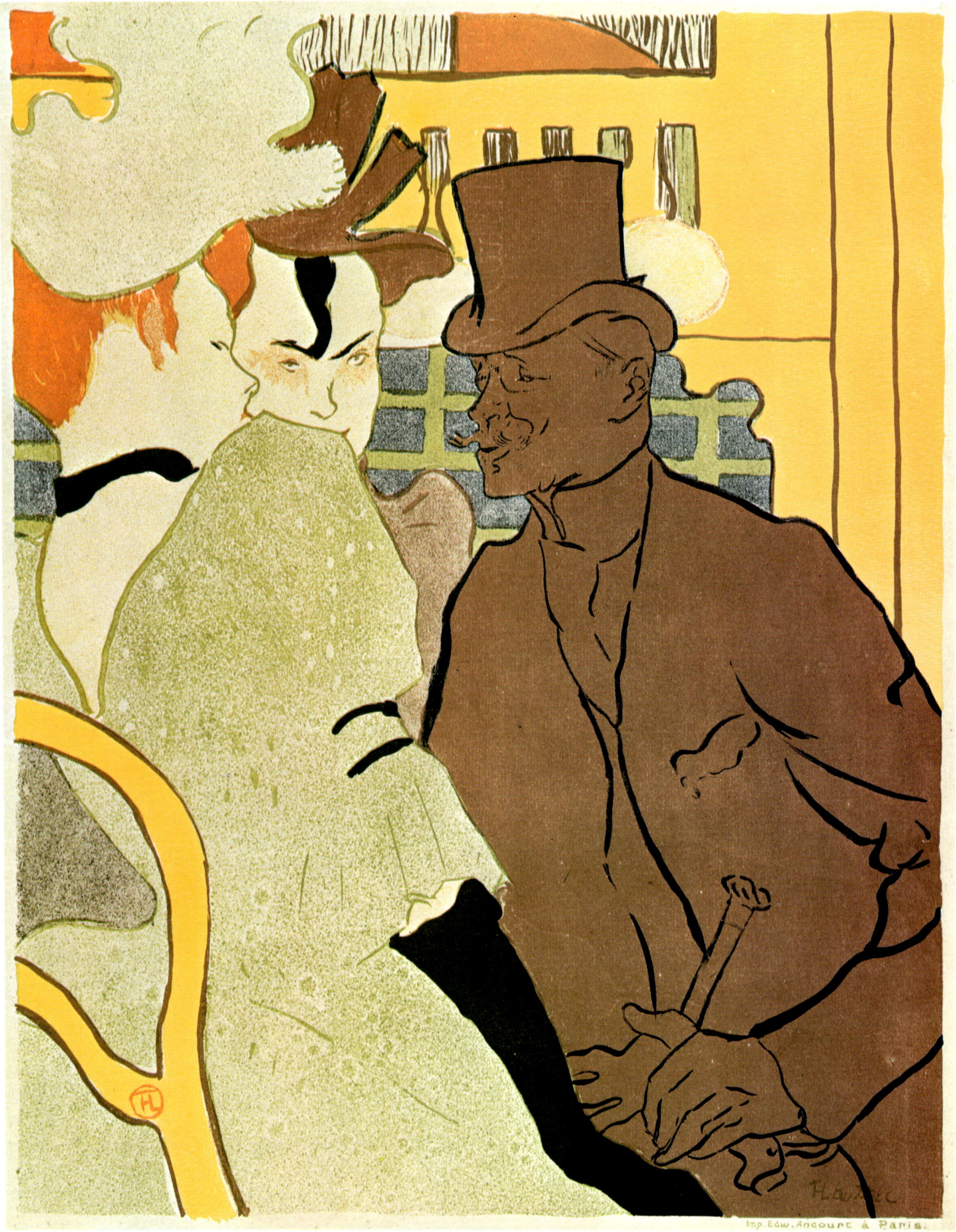

H. Lautrec
Imp. Edw. Ancourt à Paris.

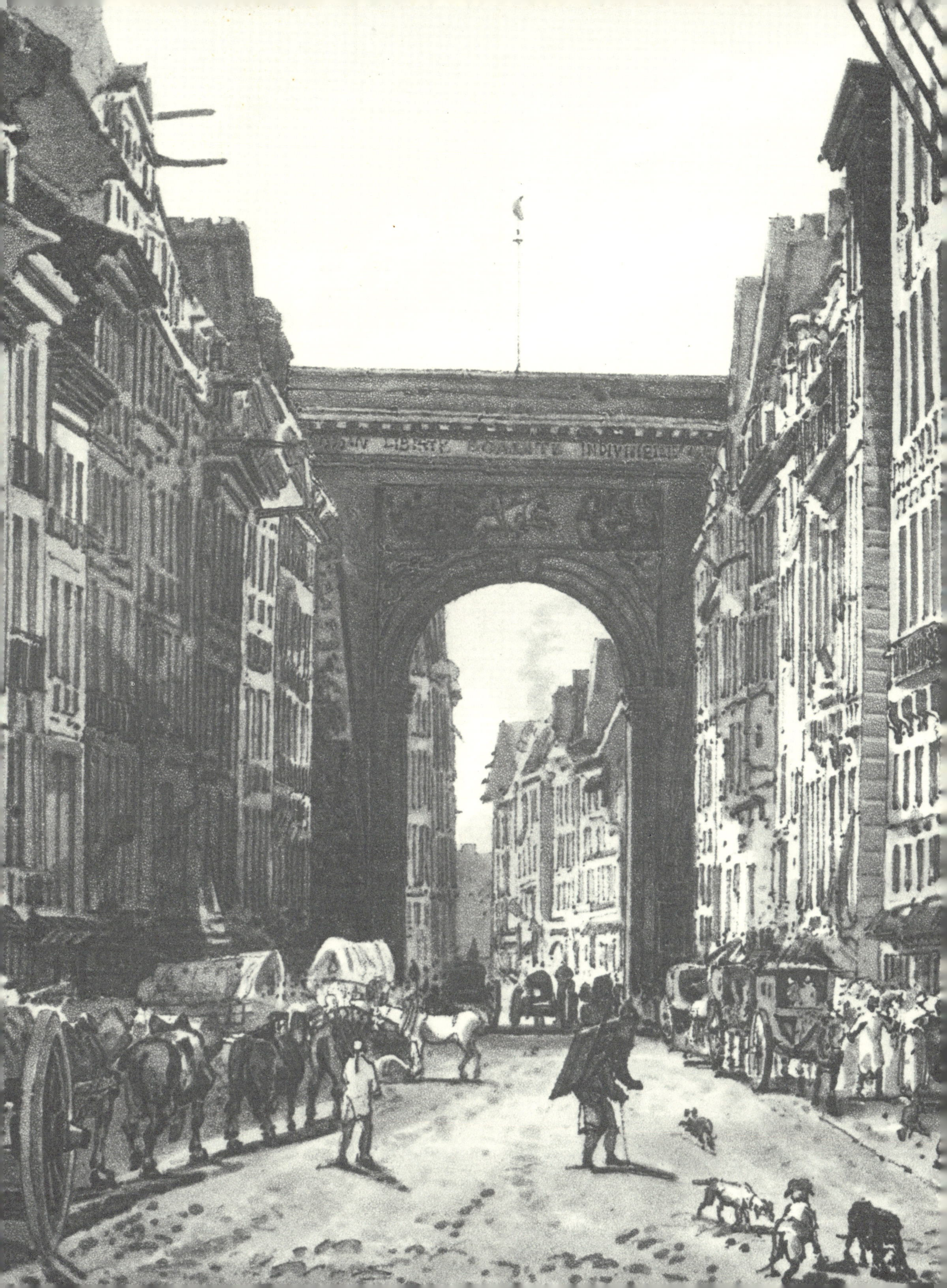

THE SMITHSONIAN ILLUSTRATED LIBRARY OF ANTIQUES

General Editor: Brenda Gilchrist

Prints

Donald Karshan

COOPER-HEWITT MUSEUM

The Smithsonian Institution's National Museum of Design

ENDPAPERS

Thomas Girtin (1775–1802). English. *View of the Gate of St. Denis.* Etching and aquatint from *A Selection of Twenty of the Most Picturesque Views of Paris*, 1802. 30 x 55.8 cm. (11¾ x 22 in.). Detail. Cooper-Hewitt Museum, gift of The Museum of Graphic Art

FRONTISPIECE

Henri de Toulouse-Lautrec (1864–1901). French. *The Englishman at the Moulin Rouge*, 1892. Lithograph. 47 x 36.8 cm. (18½ x 14½ in.). Metropolitan Museum of Art, New York, gift of Mrs. Bessie Potter Vonnoh, 1941

Printed in the United States of America
Library of Congress Catalog Card Number: 78-62726

Art Direction, Design: Joseph B. Del Valle

Text Editor: Joan Hoffman

Picture Editor: Lisa Little

Contents

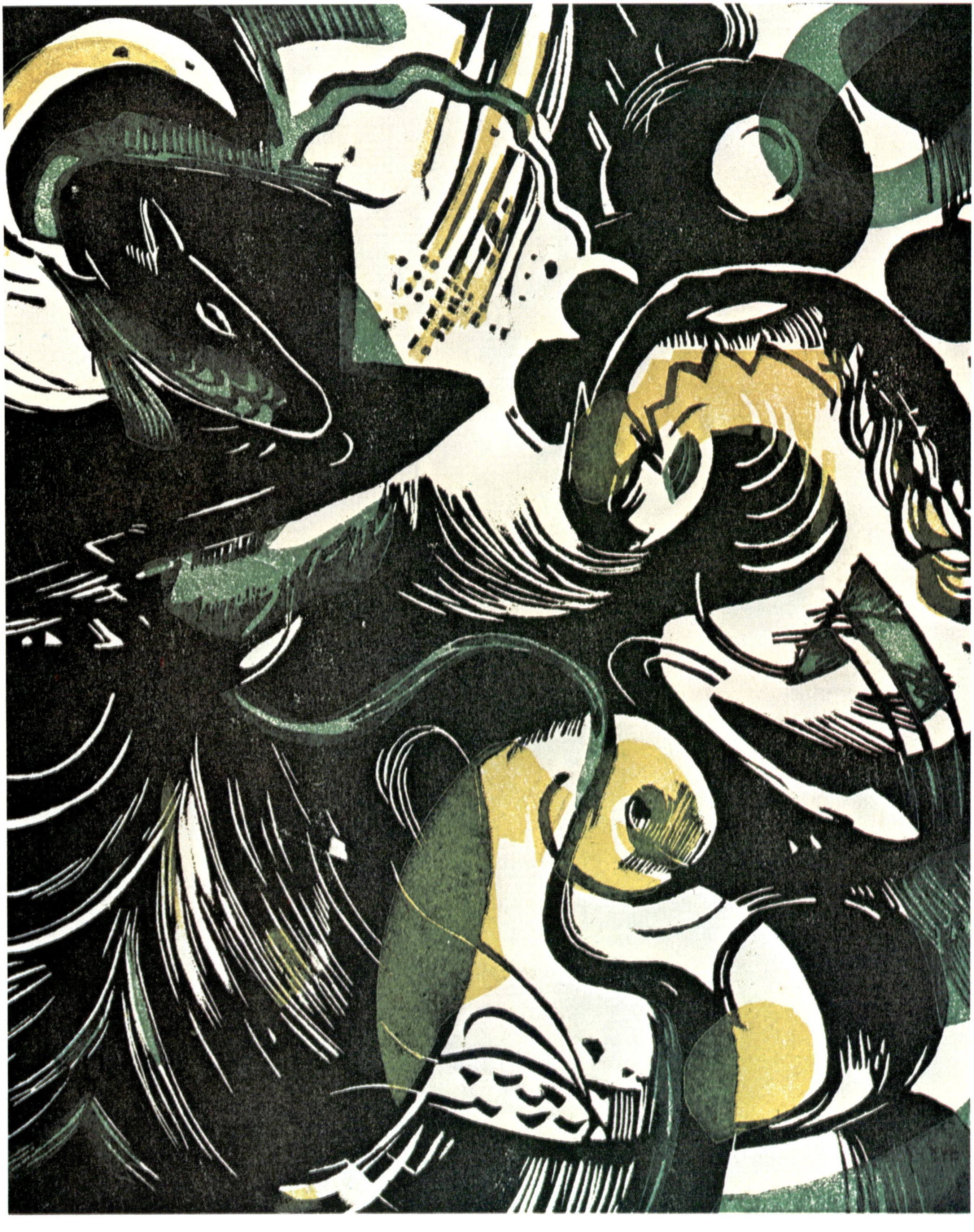

1 Introduction

The making of prints, like the painting of pictures or the carving of sculptures, is a major form of artistic expression. In the West it has evolved over a five-century span from the primitive medieval woodcut as other graphic techniques, such as metal engraving and lithography, have been invented. Any discussion of the development of printmaking is thus a discussion of an important aspect of art history, and the body of work accumulated during these centuries represents an impressive part of the West's artistic heritage.

Prints also reflect the course of Western history during this period. From the demise of the illuminated manuscript in the late Middle Ages until the arrival of photography in the nineteenth century, books, if illustrated at all, were illustrated with prints, and prints were the principal means of disseminating pictures of any kind, sacred or profane, to the general public. As a result, the many prints that survive constitute a matchless source of information on Western man's social, cultural and technological history for some four hundred years. The sheer number of prints to be found in the world's museums compared with other forms of art is staggering: in a single great collection alone, that of the Metropolitan Museum of Art in New York, there are several million prints.

Over the centuries the print medium has offered artists several advantages. One is the medium's ability to yield, with relative ease, multiple renderings, or *impressions*, as they are called, of an artist's work. (Such impressions can number in the hundreds, depending on the technique employed.) Thus, it is possible for the work to be seen and owned by many persons in what is in effect its original state, in the production of which the artist has participated almost as fully as if he or she had created a drawing or a painting instead of a print. Printmaking is the only two-dimensional visual medium besides photography in which high-quality duplications can be made in quantity.

Colorplate 1.
Franz Marc (1880–1916). German. *Genesis II*, 1914. Woodcut. 24 x 20 cm. (9½ x 7⅞ in.). Museum of Modern Art, New York, Katherine S. Dreier Bequest

A second advantage of the print medium for the artist is the capacity of the process to create certain unique and desirable surface effects. These effects are not merely incidental qualities but derive directly from the printmaking techniques involved. They are effects so singularly expressive that artists are often lastingly attracted to them, as was Rembrandt when he came under the spell of the extraordinary qualities of drypoint.

Just what constitutes a print should perhaps be defined. Printmaking is one of the graphic arts, but the basic process of printing—that is, of taking an impression from a block, plate, die, screen or mold of some kind—can produce also photographs, patterned fabrics, currency and the pages of a book or newspaper. These too are "prints" in the broadest sense, though they obviously differ from the prints we are discussing here. Essential to what is known as an *original print* are the eye and the hand of the artist, of the person who has formed the initial image and executed or overseen its replication.

How do we determine, then, whether a print is an original print? Prints of any kind all begin with some sort of *matrix*, or mold. The mold is the progenitor, the parent; it is the source from which each impression emerges. A coin pencil-rubbed through a sheet of paper; a cookie cutter biting star shapes from slabs of dough; a pail repeatedly filled with sand and inverted to form the towers of a play fortress on the beach—all are familiar types of molds. Woodcut blocks, engraving plates, etching plates and lithographic stones are molds, or matrices, and they, like the sand pail, whose concave, inner form is the negative of the article it shapes, produce images in reverse.

Two features establish such an image as an original print: (1) the artist conceived and directly carved, etched, engraved or drew the reverse image in or on the matrix; (2) the artist did his or her own printing, which includes the vital preparatory inking of the matrix, or was in close enough contact with a skilled professional printer for this operation (which can easily alter the final printed image) to be said to have been carried out "under the artist's supervision." We should note here that the handwork that guides the making of each original print inevitably introduces variation, which can range from the barely perceptible to the highly distinct.

Certain technical factors can affect the final quality of an impression and must be carefully monitored to ensure that artistic standards are being met. With some print processes the matrix becomes worn from repeated preparations and printings. Such wear causes alterations in the printed image. Some collectors maintain that these alterations compromise the claim of originality because the variant impressions are no longer faithful to the initial image. A more elusive criterion for applying the term "original print" is the size of the *edition*, or printing—that is, the number of impressions made, or "pulled," from the matrix. If one assumes no wear of the matrix, how many impressions will render the entire edition "unoriginal"—and thus of diminished value—just because of the quantity produced? At present, a print edition (also called *tirage*) approaching one thousand may raise some doubts in conservative circles, but resistance to such large printings is generally lessening.

Strictly speaking, the size of the edition per se bears no relation to any judgment of originality; no matter how many impressions are taken from the matrix, each is an original print. Until the mid-nineteenth century—when relatively small editions (they seldom exceeded two hundred) were first contrived by publishers and dealers, and artists began to number and pencil-sign their prints, thus establishing a synthetic rarity—graphic works were printed in numbers limited only by the apparent demand for them in the marketplace or until the wear on their matrices became sadly noticeable. A result of this exploitation is that countless bad impressions now survive as testimony to overused blocks and plates. The modern practice of limiting the size of editions, of artificially inducing rarity, tends to ensure the quality of the impressions, and worn impressions of modern prints seldom appear on the market.

Questions of plate wear, edition size and other such matters should not distract us from an appreciation of original prints, with their superb aesthetic potential, as major vehicles of art. It is a print's visual and spiritual impact that is of central importance, not the process, however long and meticulous, by which its creator brought it into being.

Printmaking is closest to drawing among all the visual arts. In fact, in many of the world's great museums, prints and drawings are stored and studied in the same department, or *cabinet*. Both prints and drawings are classified as "works on paper," a grouping that also includes collage, watercolor and gouache on paper. Printmaking, indeed, can involve the use of drawing: often the preliminaries for a print (and also for a painting) are drawings of some sort—everything starts with a line, as artists will affirm. Printmakers frequently glue a detailed drawing right onto a woodblock to guide their cutting. At such times the relationship between prints and drawings becomes most direct.

Despite these evident connections, however, prints and drawings differ for a variety of reasons. The drawn image is produced when particles of drawing material (pencil, charcoal and watercolor, for example) are made to adhere to the paper by friction or coagulation, whereas the printed image is pressed onto the paper from an inked matrix. In the *intaglio* process the paper is forced under pressure into lines incised, or cut, in the matrix in order to absorb the ink within these incisions. Engraving, drypoint and etching are examples of this process. In the *relief* process, of which woodcutting is typical, the reverse takes place: it is the uncut surface of the block—the level left in relief—that is inked, and the paper is pressed into the uninked grooves or incised sections. With the intaglio method the areas of the paper forced into the incised crevices emerge as accentuated inked lines, almost like the raised lettering of embossed stationery. With the relief method the uninked portions of the paper are raised, particularly those close to the inked contours. In both instances the effect, heightened by the dark density of printer's ink, can be startling in its clarity and forcefulness.

Because of the penetrating power of the printing press used for intaglio, not a scratch, not a dot, on the matrix need be lost in the reproduction. One of the most exciting visual experiences is to hold a well-executed intaglio work in a raking, or oblique, light—the best light for examining prints. The faint shadows cast by the raised lines enhance the visual effect, and when these shadows are joined with the illusionism of the composition itself, an extraordinary range of contrasts may be perceived. To the printmaker and the connoisseur of prints, the raking-light perspective is invaluable in the appraisal of intaglio prints.

A third process is that of lithography, which is termed a *planographic* process because the surface of the stone on which the image is realized remains essentially flat. The preparatory steps in printing a lithograph include applying the image to the stone, ensuring that it will remain intact during the printing process and inking the stone with a particularly dense and sticky ink. These preparations and the force of the printing press in tandem with the pliability of the handmade paper often used combine to produce a brilliant velvety image. Even the most minute detail is captured with precise definition. The final effect is dramatically different from a drawing, notwithstanding the old adage that lithography is simply drawing on a stone.

Another characteristic that distinguishes printmaking from drawing is a carefully planned, or "calculated," imagery and a sort of schematization born out of the printmaking process itself. In drawing, the artist need apply little friction or pressure to leave a mark. The same is generally true of lithography; but with the other printmaking techniques there is decided resistance from a woodblock or metal plate as lines are gouged, grooved or incised into it. It is true that in etching, the incisions are created by an acid that eats away the metal, yet the lines for the entry of the acid must first be scraped through the plate's applied protective layer. Furthermore, the quality of the etched line is controlled by the type of acid selected and the time allowed for appropriate "biting." On the whole, then, printmaking requires deliberate and painstaking effort, while the tendency in drawing is toward speed and autographic flourish.

Line rather than tone is predominant in printmaking. When tone is desired, the artist is usually inclined to schematize the image somewhat —to establish its elements and specific areas with simple lines. This inclination is reinforced by the multistep nature of printmaking and by the need for a separate matrix and printing cycle for each color when color is used. Throughout the production of a print, successive *states*, or stages, of the impression are pulled for proof purposes (and are often referred to as *work proofs*), since this is the only way the artist can view and check the image as it develops.

Still another distinction can be made between printmaking and drawing. Drawing tends to be spontaneous, notational and expansive. Graphic art tends toward contraction, reduction of scale; it encourages a small format and the elaboration of extraordinary detail. Though minutely detailed prints hardly display quite so exaggerated a compression as does the fabled Lord's Prayer engraved on the head of a pin, they can still represent much within amazingly small areas.

A final distinction between the two mediums is that drawings are often studies or preliminary sketches, not intended to be seen by others. Prints on the other hand unquestionably are intended for public viewing and even acquisition. The printing of multiple examples—the act of publishing an edition—clearly certifies this intent. To be sure, many drawings—some of them works so tentative as to be near-doodles, others perhaps deemed failures by their creators but casually saved for another day—have appeared on the market. Although such drawings may be fascinating and can add to our knowledge of an artist's creative impulses, they are rarely finished statements. Drawings that can be considered such are usually signed, and their completeness speaks for itself. So, too, with original prints—they are complete and finished works of art, as much so as signed original paintings.

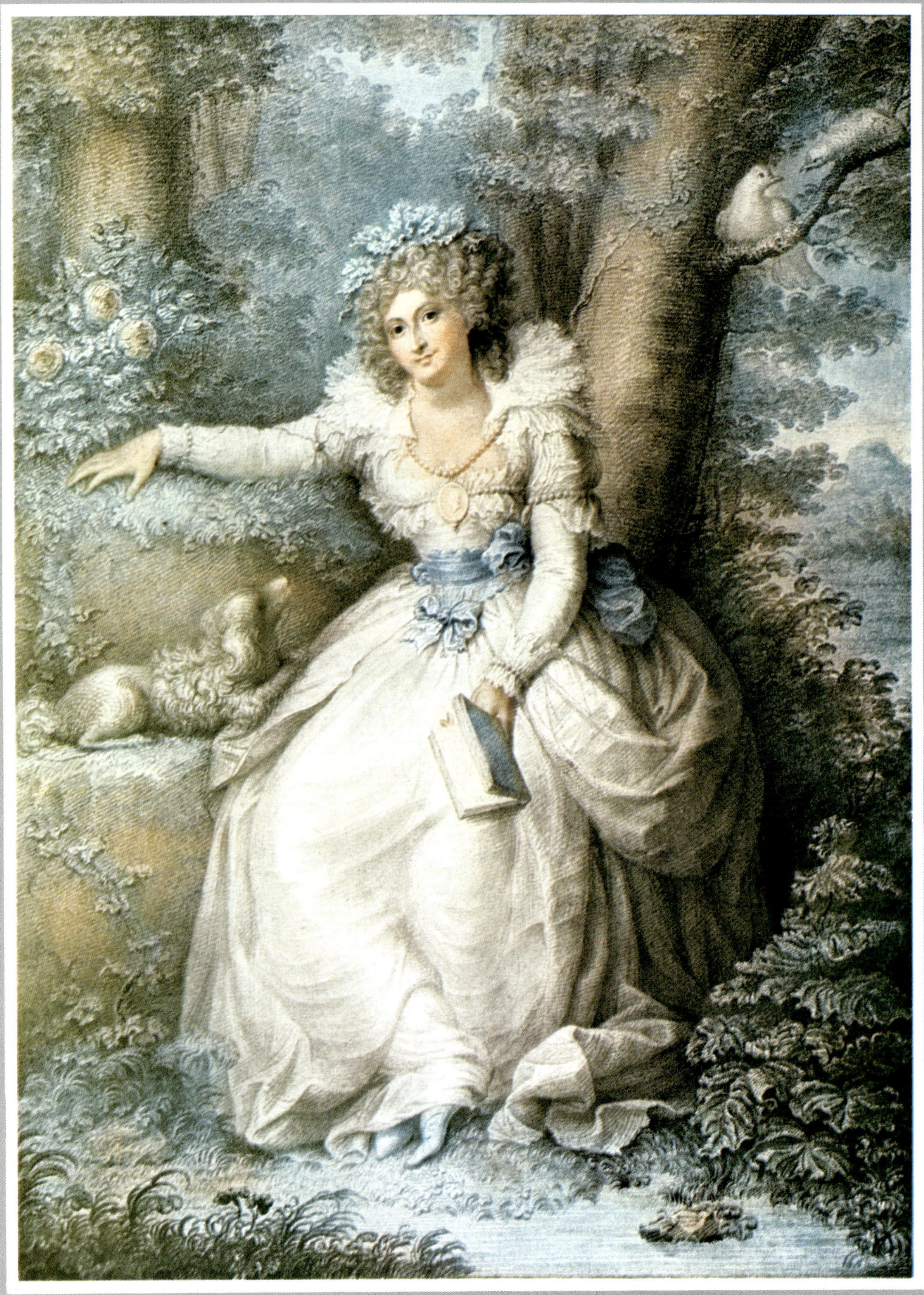

2 Techniques of Printmaking

This section serves as a guide to important techniques used by Western printmakers through the first third of the present century. (Since serigraphy and linoleum cutting were not widely used until later, prints in those techniques do not qualify as antiques; thus serigraphs and linocuts are omitted from this discussion.) Included is a concise description of each technique and of the tools used for each, and the individual processes are illustrated with a highly enlarged detail from a work that is also included in its entirety. With this information the reader can grasp the type of line and texture peculiar to each technique and, by consulting the corresponding illustration, understand more readily how those elements contribute to the aesthetic and expressive statement of the finished work of art.

Woodcut (colorplate 1 and plates 1–2). The history of printmaking begins with the appearance of the woodcut in China; exactly when this occurred is not known, but by A.D. 800 woodcuts were being produced there in great numbers. Before there could be printmaking, there had to be paper, and the Chinese are credited with its invention, too, about A.D. 100. It took eleven hundred years for the practice of papermaking to reach Europe, and the art of woodcutting arrived even later. The oldest surviving woodblock in the Western world, which was found in eastern France, dates from about 1370.

Of all printmaking methods, the woodcut technique requires the least apparatus. A multiple work of art can be made virtually on the run and with less than ten dollars' worth of tools: (1) a woodblock, whose cutting surface is the relatively soft, more easily workable long grain, rather than the harder and more resistive end grain; (2) two different-width gouges for scooping out large and small areas and a knife (a penknife could actually suffice for all cutting); (3) a small inking roller; (4) a spoon-shaped wooden burnisher.

Colorplate 2.
John Condé (d. 1794). English. *Mrs. Fitzherbert*, 1792. Engraving after Richard Cosway. 38 x 30.2 cm. (15 x 11⅞ in.). Private collection

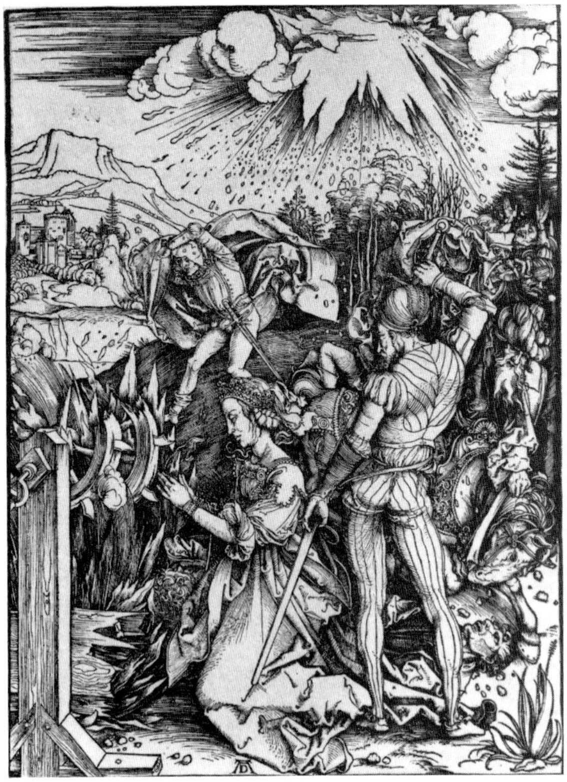

1

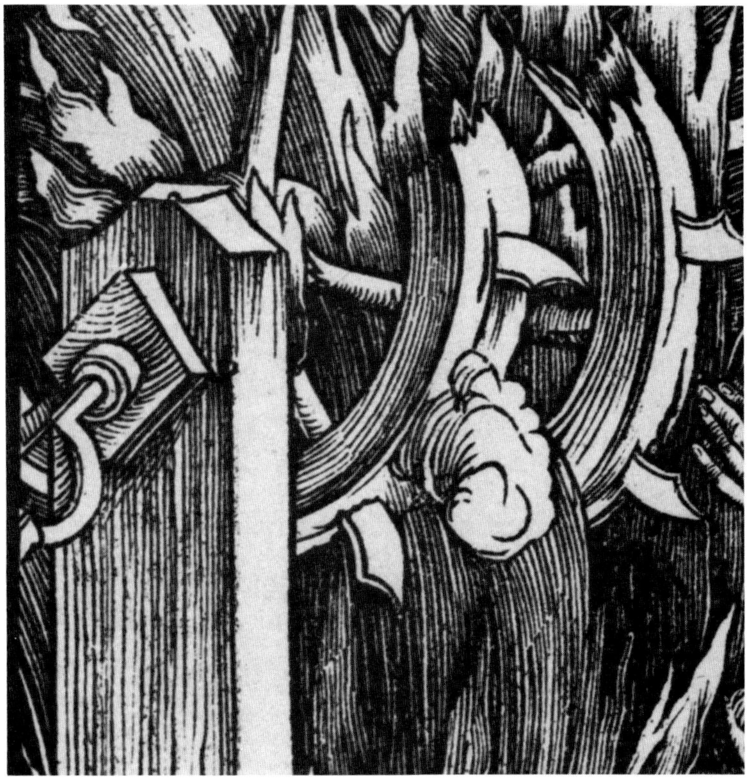

2

1.
Albrecht Dürer (1471–1528). German. *Martyrdom of St. Catherine of Alexandria*, c. 1498. Woodcut. 38.8 x 28.3 cm. (15¼ x 11⅛ in.). Private collection

2.
Detail from plate 1

If there is to be a preliminary drawing for the woodcut, it is executed on thin rice paper and pasted facedown onto the block; thus its reverse image can be seen clearly through the mounted paper. All the white, undrawn areas are cut or gouged away to a depth of about one-eighth of an inch—a safe, workable depth for the next printing step. Ink is rolled onto the raised, uncut areas after any remnants of pasted-down pattern paper are removed. After the paper for printing is laid over the inked block and carefully hand-burnished, it should have absorbed enough of the ink so that, when the woodcut is pulled (that is, when the paper is slowly peeled away from the block), the resulting printed image approximates the image as originally drawn. The distinction between these two images is what defines the woodcut's special character: since a line in relief, regardless of its thickness, is produced by cutting away from it on both sides, the printed line reveals the many cutting gestures involved in its discontinuous, often jagged rectilinearity. Large intact areas print flat and solid, giving a certain rugged planar simplicity to the final image. Any grain patterning or other natural roughness on the block's surface is transferred in the act of printing, producing a textural effect that can also be obtained on an ordinary mechanical printing press. An advantage of hand-printing by burnishing is that the artist can vary the pressure while doing it, thereby varying the depth or intensity of inking, and can also burnish ever so slightly within the scooped-out open areas, thus picking up some of the inked high points left in those areas.

Engraving (colorplate 2 and plates 3–7). Although the Renaissance painter and art historian Giorgio Vasari claimed that Maso Finiguerra invented the engraving about 1460, the earliest dated engraving to have survived, *The Flagellation*, is attributed to a northern artist who is known only by the date of the engraving: the Master of 1446. The most accomplished and important of the early anonymous engravers whose works survive in small numbers is the so-called Master of the Playing Cards, active around Basel from 1430 to 1445.

The following equipment is needed for making line engravings: (1) a beveled and polished copperplate; (2) a burin (a steel tool with a sharp end and a wooden handle); (3) a metal burnisher; (4) an ordinary printer's press.

Incised lines, which are actually V-shaped trenches, are cut in the plate by guiding the burin over its surface with sufficient pressure to gouge out shavings or slivers of metal, which are then brushed away. The depth and width of the trench can be modified with hand pressure and motion, which will thus vary the visual quality of the printed line. Scratches or other unwanted markings on the plate, all of which would print after inking, are polished away with the burnisher. Next, the plate is heated, and printer's tacky ink is pressed into the incised lines. The plate surface is then wiped clean, first with a pad of folded cheesecloth and finally with the palm of the hand—still the best tool for that extra touch of brilliance—since the slightest film of excess ink will also print. Faceup, the plate is set on the press bed and readied for printing. The dampened paper is laid on the plate, and over this are placed pieces of felt or blankets. The bed is hand-cranked between the two heavy rollers of the press; their enormous pressure forces the pliable paper into the plate's incised lines to absorb the ink trapped there. When the engraving is pulled, these printed lines remain slightly raised. The beveled edge of the printing plate leaves an embossed inkless *plate mark*, which adds a visual accent to the composition by its four-sided border, a kind of subdued, integral framing device for the printed image within. (It should be noted that dimensions given for all prints with a plate mark—thus excluding the woodcut, wood engraving and lithograph—are measured to the outer edge of the plate mark, not merely to the extent of the printed image itself.)

The unique quality of an engraved line lies in its literally clean-cut look and smooth, fluent contours. Since the artist must steadily exert considerable pressure on the burin and at the same time carefully control its direction, a sharply defined, continuously flowing line results.

3.
Jean Duvet (1485–c. 1570). French. *The Fall of Babylon*, c. 1545–55. Engraving from *L'Apocalypse figurée*, 1561. 30.2 x 21.3 cm. (11⅞ x 8⅜ in.). Private collection

4.
William Hogarth (1697–1764). English. *The Times*, Plate 1, 1762. Engraving. 25.8 x 30.8 cm. (9¾ x 12⅛ in.). Private collection

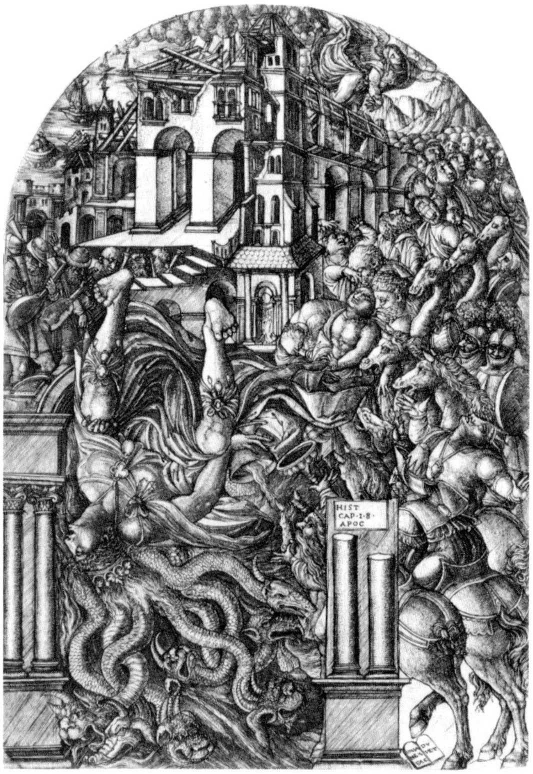
3

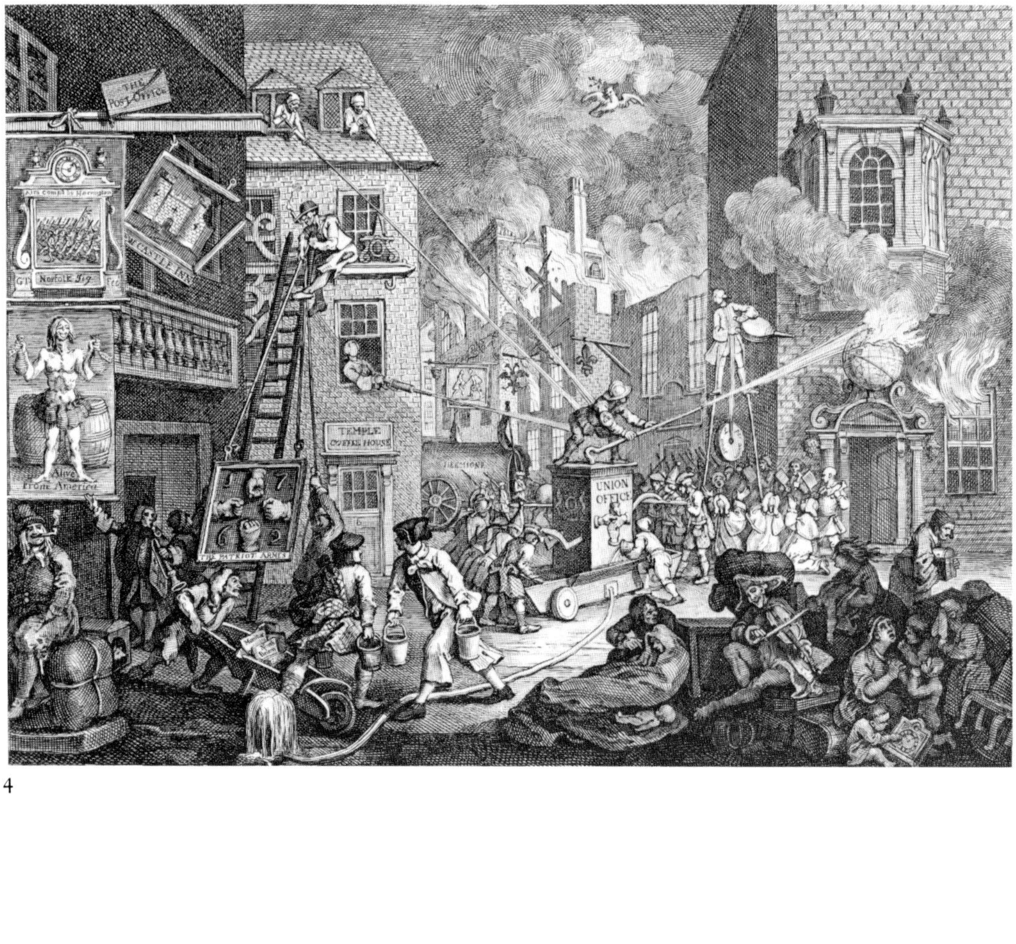

4

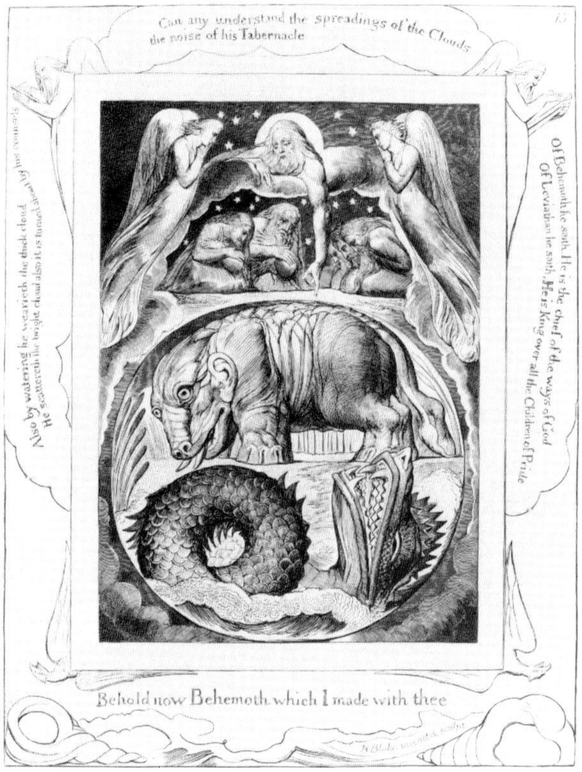

5

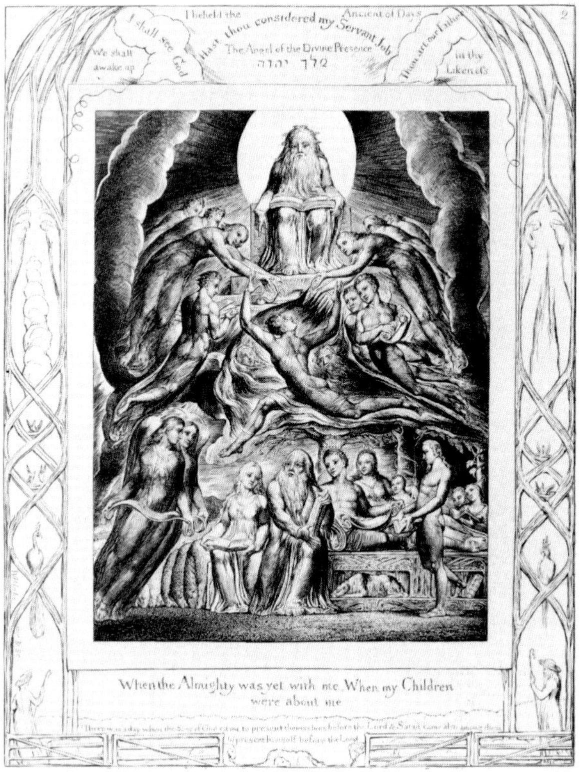

6

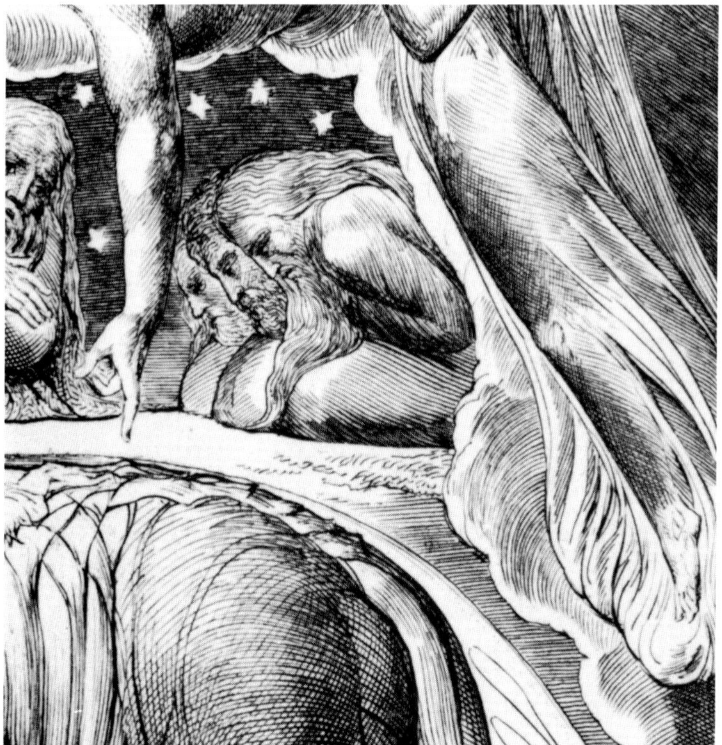

7

5.
William Blake (1757–1827). English. *Behold now Behemoth which I made with thee.* Engraving from *Illustrations of the Book of Job*, 1825. 21.5 x 16.9 cm. (8½ x 6⅝ in.). Private collection

6.
William Blake (1757–1827). English. *When the Almighty was yet with me, When my Children were about me.* Engraving from *Illustrations of the Book of Job*, 1825. 21.5 x 16.9 cm. (8½ x 6⅝ in.). Private collection

7.
Detail from plate 5

Drypoint (plates 8–11). Drypoint was invented about 1450 by an anonymous Netherlandish painter called the Housebook Master. For a new medium it was a spectacular beginning. The ninety-one surviving drypoints of this unknown artist remained unsurpassed in their exquisite sensitivity until Rembrandt took up the technique two hundred years later. Dürer had experimented briefly with the medium about 1500, but not until its prolific—and matchless—use by Rembrandt in the mid-seventeenth century did drypoint again become a major vehicle of expression.

Although so closely associated with etching that it sometimes is regarded as an etching technique, drypoint is in fact a form of engraving. Instead of the burin, which disengages the metal it cuts into, a steel needle is used in drypoint. The needle creates a delicate furrow by pushing the metal into minute ridges on either side of the scratched line. When the plate is prepared for printing, these slightly ragged, raised edges—called *burr*—trap some of the ink. The result is a unique printed line: raised, since it is made by an intaglio procedure, but looking, as one expert has said, "as if it were wearing a fur coat." This vaporous blur of ink enriches the line from which it emanates and creates perhaps the most bewitching effect obtainable in the whole wide realm of printmaking. Enhancing this mysterious presence is its transient nature, for the fragile ridges begin to crumble after only

8.
Rembrandt Harmensz. van Rijn (1606–1669). Dutch. *Faust in His Study*, 1652. Etching and drypoint. 21 x 16.1 cm. (8¼ x 6⅜ in.). Private collection

9.
Detail from plate 8

10.
Georges Braque (1882–1963). French. *Bass (Still Life: Wine Glasses, Bottles, Cigarettes)*, 1912. Drypoint and etching. 45.5 x 32.7 cm. (17⅞ x 12⅞ in.). Private collection

11.
Marc Chagall (b. 1887). French. *Acrobat with Violin*, 1924. Etching and drypoint. 41.3 x 31.5 cm. (16¼ x 12⅜ in.). Private collection

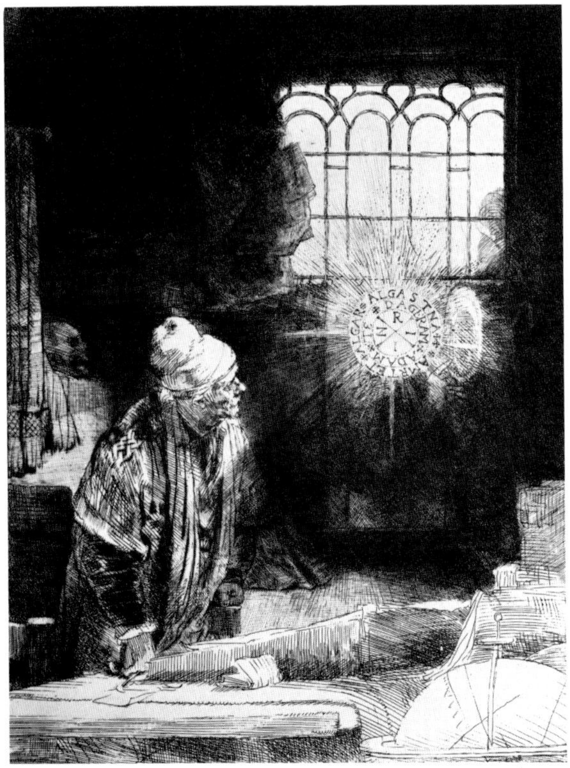

8

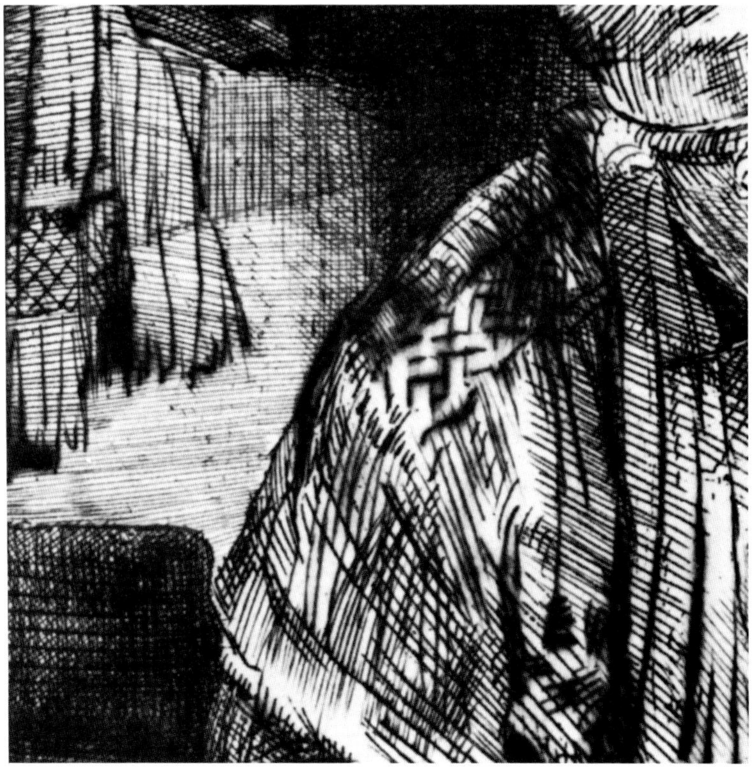

9

a few impressions have been taken, and the printed line then loses its fur coat. The number of impressions that can be made retaining the evocative burr effects is therefore extremely limited.

Etching (plates 12–16). Daniel Hopfer, an armor decorator in Augsburg, is credited with having pulled some of the first etchings (from iron plates) about 1510. The invention of the etching process was a breakthrough of great importance in printmaking, since the new technique gave the artist an unprecedented ease of line after more than a century of difficult manual work against resistive material. This significant technical advance was unrivaled until the development of lithography nearly three centuries later gave printmaking an even greater freedom of expression and range of aesthetic effects.

To produce an etching the artist needs (1) a beveled and polished copperplate; (2) an etching needle; (3) a blackish acid-resistant material containing wax, which is called the *ground*; (4) an acid bath (dilute nitric, for example); (5) a printer's press.

The plate is first covered with the ground. The image to be printed is drawn freely in the ground with the needle, with just enough pressure to scratch through the waxy layer; there is no need for digging into the plate itself. The incised lines stand out as bright glints of metal against the black ground. The prepared plate is then placed in the

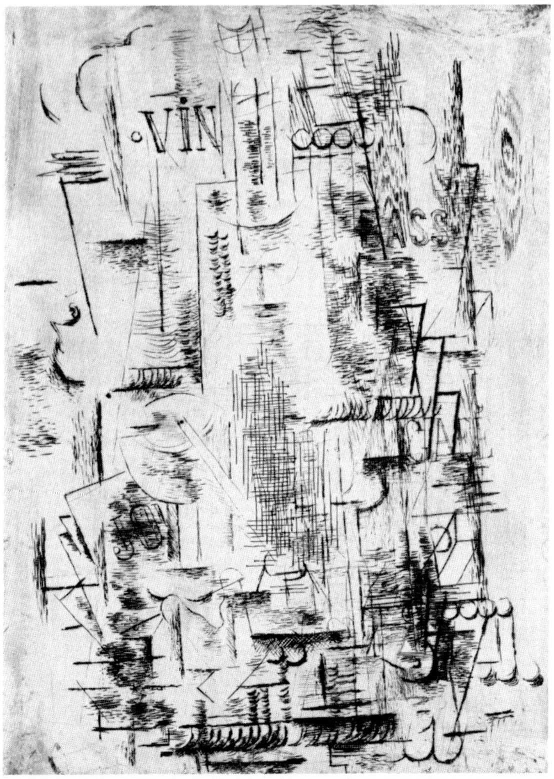

10

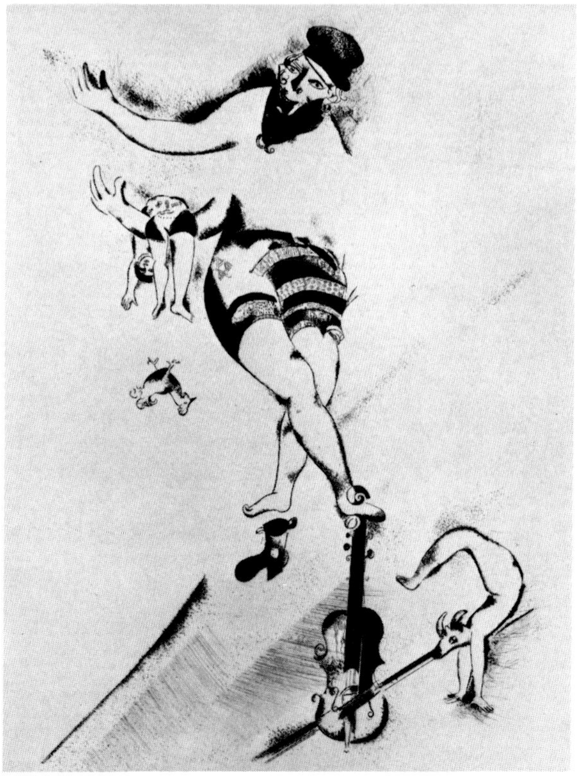

11

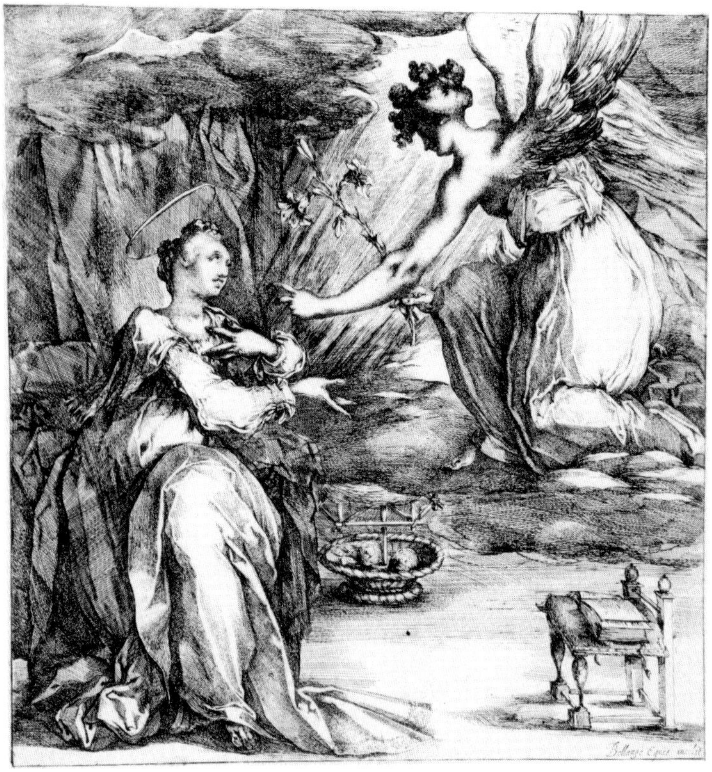

12

12.
Jacques Bellange (1594–1638). French. *The Annunciation*, c. 1616. Etching. 33 x 31.8 cm. (13 x 12½ in.). Pennsylvania Academy of the Fine Arts, Philadelphia

13.
Giovanni Battista Tiepolo (1696–1770). Italian. *Beggar Seated and Seen from Behind*, c. 1765. Etching from *Scherzi di Fantasia*. 22 x 17.3 cm. (8⅝ x 6¾ in.). Cooper-Hewitt Museum, gift of Eleanor and Sarah Hewitt

14.
Detail from plate 13

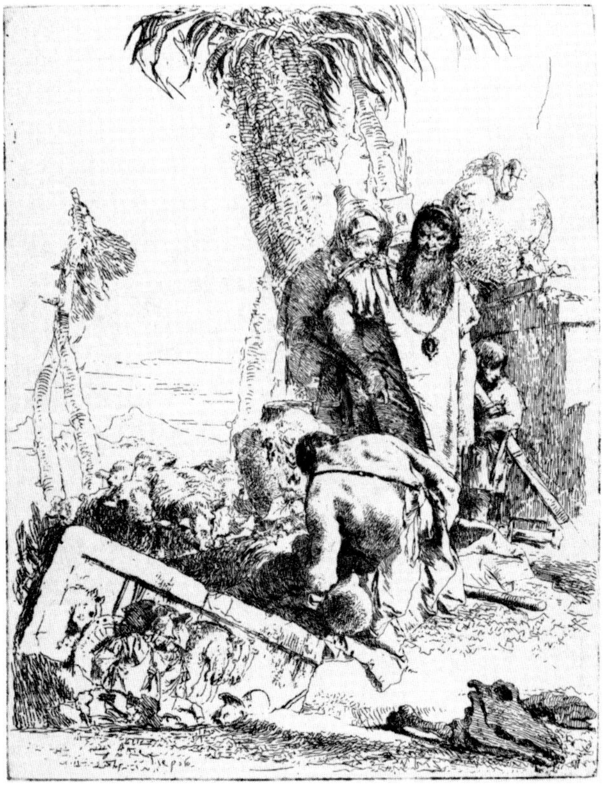

13

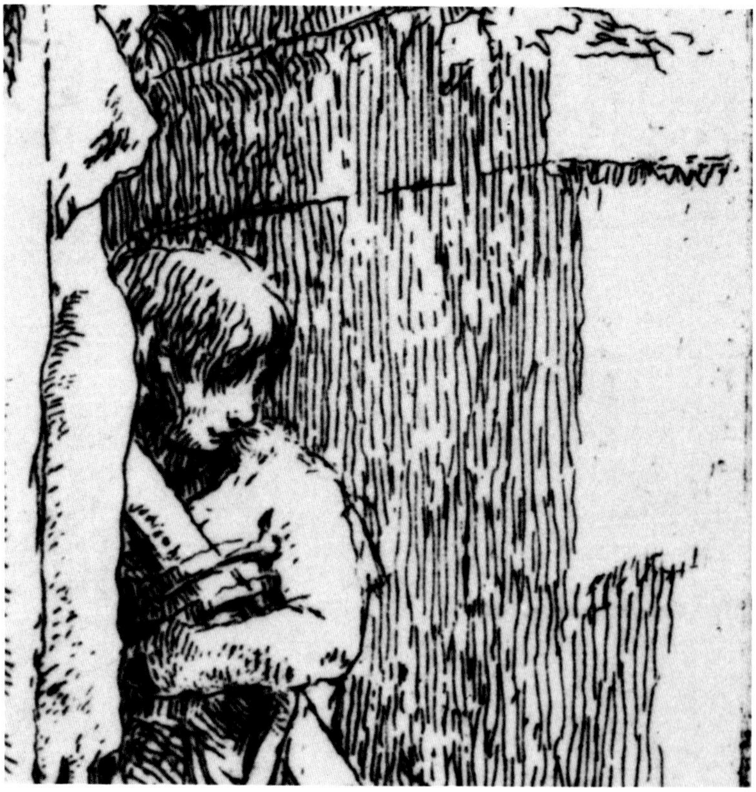

14

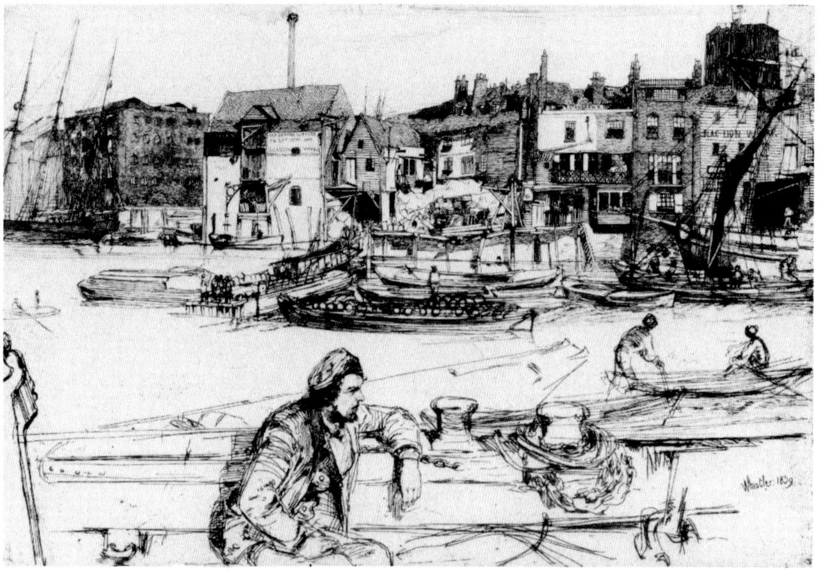

15

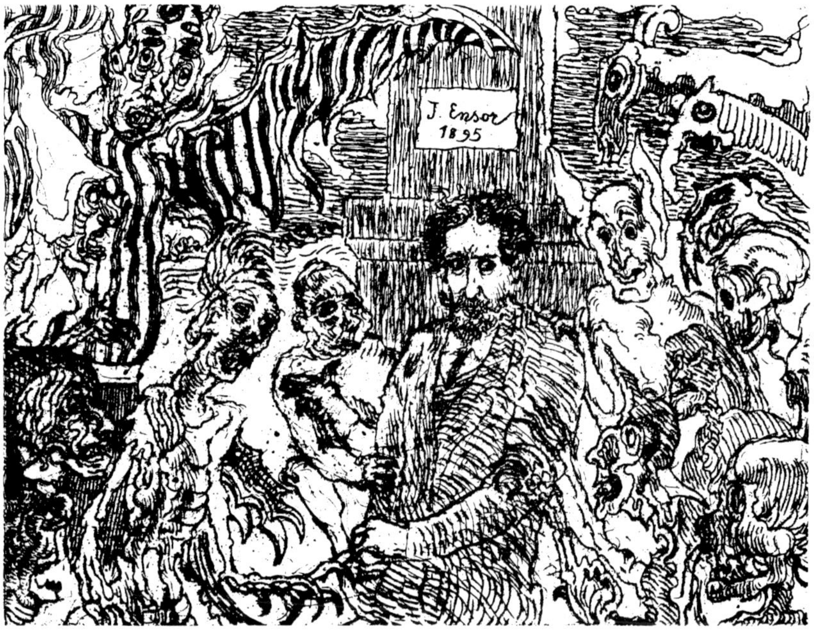

16

acid bath, where the acid bites into, or erodes, the metal exposed within the lines but does not penetrate the bordering ground. The eventual width of the printed line depends on the amount of time allowed in the bath. Since the erosive activity of the acid occurs in all directions, it widens as well as deepens the crevice it creates in the metal. Next, the protective ground layer is removed with a solvent. The inking and printing procedure for etching is identical to that for engraving.

The most pronounced characteristic of the etched line arises from the technical procedure itself: in strong contrast with the smoothly flowing, sharply defined engraved line, the more irregular or jagged etched line discloses that a process of erosion has taken place, giving rise to numerous microscopic, ink-holding rivulets.

15.
James McNeill Whistler (1834–1903). American. *Black Lion Wharf*, 1859. Etching. 15 x 22.3 cm. (5⅞ x 8¾ in.). Private collection

16.
James Ensor (1860–1949). Belgian. *Demons Torment Me*, 1895. Etching. 11.8 x 16 cm. (4⅝ x 6¼ in.). Private collection

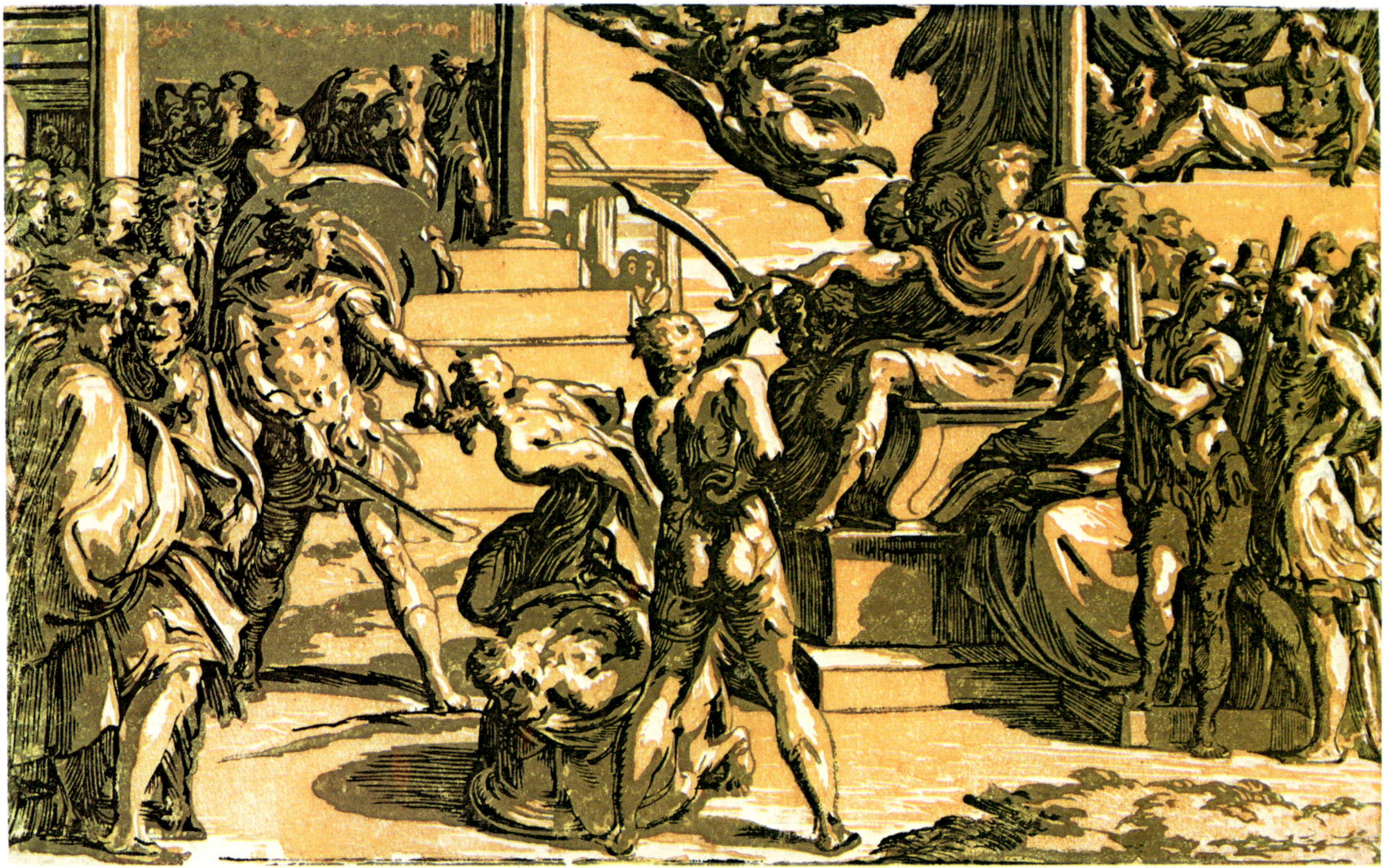

Colorplate 3.
Antonio da Trento (flourished first half of the sixteenth century). Italian. *The Martyrdom of SS. Peter and Paul*, c. 1525. Chiaroscuro woodcut after Parmigianino. 28.9 x 47.3 cm. (11⅜ x 18⅝ in.). Metropolitan Museum of Art, New York, Joseph Pulitzer Bequest, 1917

Chiaroscuro Woodcut (colorplate 3 and plate 17). The painterly term *chiaroscuro*, meaning the play of light against darkness, is also used to describe a short-lived type of woodcut that first appeared in Germany before 1510, with the works of Hans Burgkmair of Augsburg. Perfected in the early sixteenth century, the chiaroscuro woodcut was inspired by and imitated a type of drawing prevalent at the time. Renaissance artists often drew on a toned paper that served per se as the middle tone (first color). They next laid in shadows with a darker tone (second color) and then the highlights with white (third color). Similarly, for the chiaroscuro woodcut a first block was cut and printed, say, in light umber, representing the middle tone (first color); the unprinted areas—the original white of the paper—served as highlights (third color). Lastly, a second block was cut and printed over the first impression, say, in dark sienna (second color). This second block is called the *key block* because the dark contours realized from its linear printing are the key to the image, the backbone of the composition that defines and brings its figuration into proper focus.

The same equipment is required for a chiaroscuro woodcut as for a monochromatic one, except that more than one woodblock is used. The characteristics of both techniques are the same, except that in the chiaroscuro woodcut the telltale effects of the relief process are multiply impressed and are multicolored.

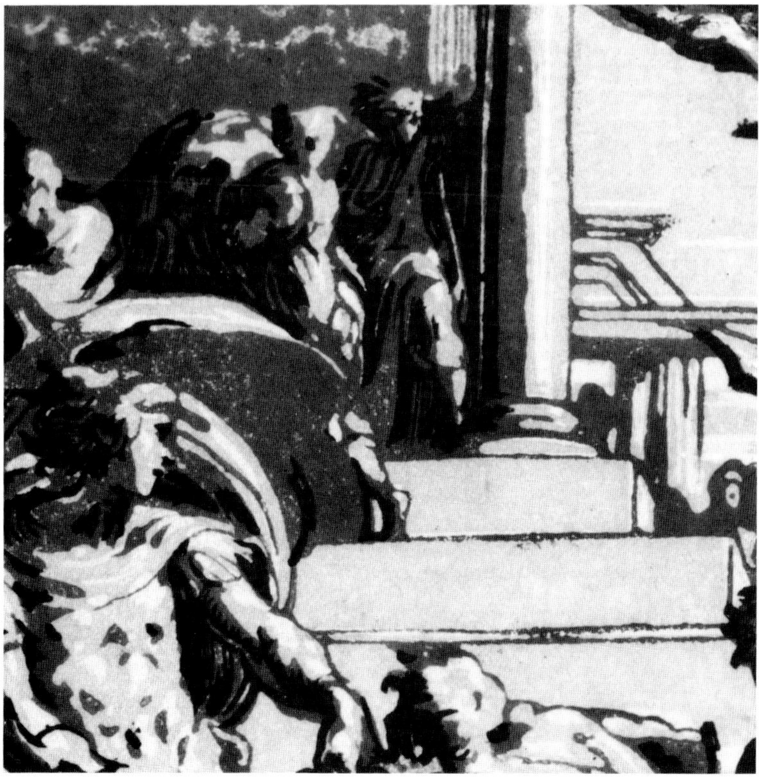

17.
Detail from colorplate 3

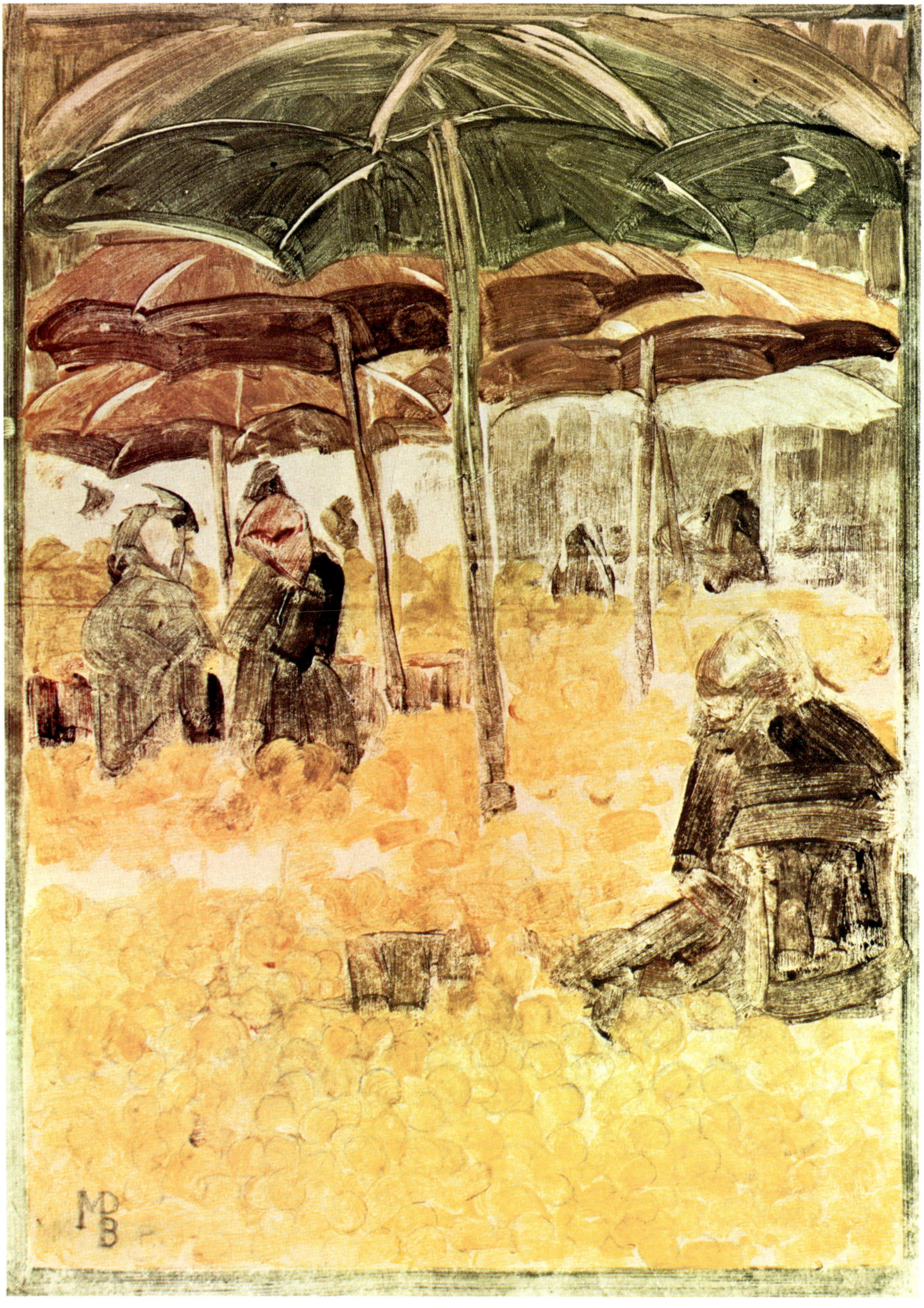
MB

Colorplate 4.
Maurice Prendergast (1859 1924). American. *Orange Market*, c. 1900. Monotype. 31.5 x 23.2 (12 3/8 x 9 1/8 in.). Museum of Modern Art, New York, gift of Abby Aldrich Rockefeller

Monotype (colorplate 4 and plate 18). The one printmaking technique that cannot produce multiples from its matrix is the monotype, which permits only a single impression and is named for that distinctive trait. Invented by Giovanni Benedetto Castiglione of Genoa about 1640, the process involves brushing (painting) an image with printer's ink or painter's colors onto a nonabsorbent surface such as copper, glass or varnished cardboard. Printing is accomplished by hand (the essential method in the case of a glass surface) or on the type of press used for engravings and etchings. Since the single printing cycle picks up most of the ink or paint from the smooth surface on which the original image is set down, the process is not repeatable from this same "matrix." Although there is a distinct advantage to its painterly directness that offsets the loss of duplicability, artists generally took scant advantage of this process until Edgar Degas, between 1874 and 1893, produced the first major oeuvre of monotypes (about four hundred) since Castiglione. These richly suggestive daubed and smudged images, many resembling marvelously virtuoso finger paintings, are among the most haunting and dramatic works in the great French artist's entire output.

A monotype's technical characteristics and aesthetic effects are outstanding: no grainy texture, no pronounced lines or contours, just evocative streaks of softly modulated tone indicating the passage of the artist's brush or finger or some wiping motion across the printing surface. And, of course, there are no tactile raised or recessed areas; image and paper are fused in one smooth surface.

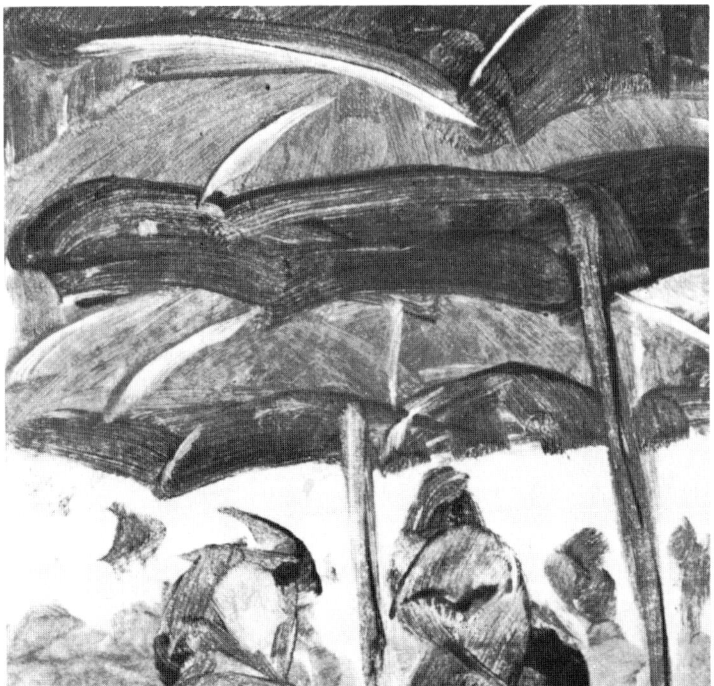

18.
Detail from colorplate 4

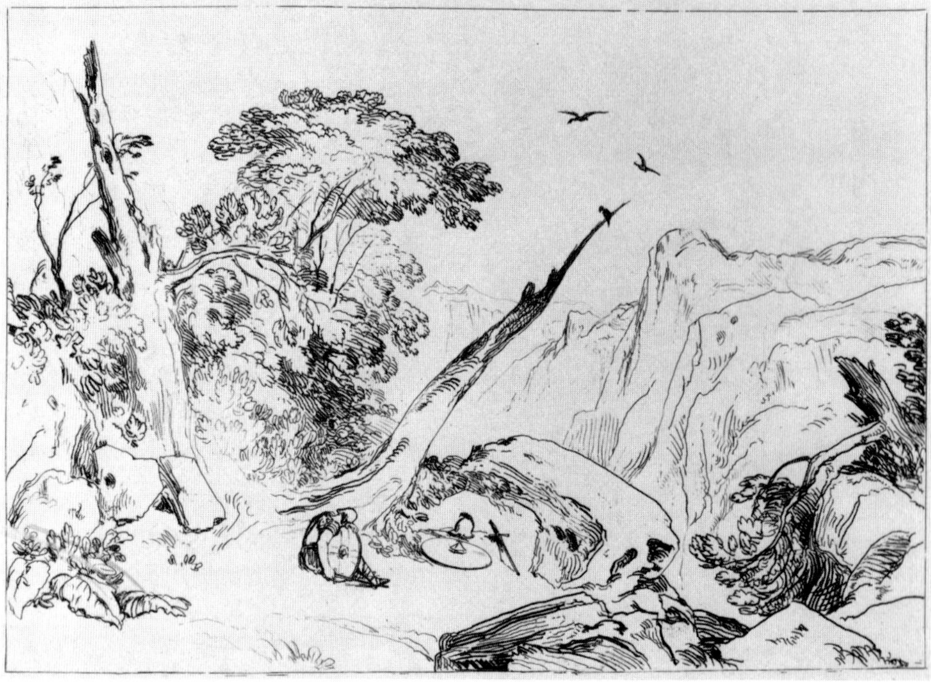

19

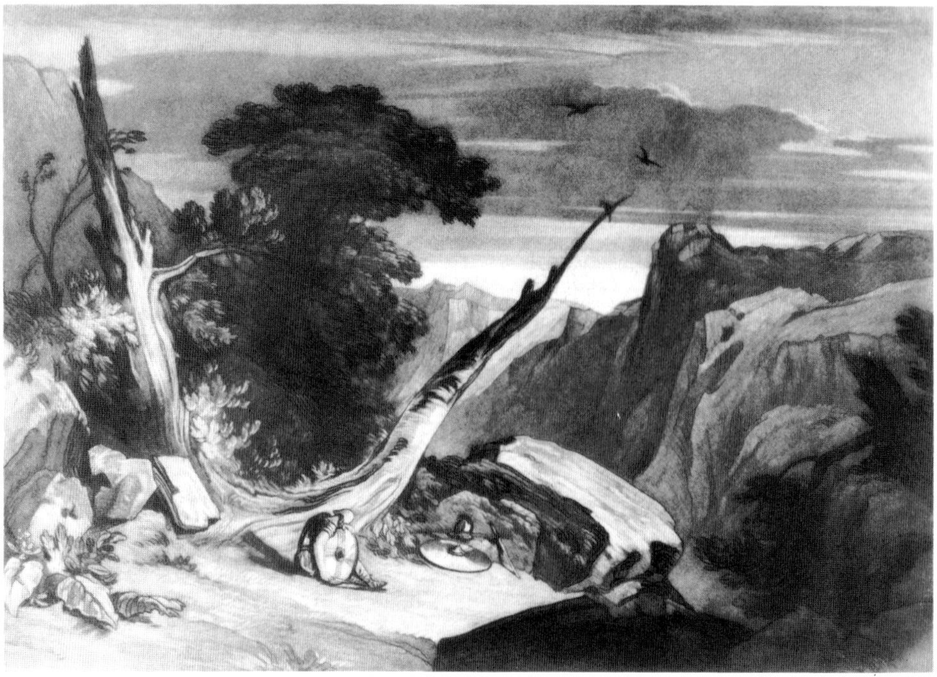

20

19.
Joseph Mallord William Turner (1775–1851). English. *From Spenser's "Faerie Queene,"* c. 1810. Etched state before publication in *Liber Studiorum*, 1811. 20.6 x 28.6 cm. (8⅛ x 11¼ in.). Private collection

20.
Joseph Mallord William Turner (1775–1851). English. *From Spenser's "Faerie Queene."* Etching and mezzotint, published state, in *Liber Studiorum*, 1811. 20.6 x 28.6 cm. (8⅛ x 11¼ in.). Private collection

Mezzotint (plates 19–21). By 1642, in Amsterdam, the German Ludwig von Siegen had developed the most painterly of printmaking's multicopy techniques, the mezzotint (meaning "half tint"—an apt description). The engraver's line can go just so far in simulating tone; by rolling a spiky *roulette* over the copperplate, however, a certain trail of roughness can be created. When a plate worked in this way is printed, a lush, velvety tone is achieved; the coloristic effect ranges from the deepest black to the softest gray, depending on the density and depth of the rouletting. In 1657 Prince Rupert, nephew of England's Charles I, who probably knew von Siegen (curiously, both were military officers), further perfected the technique. By working the plate with a sawtoothed *rocker*, he transformed its entire surface into a veritable "bloom" of thrown-up metal, or burr. Subtly graded highlights were then meticulously scraped and burnished into the plate, extracting light from dark in a manner similar to the working method of a painter. This sort of printed image was thus ideal for reproducing oil paintings—mezzotint's primary role for two centuries. The "dark manner," as this process was sometimes called, spread to England, where a whole industry for printing inexpensive, painterly portraits in mezzotint thrived.

The equipment for making a mezzotint is largely the same as that for line engraving, except that a roulette and/or rocker replaces the burin, and a metal scraper and burnisher are also required. A mezzotint is characterized by the patterned trails left by manipulation of the roulette over the plate surface and by the soft, almost fuzzy highlights that are clearly visible as the result of burnishing.

21.
Detail from plate 20

Aquatint (plates 22–24). Although the aquatint process emerged as early as the 1650s in Amsterdam, it was Jean-Baptiste Le Prince's treatise on the subject, published in Paris in 1780, that popularized the aquatint. Before the invention of the process, the appearance of tonal gradations in etching was simulated by many closely spaced parallel lines, or crosshatching, and by such other conventional devices as dots and flicks worked into the plate.

The term *aquatint* is itself misleading, since the reproduction process does not involve water, nor does a true tint result. It is simply a convenient, loosely reminiscent description of the visual effect, harking back to the brushed-in tints of watercolors (*aquarelles*). Aquatint extended the capabilities of etching significantly by creating a granular field of entry for the biting action of the acid, which produces a textured tone in printing. The full potential of the technique in combination with etching, as a distinct medium with aesthetic merits of its

22.
Francisco Goya (1746–1828). Spanish. *A Bad Night*, 1797. Etching and aquatint from *Los Caprichos*. 21.5 x 15.2 cm. (8½ x 6 in.). Private collection

23.
Edgar Degas (1834–1917). French. *At the Ambassadeurs*, 1875. Etching and aquatint. 26.7 x 29.5 cm. (10½ x 11⅝ in.). Private collection

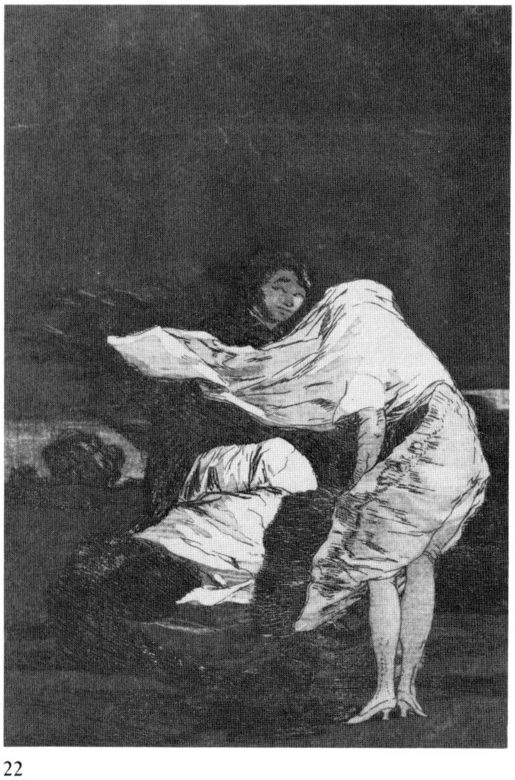

22

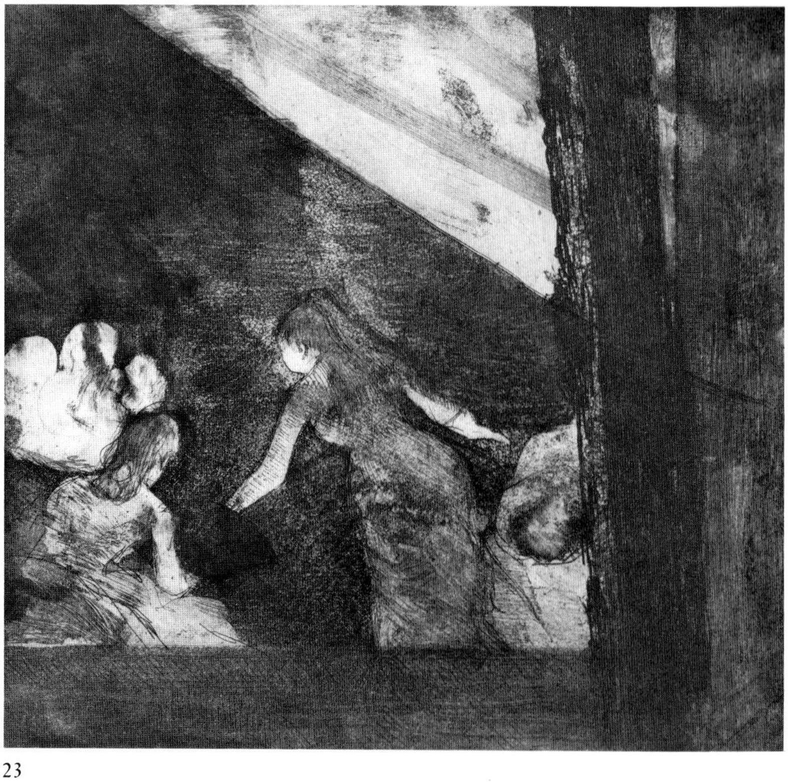

23

own, was realized by Francisco Goya in 1797, in the eighty plates of his great *Caprichos* series.

The equipment for aquatint is the same as for etching per se, with which it is usually combined. The only additional element is the material for the aquatint ground, a substance that contains salt or sugar or is a dissolved rosin. When heated, this rough ground—in contrast to the smooth waxy compound in etching, which completely blocks the acid—permits the acid to enter the copperplate through numerous microscopic openings. The length of time the plate is immersed in the acid bath determines the depth of biting and, consequently, the density of the printed texture. The identifying characteristic of aquatint is the raised surface impression—the result, of course, of the intaglio process—which has a somewhat random granular tone.

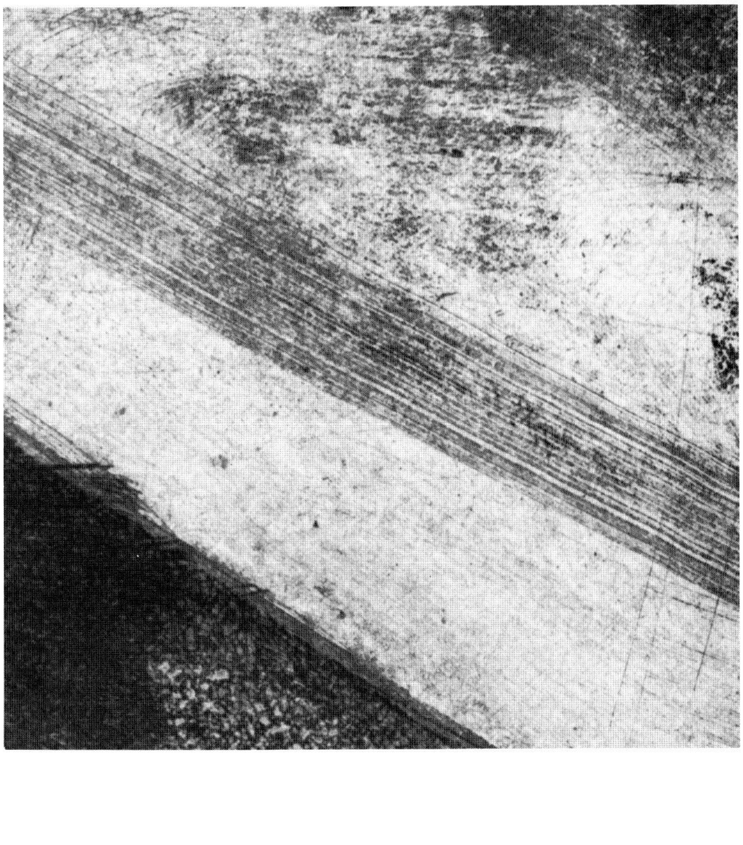

24.
Detail from plate 23

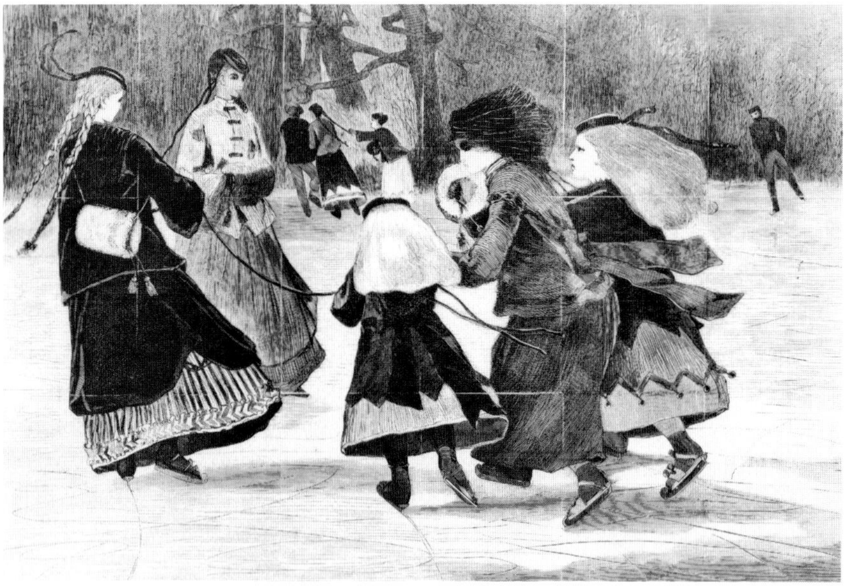

25

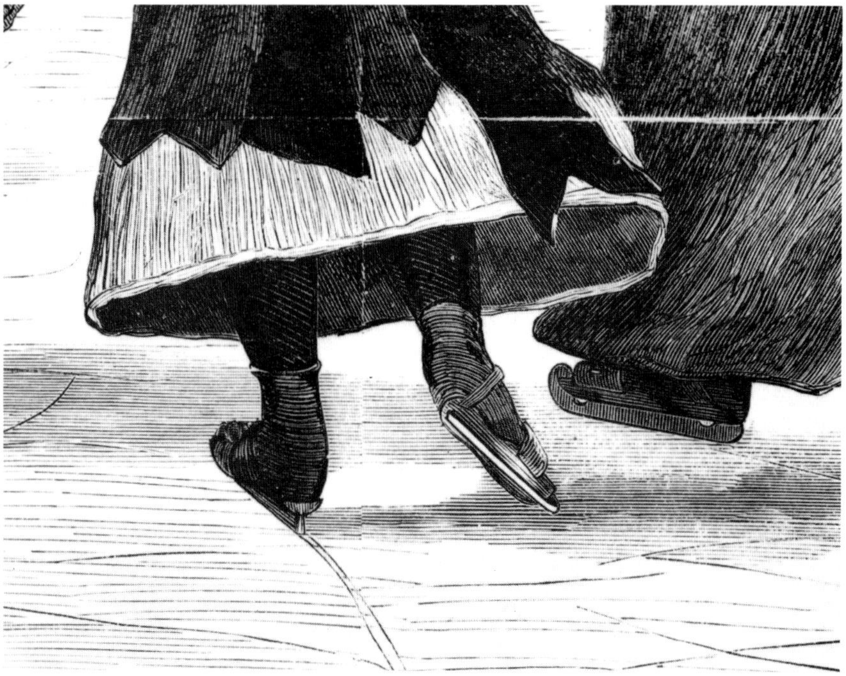

26

25.
Winslow Homer (1836–1910). American. "*Winter*"—*A Skating Scene*. Wood engraving in *Harper's Weekly*, January 25, 1868. 22.6 x 34.3 cm. (8⅞ x 13½ in.). Private collection

26.
Detail from plate 25

Wood Engraving (plates 25–27). Thomas Bewick of Newcastle is credited with having refined the technique of wood engraving about 1780. A copperplate engraver, Bewick had the inspiration to apply the engraver's tool to the extremely hard end grain of boxwood. As a guide for cutting, he darkened the polished surface of the block so that as he worked, his engraved line would stand out keenly, almost glistening white. He made this line with two close parallel cuts that left between them a level of uncut wood. When inked and printed, this surface produced a very fine black line. Since this uncut level was so extraordinarily durable because of the upstanding end fibers of the wood, countless impressions could be pulled without noticeable block wear. The fine detail attainable with this technique was brought out even further by printing on very smooth machine-made paper. Because the cuts themselves became the unprinted, or white, areas of the final impression, this technique is sometimes referred to as *white-line engraving.*

Wood engraving soon rivaled metal engraving as an inexpensive means of turning out facsimiles of drawings, and a veritable torrent of images done in this medium filled nineteenth-century periodicals. Indeed, until the advent of photomechanical reproduction of news photographs, wood engraving was the principal vehicle of pictorial journalism, capable of recording the events of the day swiftly and with authentic detail.

The equipment for making a wood engraving includes (1) a woodblock with an end-grain cutting surface, preferably boxwood; (2) such cutting tools normally associated with metal engraving as burins, or gravers, and a steel needle embedded in a wooden grip; (3) a small

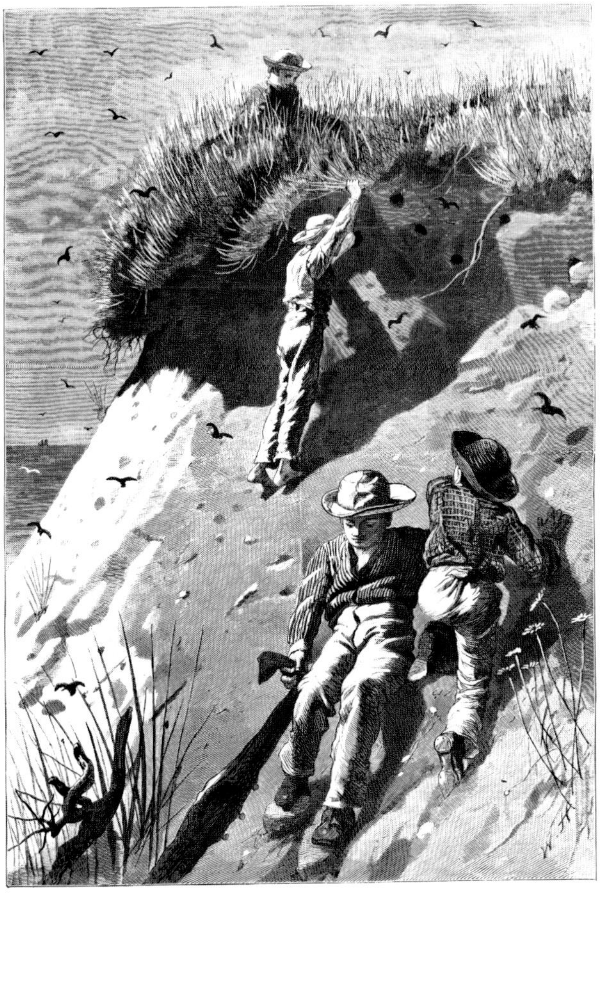

27.
Winslow Homer (1836–1910). American. *Raid on a Sand-Swallow Colony— "How Many Eggs?"* Wood engraving in *Harper's Weekly*, June 13, 1874. 34.3 x 23 cm. (13½ x 9 in.). Private collection

ink roller; (4) a spoonlike wood burnisher for hand-printing, or else a printer's press.

A wood engraving can be distinguished from a metal engraving by the predominance of what the eye interprets as white lines emerging from among the network of black lines (rather than metal engraving's black lines superimposed on a white background). Wood engravings are usually printed on very smooth paper, rather than on the absorbent, more luxurious paper used for metal engravings.

Lithograph (frontispiece, colorplates 5–6 and plates 28–32). In the late 1790s, in Munich, the inventor of the lithographic process, Alois Senefelder, pulled the first lithograph from a Bavarian limestone block (still the only stone found entirely suitable for this medium—hence the stone's rarity today). Senefelder discovered that water will rest on the surface of limestone in a thin film except in areas that are greasy. Correspondingly, greasy ink rolled onto the stone will adhere to greasy places but not to water-moistened areas. The important advantage of lithography is that the artist can draw in black what will actually print in black. Thus, while working directly on the stone, the artist sees quite faithfully (albeit in reverse) what will eventually be printed.

Equipment for making a lithograph includes (1) a polished Bavarian limestone block (or its modern counterpart, a specially prepared zinc or aluminum plate, although the limestone is still far preferable for a maximum range of effects); (2) a crayon or pencil made of a material containing grease and lampblack, or a pen or brush with a liquid form of the same compound, called *tusche*; (3) a metal scraper or polisher for producing negative (white) accents in the image; (4) a solution of nitric acid and gum arabic, called the *etch*; (5) turpentine; (6) a large ink roller; (7) a special lithographic press.

The image is drawn on the stone with the crayon, pen or brush, sometimes aided by the scraper. The stone is treated with the etch, which makes its surface more receptive to water and fixes the image so that it will remain intact throughout repeated printing cycles. The stone is then treated with turpentine, which removes the lampblack pigment from the image, thereby reducing the drawing to a faint, ghostly image. The stone is sponged down with water; the surface areas that are unmarked by the greasy drawing material partly absorb this moisture. Greasy ink is then rolled onto the stone. Since the wet portion of the stone rejects the ink but the greasy areas accept it, the image, with its normal intensities of black, reappears almost magically. The stone is then placed faceup on the press bed, and the dampened paper to be printed is placed over it. Both stone and paper are then run through the press, and the lithograph is carefully pulled. To be used again, the stone must be meticulously ground down until all traces of the old image have been removed.

Colorplate 5.
Louis Maurer (1832–1932). American. *"Trotting Cracks" on the Snow*, published by Currier & Ives, 1858. Lithograph and watercolor. 42.9 x 70.8 cm. (16⅞ x 27⅞ in.). Metropolitan Museum of Art, New York, bequest of Adele S. Colgate, 1963

Colorplate 6.
Paul Cézanne (1839–1906). French. *Bathers*, 1899. Lithograph. 43.2 x 53.3 cm. (17 x 21 in.). Museum of Modern Art, New York, Lillie P. Bliss Collection

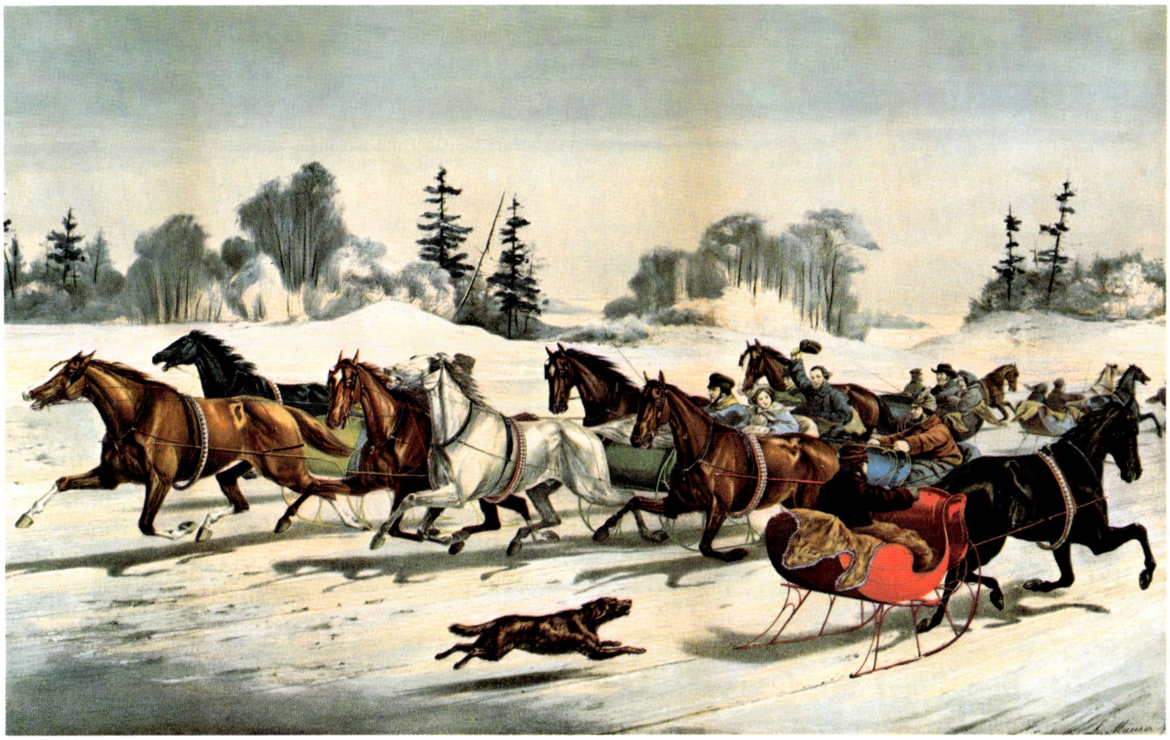

Colorplate 5

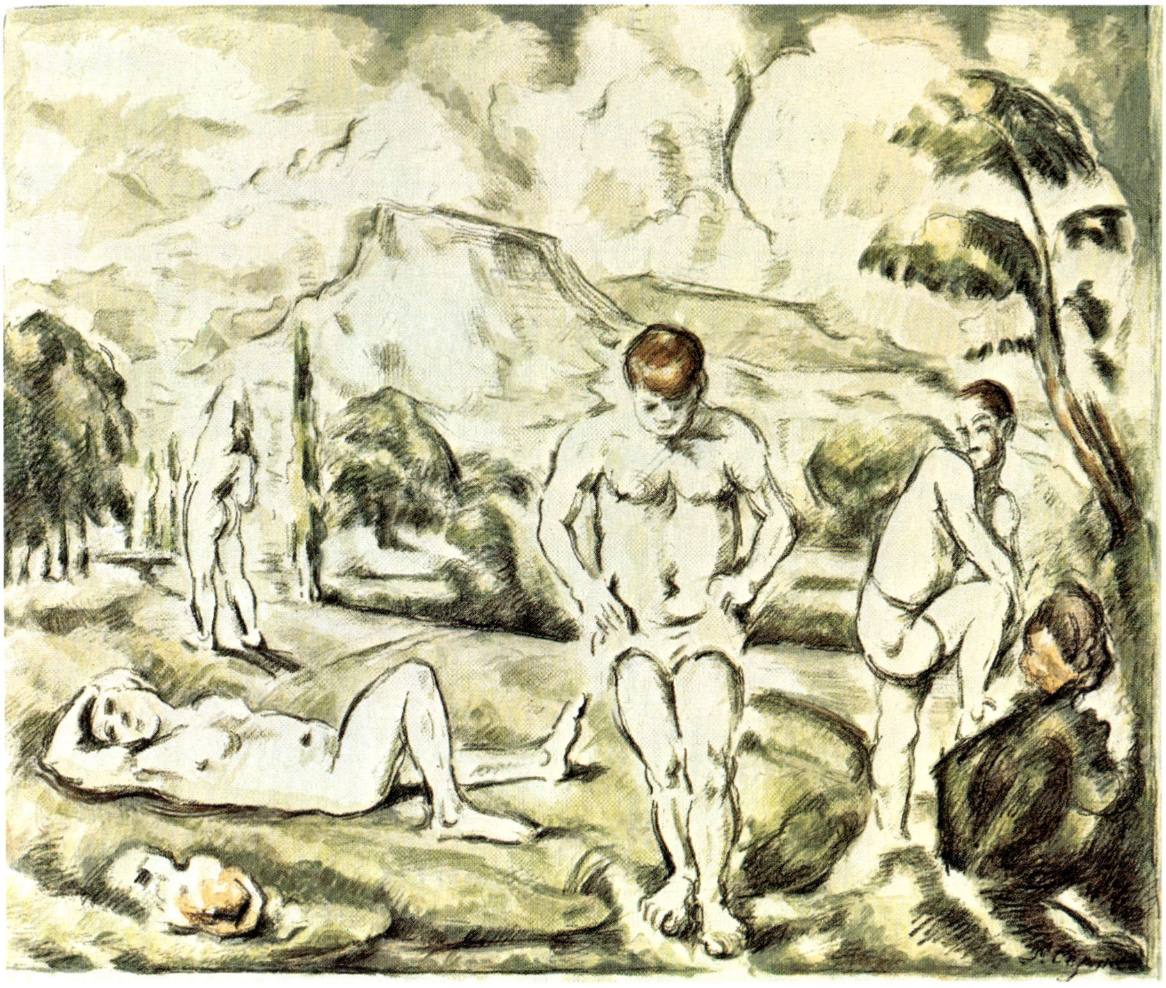

Colorplate 6

28.
Honoré Daumier (1808–1879). French. "*How Silly We Were to Be So Frightened*," 1845. Lithograph. First state before caption and publication. 27.3 x 23.5 cm. (10¾ x 9¼ in.). Private collection

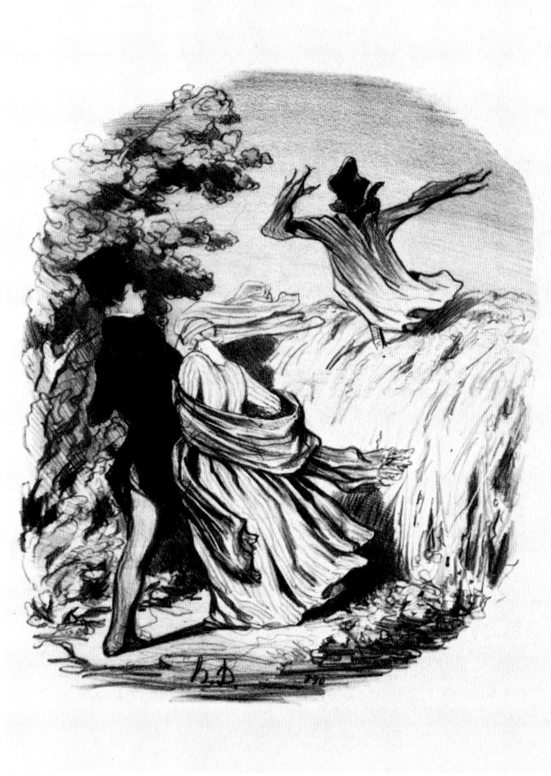

29.
Detail from plate 28

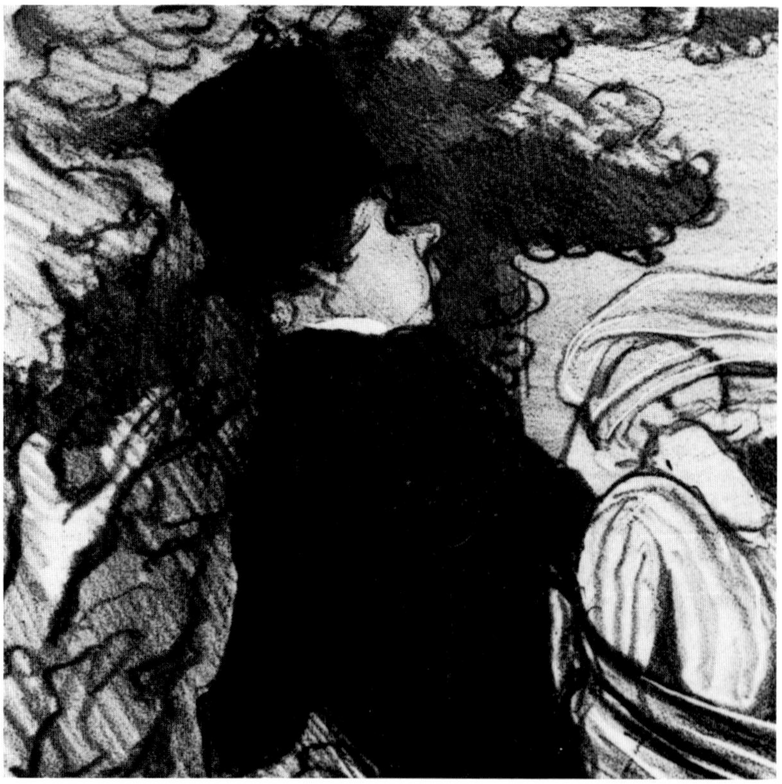

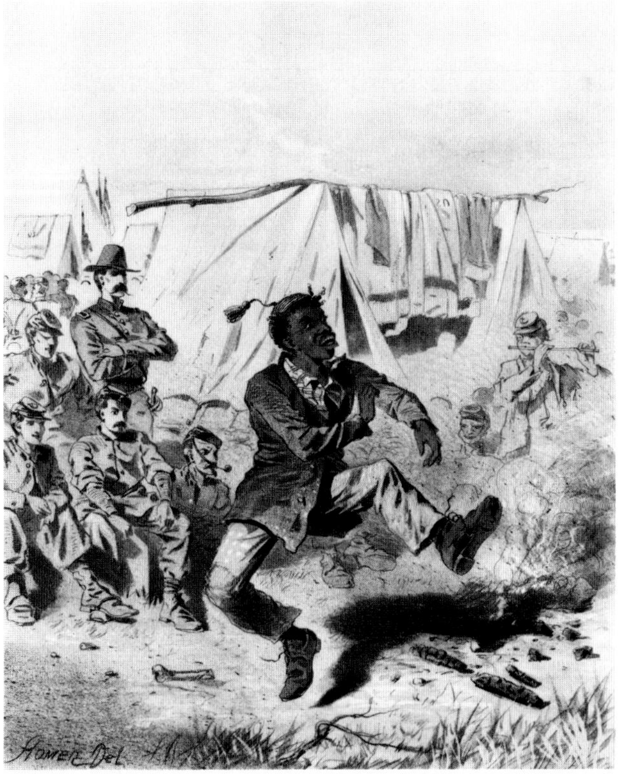

30

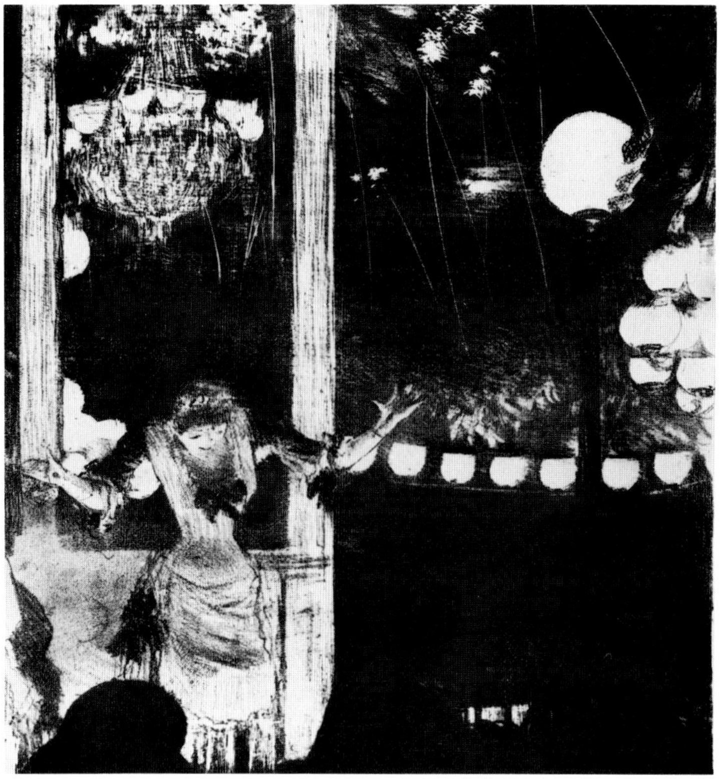

31

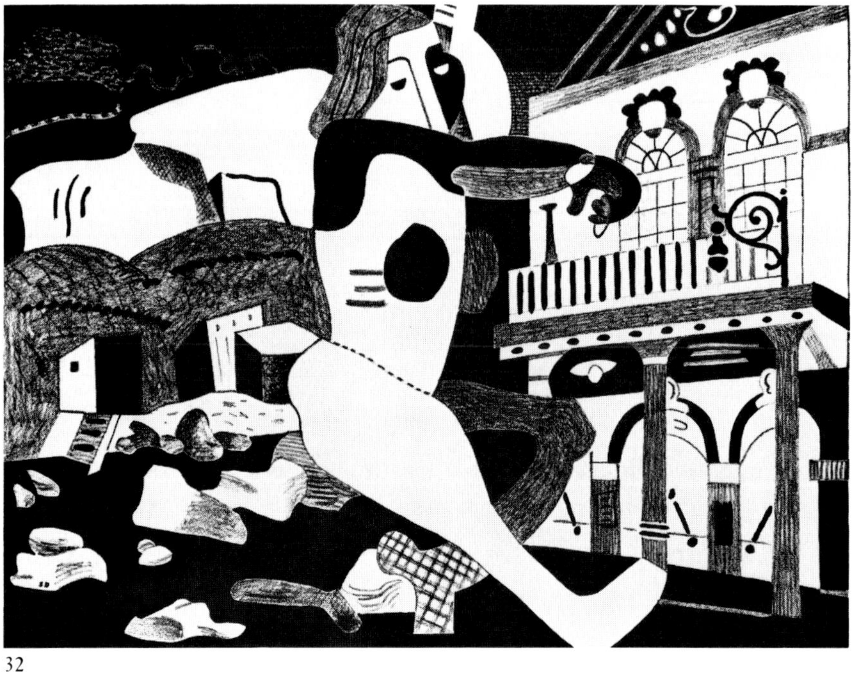

32

30.
Winslow Homer (1836–1910). American. *Our Jolly Cook.* Lithograph from *Campaign Sketches,* 1863. 30.7 x 22.6 cm. ($12\frac{1}{8}$ x $8\frac{7}{8}$ in.). Private collection

31.
Edgar Degas (1834–1917). French. *Mlle. Bécat Singing at the Ambassadeurs,* 1875. Lithograph. 20.7 x 19.4 cm. ($8\frac{1}{8}$ x $7\frac{5}{8}$ in.). Private collection

32.
Stuart Davis (1894–1964). American. *Theater on the Beach,* 1931. Lithograph. 27.7 x 38 cm. ($10\frac{7}{8}$ x 15 in.). Private collection

Lithography transmits with admirable accuracy the texture and quality of the crayon or pencil or brushed-on ink or wash. This capability gives the lithographic image its special characteristic: grain by infinitesimal grain a one-to-one transfer is made and lies flat on the paper, except for the nearly imperceptible thickness of the dried ink. The resulting surface contrasts markedly with the surface of relief or intaglio works, in which either the image or the surrounding paper is raised. If, by the way, the paper is larger than the lithographic stone, the irregular edges of the stone will leave a *stone mark*, corresponding to the plate mark of the intaglio processes. Whether or not a stone mark is discernible, measurements of all lithographs apply solely to the printed image.

Combined Processes Although the preceding description of graphic reproduction techniques deals with each separately, throughout the history of printmaking these techniques have often been used in combination; for example, woodcut with wood engraving. Other printmaking combinations employed with some frequency include (1) engraving with drypoint; (2) etching with drypoint—plates 8–11; (3) etching with engraving; (4) engraving with mezzotint; (5) etching with mezzotint—plate 20; (6) etching with aquatint—plates 22 and 23; and (7) etching with monotype—colorplate 7.

Colorplate 7.
Suzanne Valadon (1867–1938). French. *Louise, Nude on the Sofa*, 1895. Etching and monotype. 22.3 x 28 cm. (8¾ x 11 in.). Private collection

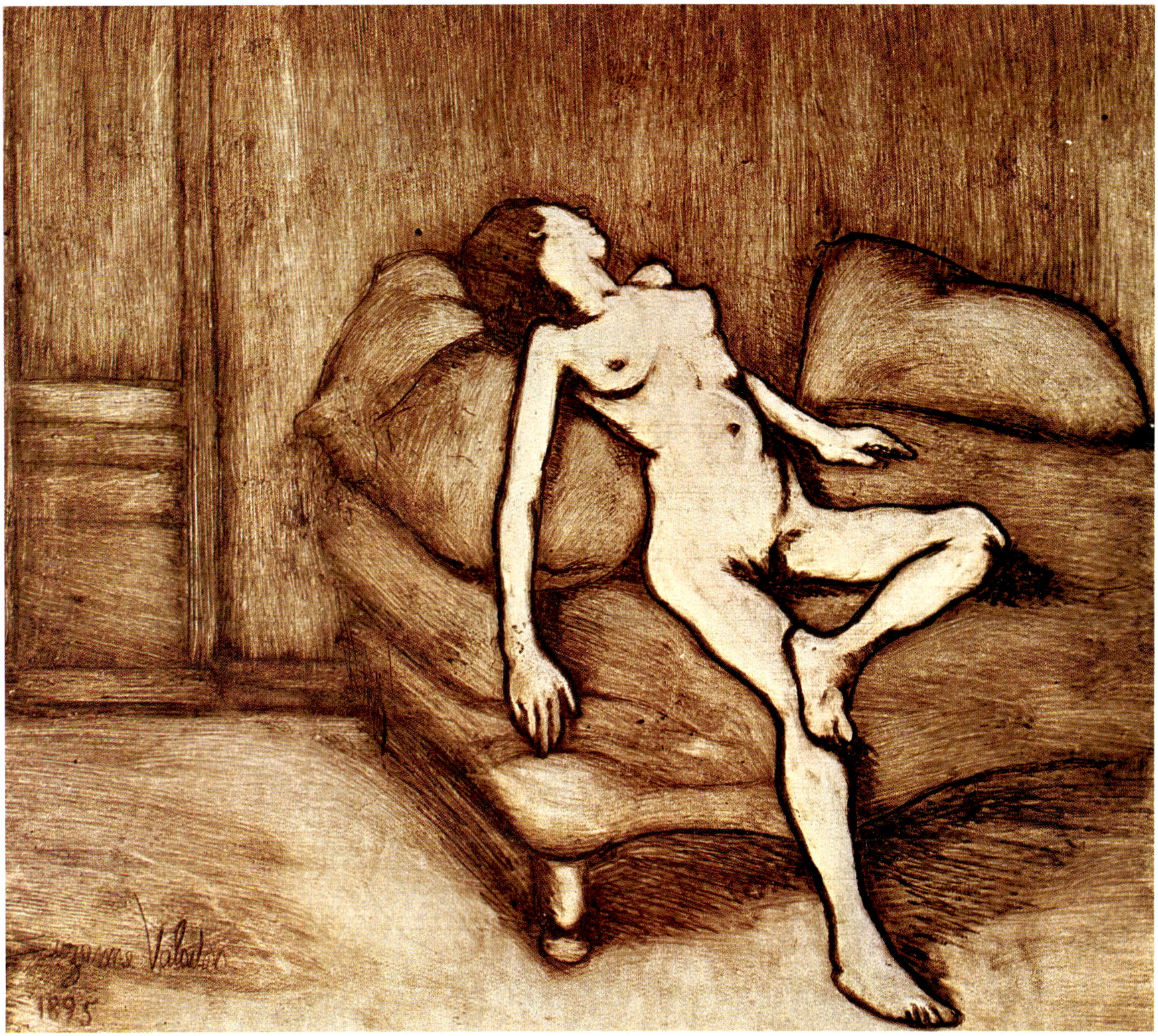
Valadon
1895

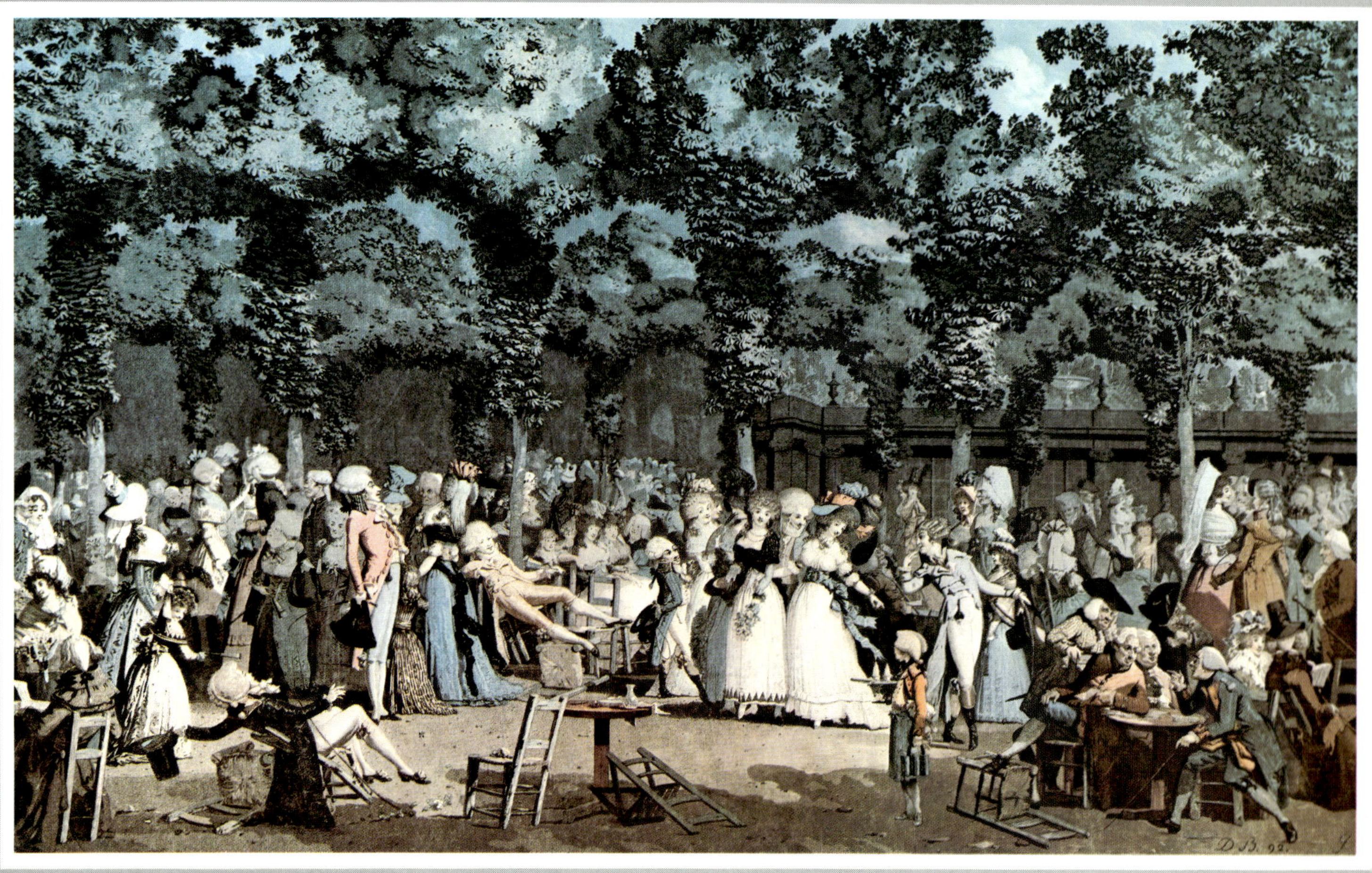

3 The Printmaker's Subjects: A Selection

The print medium has often been regarded as extremely complicated: an obstacle course of chemistry and technology that restricts creative flow. But is this really the case? The preceding chapters have described the characteristics of the print and the stepped sequences involved in printmaking with various techniques. Except for considering the special nature of these techniques and the inherent qualities that attracted artists to them, we have not examined printmaking as an art form. In this chapter we survey the vast oeuvre left by printmakers over the centuries in terms of many of the subjects they chose to illustrate. This approach—a departure from the customary chronological view of printmaking—leads inevitably to one dazzling truth: method or technology has never controlled the artist. On the contrary, it was the artist who invented, modified and reformed the act of printmaking; who learned the dangers of preoccupation with line and texture and conquered technique to create images of enduring beauty and undiminished impact.

Visions of Christianity At our vantage point, nearly twenty centuries after the birth of Christ, we are immeasurably enriched by the breathtaking imagery that Christianity has inspired. Just as it is inconceivable for Western humanism to have evolved without Christianity, so it is inconceivable that art as we know and cherish it could have emerged in the absence of Christianity. What we have to remind ourselves, since the Christian images are so imbedded in our mind's eye as to be almost real, is that they were invented by artists. Although a certain rudimentary set of images was handed down through the generations after Christ, it was not until quite late—the fifteenth century—that the vocabulary of art and the introduction of woodcutting and engraving permitted impressively realistic images to be made and disseminated to countless people. To visualize the complexities and

Colorplate 8.
Philibert-Louis Debucourt (1755–1832). French. *The Public Walk in the Garden of the Palais Royal*, 1792. Aquatint, etching and engraving. 36.5 x 59 cm. (14⅜ x 23¼ in.). Metropolitan Museum of Art, New York, Elisha C. Whittelsey Fund, 1961

extremes of passion of the Old and New Testaments and to set them down as credible printed images became a creative challenge to artists. Although many of the same artists also painted for church walls and altars, these efforts were unique and fixed images seen by relatively few at an appreciable distance. With printmaking it was at last possible to place directly in the possession of the people images on paper that could ennoble or terrify them or conjure up the most private thoughts. Like family photographs of today, these little pictures were meant to be pondered again and again; they were so superbly wrought that they could kindle and lastingly capture the imagination of the faithful.

In Martin Schongauer's engraving *The Bedeviling of St. Anthony* (plate 33), the saint's gentle ascent to heaven has been brazenly interrupted by demons whose hybridized forms were shockingly new for the 1470s. Indeed, the work's present rarity may be partly explained by the possibility that many impressions were destroyed as devil-haunted. More than five hundred years later this image's prickly effectiveness has not diminished. In what is probably the most memorable aerial confrontation in the history of printmaking, Schongauer's incessant stitching of dash, flick and crosshatch across the plate assaults our eyes. As Saint Anthony is airborne, so Christ is earthbound in the artist's other masterpiece, *Road to Calvary* (plate 35). The crushing weight of the slanted T-shaped cross—almost spiked into the earth to emphasize its immobility—is contrasted with the lighter diagonals of the spears and rods. This linear scaffold braces a multitude so detailed and compressed that our eyes must wander through the procession to discover and identify, first moving left along the strong diagonal thrust of the cross and then veering beyond the rocks.

Schongauer's biting northern explicitness contrasts with the softer, more sentimental images of the south, such as the Florentine engraving *The Adoration of the Magi* by Cristofano Robetta (plate 34). Flattened, overlapping figures frame the event in a contained, tapestrylike design. The gentle parallel strokes of the burin endow this image with a luminous gray—almost silvery—overall tone. Centuries later the great Venetian painter Giovanni Battista Tiepolo, using the more notational advantages of etching, treated the same subject (plate 36). He created an open, sun-drenched spectacle with sharp perspective and looming foreground. To achieve such grandeur with so light a touch and a minimum of modeling and contour demonstrates a truly inspired visual shorthand. Look closely at the type of line that has produced this effect: amazingly tiny flicks of the etcher's needle. In Robetta's engraving the Madonna, centrally placed in the composition, appears to float, transfixed as if the two tree trunks were celestial cables that had lifted her. With Tiepolo, scale and position are realistic, documentary. The resulting scene is far from frontally hierarchic or posed. The Madonna is seen amid a flurry of activity, surrounded by randomly

33.
Martin Schongauer (c. 1430–1491). German. *The Bedeviling of St. Anthony*, c. 1470. Engraving. 30.7 x 23 cm. (12⅛ x 9 in.). Private collection

34.
Cristofano Robetta (1462–after 1535). Italian. *The Adoration of the Magi*, c. 1496. Engraving after Filippino Lippi. 30.8 x 29 cm. (12⅛ x 11⅜ in.). Private collection

35.
Martin Schongauer (c. 1430–1491). German. *Road to Calvary*, c. 1470. Engraving. 28.5 x 42.8 cm. (11¼ x 16⅞ in.). Cooper-Hewitt Museum, gift of Mrs. Leo Wallerstein

36.
Giovanni Battista Tiepolo (1696–1770). Italian. *The Adoration of the Magi*, c. 1750. Etching. 43 x 28.8 cm. (17 x 11⅜ in.). Cooper-Hewitt Museum, gift of Eleanor and Sarah Hewitt

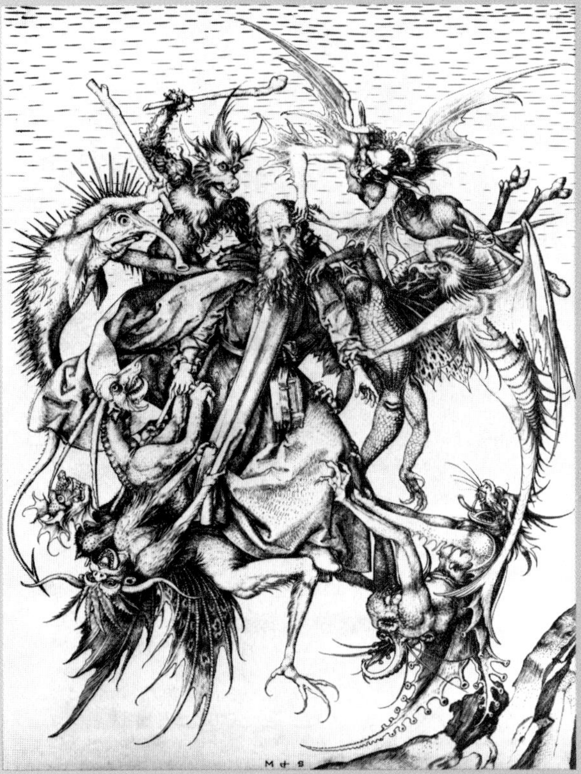

33

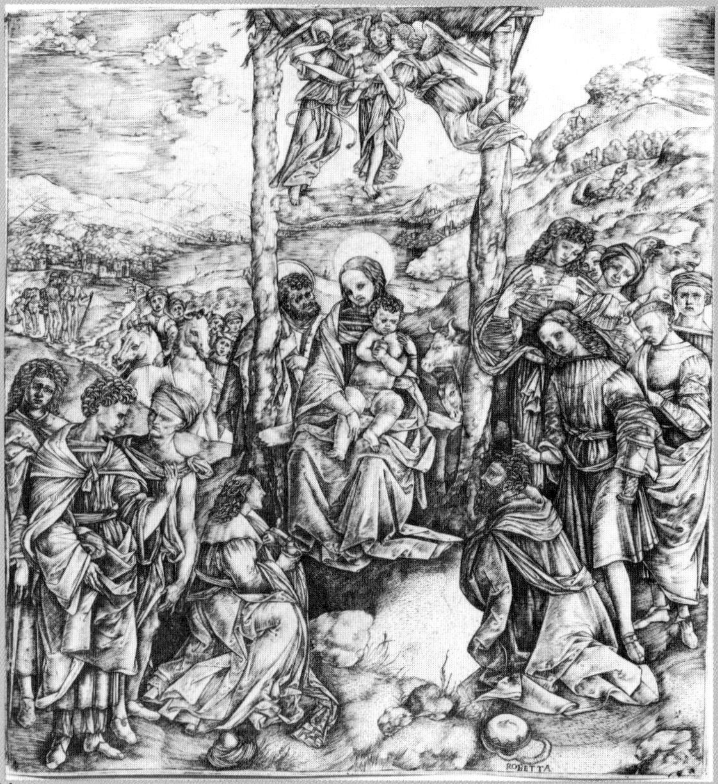

34

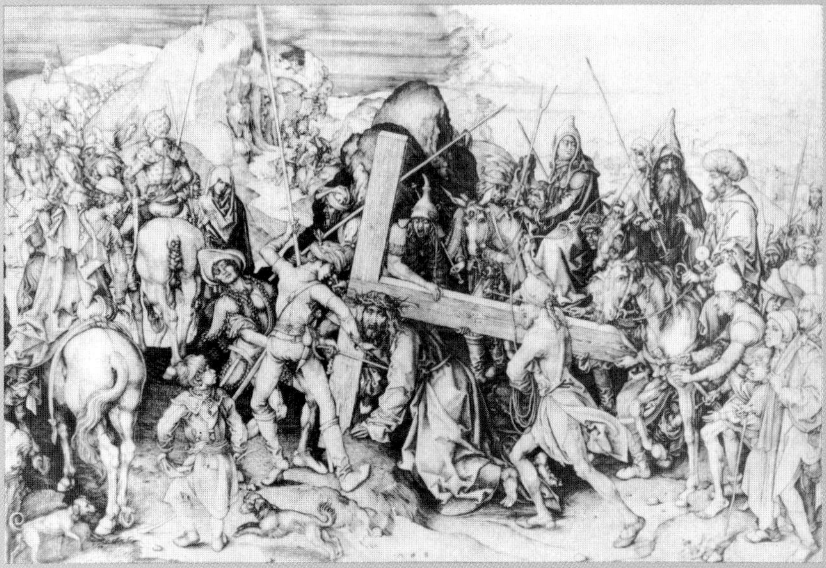
35

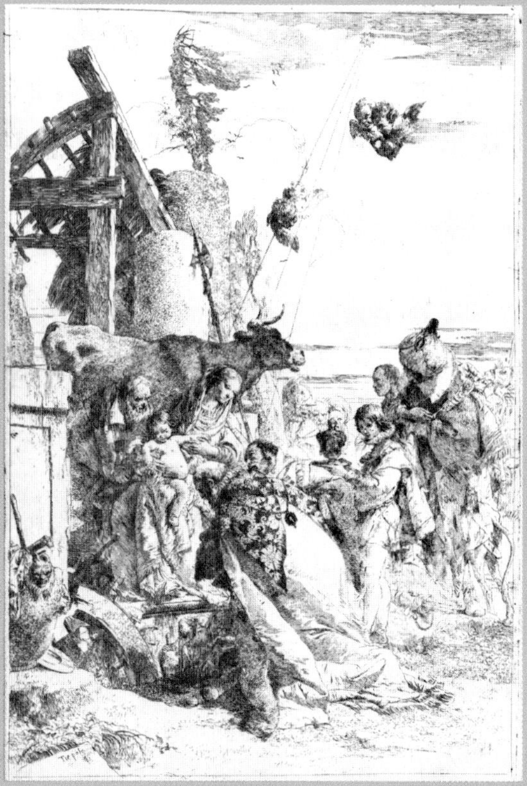
36

placed worldly objects and ancient relics—all of which add to the quivering liveliness.

The two Rembrandt etchings with drypoint, *St. Jerome in an Italian Landscape* and *The Descent from the Cross by Torchlight* (plates 37 and 38), bear some remarkable resemblances. Both are vertical rectangles divided in half by a strongly implied diagonal from the upper-left to the lower-right corner. Both have stone ledges in the foreground that serve as a stage for action, and both have brooding architecture in the background, which also serves as the horizon line. Yet there is a striking reversal of dark-and-light systems, governed by the time of day. In the daytime view the diagonal sweep is an irregular mass of dark shadows. The toned buildings are likewise realized in deep-chiseled shadow. These forms are set against a clear white sky, hilly landscape and foreground. In the nighttime view the diagonal is comprised of dramatically lighted irregular forms and structures against a black sky and heavily shadowed foreground. With these analogous compositions an uncanny sense of reality has been created. Rich accents of burr, shadow and register form throughout the Saint Jerome etching. The lion, a powerful guardian figure, his mane bristling with burr, gazes into the distance. In contrast, Saint Jerome is drawn with only a few light lines; the bulk of his form is composed of

37.
Rembrandt Harmensz. van Rijn (1606–1669). Dutch. *St. Jerome in an Italian Landscape*, c. 1653. Etching and drypoint. 26.1 x 21.2 cm. (10¼ x 8⅜ in.). Cooper-Hewitt Museum, gift of Leo Wallerstein

38.
Rembrandt Harmensz. van Rijn (1606–1669). Dutch. *The Descent from the Cross by Torchlight*, 1654. Etching and drypoint. 21.2 x 16.2 cm. (8⅜ x 6⅜ in.). Cooper-Hewitt Museum, gift of Leo Wallerstein

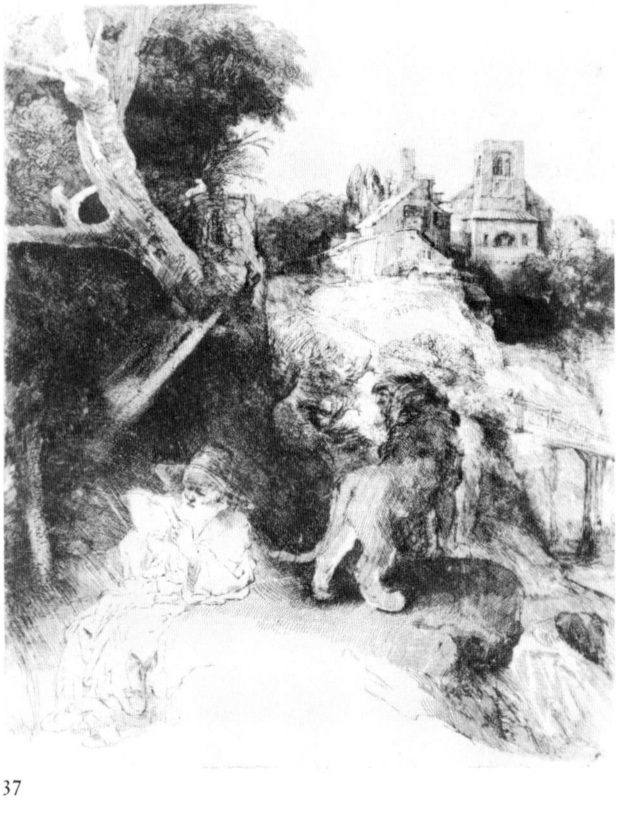

37

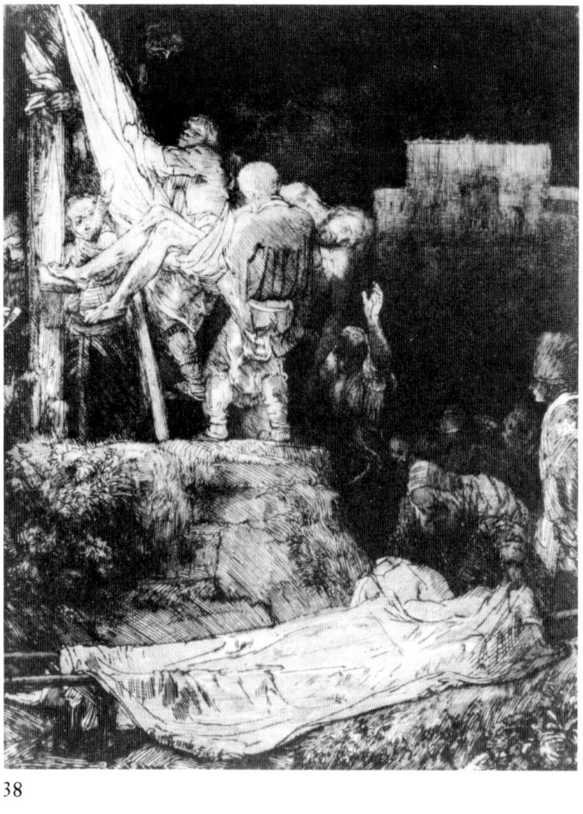

38

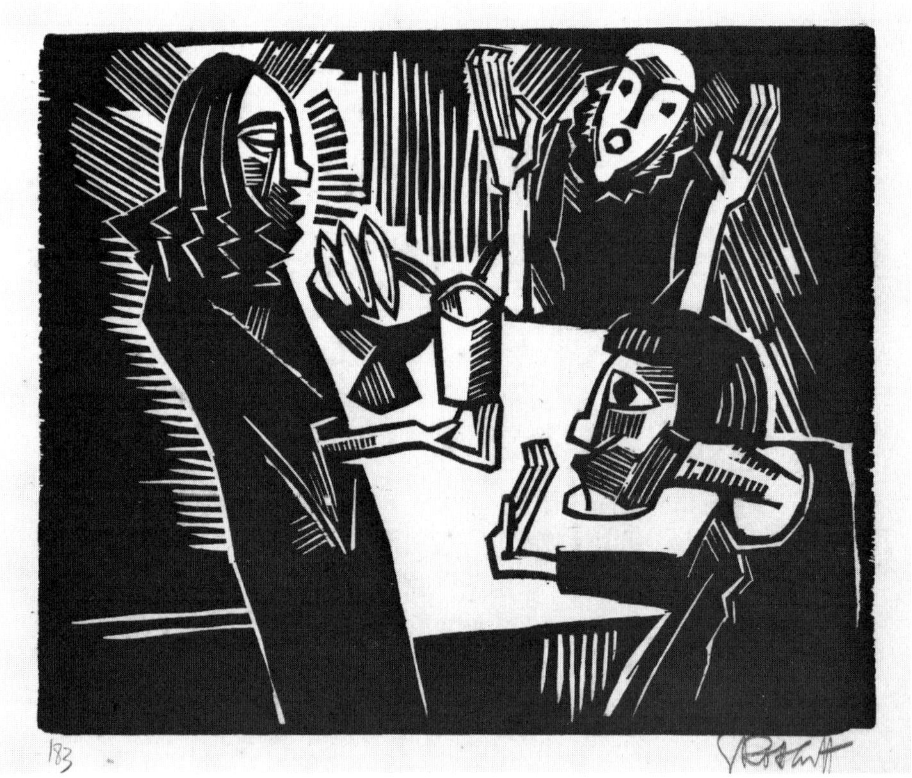

39.
Karl Schmidt-Rottluff (1884–1976). German. *Christ at Emmaus*, 1918. Woodcut. 29.5 x 36 cm. (11⅝ x 14⅛ in.). Museum of Modern Art, New York, Purchase

uninked white paper. In *The Descent* Christ's body is heavy and strongly worked; weight is accentuated by the parallel vertical lines with burr in the cloak of the central figure supporting him. Christ is caught midway on a space-time journey down the diagonal from the cross to the bier.

The German expressionists of the early twentieth century knew full well the expressive attributes of primitive woodcarvings: their directness, simplicity and animation. In *Christ at Emmaus* (plate 39) Karl Schmidt-Rottluff fused this aesthetic awareness with his admiration for the fifteenth-century northern woodcuts that share these characteristics. In a natural disposition of the relief process, he has boldly worked his whites out of a black field. With probably only a few hundred individual jabs of the carver's knife, the artist has created an electrifying composition. Surprise and submission are simultaneously achieved with sawtoothed ferocity and flashbulblike glare.

Whether viewed in a museum or in one's personal collection at home, the visualization of Christianity conveyed in printmaking through the ages holds a profound emotive potential. This subject matter is the oldest, the most durable, in the history of printmaking. Because of the range and the depth of emotions portrayed, these religion-inspired works can have formidable impact.

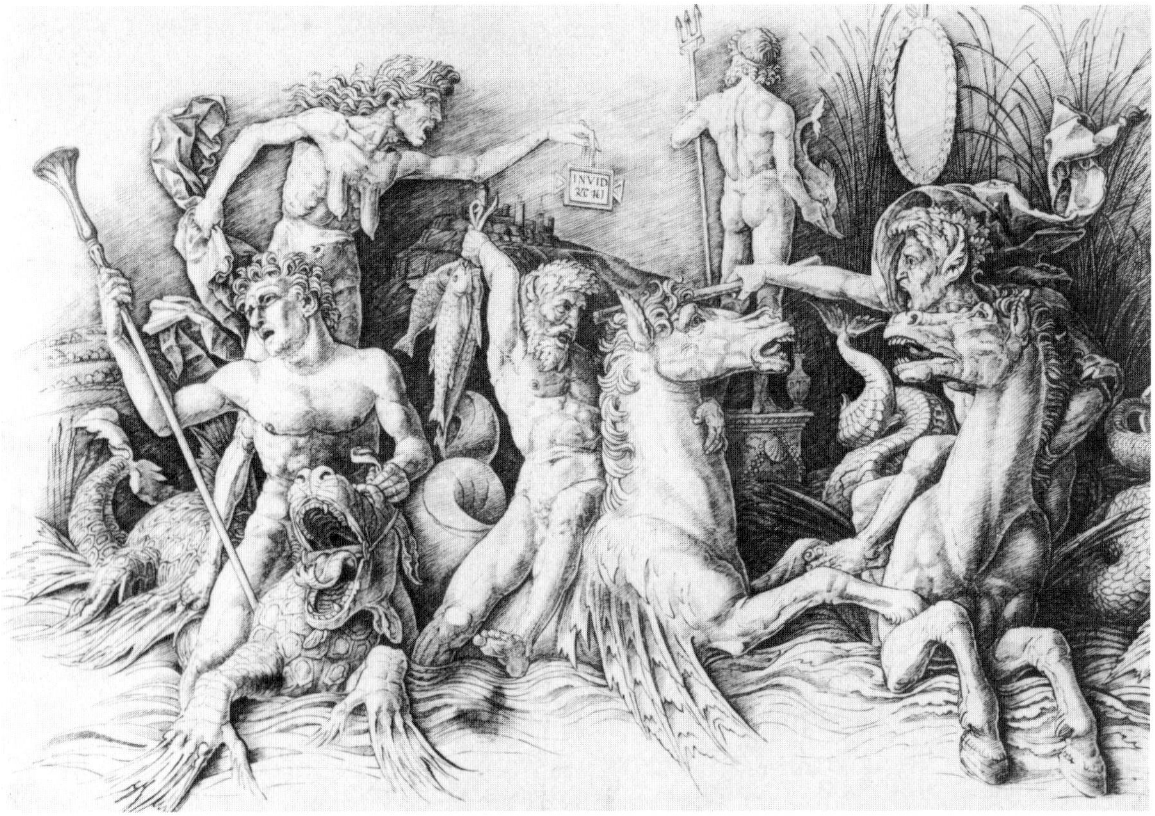

40

Antiquity and Myth The first great Renaissance print of a mythological subject is Andrea Mantegna's engraving *Battle of the Sea Gods* (plate 40). The painter's interest in sculpture led him to Roman antiquities and their Greek sources. Mantegna chose an obscure Greek myth and represented it with unusual sculptural clarity and definition: a gentle fish-eating people are visited by Envy, in the form of a shrieking hag; as the gods turn their backs, these docile creatures of the water become enraged and a battle ensues. In addition to relating the story, the engraved image presents much anatomical information that was then difficult to obtain. As a result, other artists became a principal market for the prints, and some surviving impressions bear the telltale paint and ink of artists' studios where the engraving had served as a guide for figural compositions. No ancient classical sculpture was known to have encompassed such an ensemble. At least one Italian sculptor—appropriately, the creator of a fountain group—plagiarized Mantegna's design rather than the oft-used Roman-Greek models, which suggests that the recent work on paper offered more detailed guidance. The composition virtually crackles with unleashed energy. Mantegna has used a fluid line in imitation of his quill and brush drawings. The impressions, combining the autographic flow of drawing

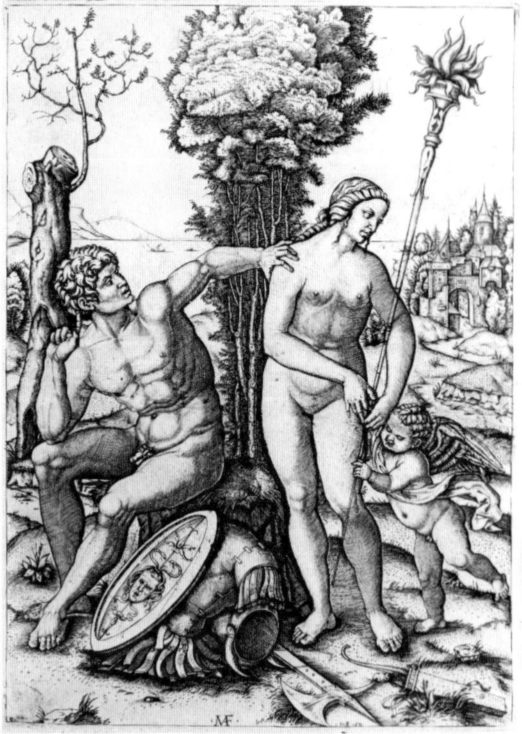

41

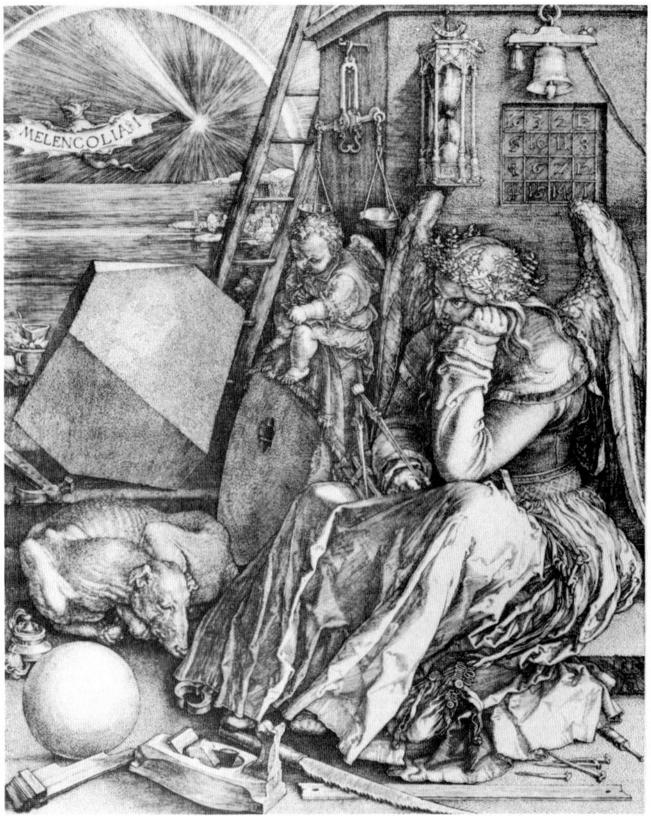

42

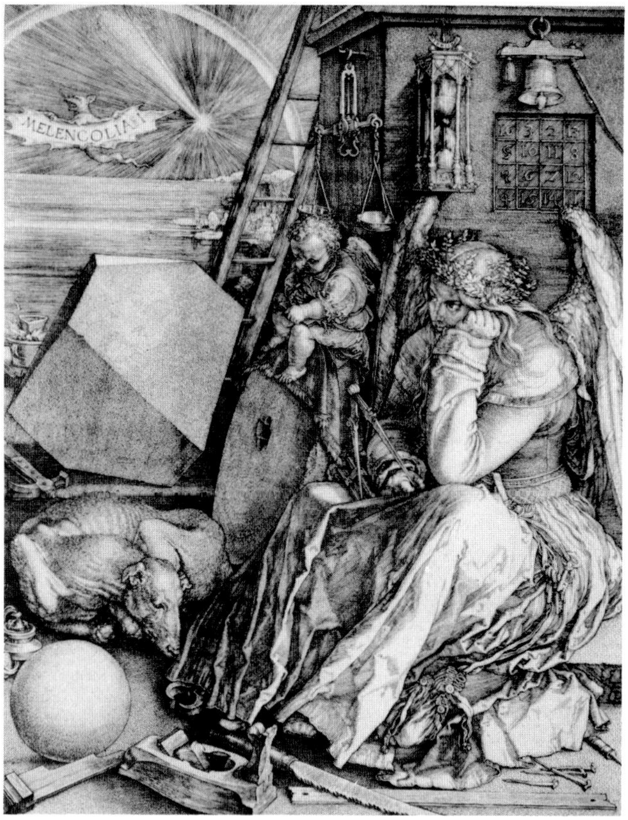

43

with the lucidity and depth of engraving, are startlingly vigorous. A certain unfinished, made-on-the-spot aspect of the work, arising from the unprecedented unworked areas that surround and fuse with the action, makes the viewer feel like a witness to mythology in the making.

Marcantonio Raimondi engraved many mythological subjects after drawings by others. His *Mars, Venus and Cupid* (plate 41) reveals Dürer's influence in the dense clump of trees and the northern-style castle and Mantegna's in the figure of Mars. The pervasive mood of calm, however, is native to the engraver. Our eyes travel smoothly from left to right: from the musculature of Mars, along the curve of his arm that touches Venus, then down the curve of her arm to Cupid. The linear accent created by the right arm of Mars is continued upward in the tree trunk behind him. One of those minor but fascinating aspects of printmaking history occurs in this work: the date near the bottom of the engraving includes even the month and day—the first time such specific data were graven in a plate.

Seeing double can sometimes be illuminating, as in the two versions of Albrecht Dürer's *Melencolia I* reproduced here (plates 42 and 43). In the darker impression, one of the earliest pulled from the plate,

40.
Andrea Mantegna (1431–1506). Italian. *Battle of the Sea Gods* (left portion), c. 1485–88. Engraving. 30.8 x 42 cm. (12⅛ x 16½ in.). Private collection

41.
Marcantonio Raimondi (c. 1480–c. 1530). Italian. *Mars, Venus and Cupid*, December 16, 1508. Engraving. 29.6 x 21.1 cm. (11⅝ x 8¼ in.). Private collection

42.
Albrecht Dürer (1471–1528). German. *Melencolia I*, 1514. Engraving. Early impression. 23.8 x 18.8 cm. (9⅜ x 7⅜ in.). Private collection

43.
Albrecht Dürer (1471–1528). German. *Melencolia I*, 1514. Engraving. Later impression, showing effects of plate wear. 23.8 x 18.5 cm. (9⅜ x 7¼ in.). Cooper-Hewitt Museum, bequest of George Campbell Cooper

the clarity of detail and depth of modeling are astounding. The other version, despite being fully comprehensible, shows the deleterious effects of plate wear—the countless incisions could no longer hold the optimal amount of ink. Without the advantage of comparison, one might erroneously conclude that the lighter impression is a satisfactory transfer of the artist's imagery; this underscores the value of access to better-executed early impressions in museums.

A forbidding twilight of antiquity permeates the image, whose concentrated symbolism must be understood in order to appreciate fully the reasons for engraving one of the most detailed intaglio works ever made.

Instead of aspiring to sublime heights, this winged creature is grounded; she is portrayed sitting awkwardly on cold stone. Her fixed gaze and empty fist betray her state: some deep quandary has rendered her immobile. The babe alongside her is active, writing on a tablet while perched on an unused grindstone; yet its position echoes hers, as do its limp little wings. The infant can act, but without the power to reason, its effort is meaningless. Conversely, the adult is well within the age of reason yet cannot act. The rest of Dürer's vision makes similar dichotomous statements, like a surrounding chorus of dread. The background ladder is a merciless triple symbol: its disuse, a reminder of inaction; its very presence, a signal that construction was under way but has stopped; and, finally, its mundane, clumsy means of ascent, a contrast to the release of winged flight. A visual vocabulary of builder's tools and symbols strewn about echoes the disarray of the allegorical figure's hair and personal effects. These objects are pitifully still; the conceptual glue holding them down is not their physical weight or the pull of gravity but the absence of a purposeful activator. Visible are a plane, clamp, saw, rule, hammer and nails. A pot for melted lead is flaming uselessly, since the crucible nearby does not tilt. An empty scale is shown in balance as if equivalents of air were being weighed. Timing nothing, the sand in an elaborate hourglass is halfway down its course; the clapper of a bell hangs vertical, with no contact, soundless. A perfect stone sphere rests inert on a flat plane. The facets of the prismatic stone farther back seem to repeat the stony seated figure. Attached to her belt is a loop of keys that go unused, despite the property and power they represent. Near her feet is an impressive pouch holding unspendable money—unfulfilled fortune. The normally fleet, intent hunter, the companion hound dog, is immobile in slumber, save perhaps for a barely perceptible shiver; curled within itself, the wretched animal seeks a warmth unobtainable from the stone. The figure holds a large compass in a spread-out position: little action is required to operate such an instrument, only a slight pivot of its head. Yet no such action occurs, and the compass rests incongruously on her deeply furrowed garment, the pointer held aimlessly like a writing instrument. A magic square of numbers below the silent bell adds up to 34 in all directions, its purpose nonutilitarian, in contrast with the practical use made of mathematics and geometry by a builder. But even as an amusement the square is useless, since the potential viewer gazes in the other direction. There is evidence that Dürer was sufficiently concerned with his own melancholic nature to alert his doctors. This biographical fact has given rise to the interpretation of *Melencolia I* as a form of symbol-laden self-portrait.

In Italy mythological images proliferated during the sixteenth century and evocations of antiquity during the eighteenth, when Italian excavations produced a renewed interest in the classical past. In the late nineteenth century, mythology became one of the favored vehicles of the French symbolists, in whose hands such legends took on strange, personal and often ambiguous forms that would attract their spiritual inheritors—the surrealists—a generation later. The most powerful of these images is Odilon Redon's lithograph *Captive Pegasus* (plate 44). The great winged horse, symbol of poetic inspiration, is seen at the moment he is forcefully bridled—a stirring portrait of arrested energy. Though Pegasus' arched neck is bent low in submission, his wings are still aflutter in a haze of light, like a butterfly's. The glistening highlight on his head leads the eye down through a succession of such highlights into the vertical of his captor's uplifted forearm. It is as if a kind of unearthly transfer of power were being made from beast to man. As the winged Melancholy is silvery in her finely engraved lines, so the winged Pegasus is deep velvet in his softly modulated lithographic strokes and scrapings.

44.
Odilon Redon (1840–1916). French. *Captive Pegasus*, 1889. Lithograph. 33.6 x 29.5 cm. (13¼ x 11⅝ in.). Private collection

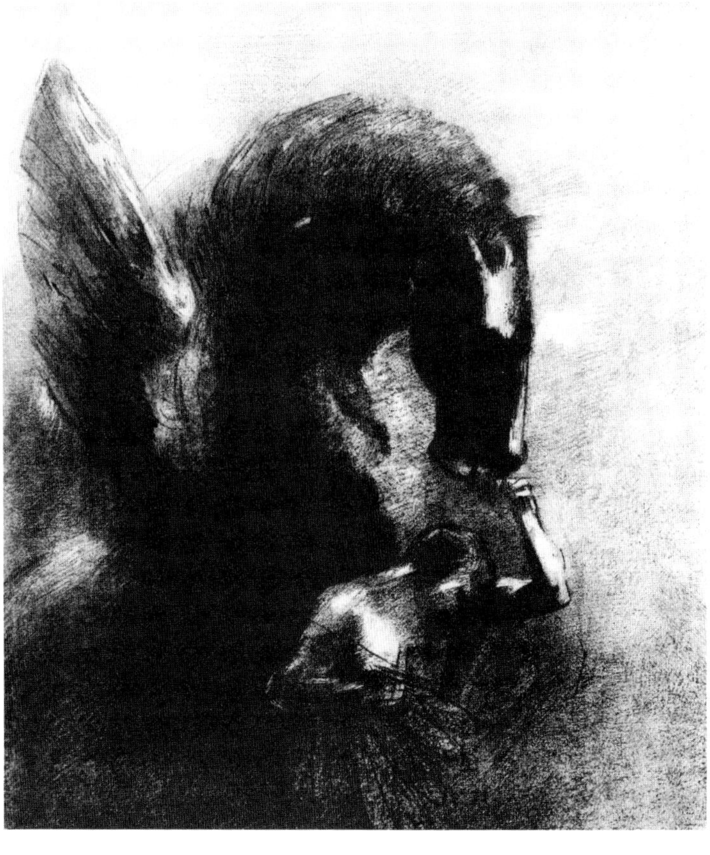

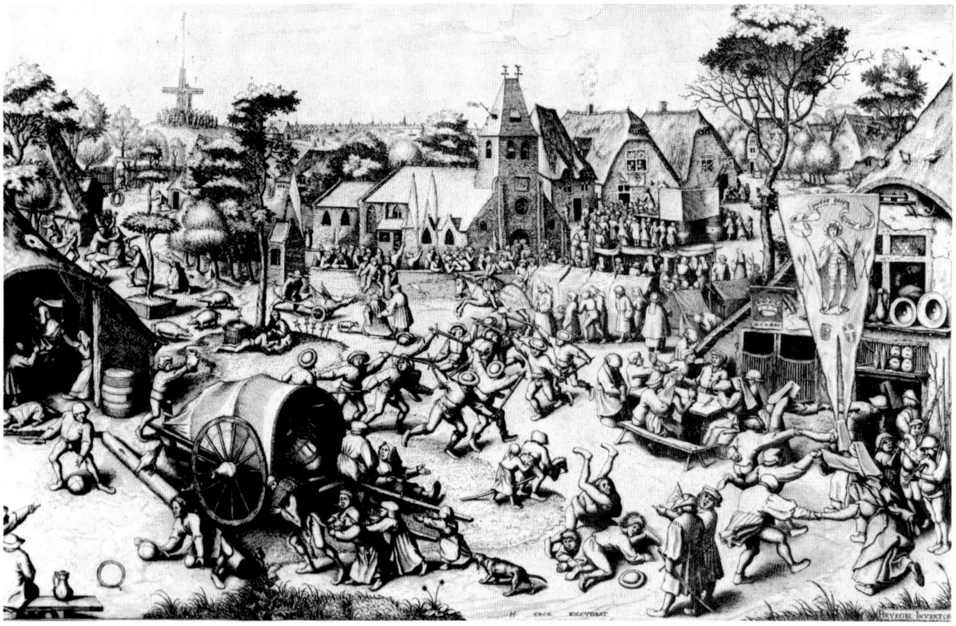

45.
After Pieter Brueghel the Elder (c. 1525–1569). Netherlandish. *The Fair of St. George's Day*, c. 1553. Engraving. 33 x 52 cm. (13 x 20½ in.). Private collection

The Public Meeting Place Where we gather publicly and what we do there have been fertile subjects for printmakers since the sixteenth century, when artists began in earnest to engage in social commentary. The gradual secularization of printed images can be broadly traced from Christianity in the fifteenth century, to mythology in the early sixteenth century, to daily communal life as that century passed its midpoint. One of the earliest masterpieces of this genre is Pieter Brueghel the Elder's image *The Fair of St. George's Day* (plate 45). The emergence of this theme reflected both an expanding freedom in subject matter, as artists more and more were permitted to express their individuality, and the growing power of the peasantry and townspeople. If any one common element can be perceived as we view these great "peoplescapes" over the centuries, it is a groundswell of collective energy at once exalting in its life-supporting assertion and frightening in its potential for group blindness and manipulation. Brueghel places us at a vantage point where we can scan his crowded scenes like helicopter-borne reporters four centuries later. We look down on a bewildering maze of activity as the village populace breaks out in celebration of a saint's day: dancing, swinging, chasing, wrestling, ball playing, musicmaking, drinking, fighting, playacting and churchgoing. Children's and adults' games and pleasures become sardonically interchangeable. Brueghel has coalesced this diverse, swarming activity into a serpentine pattern that coils with whiplash energy, and the surrounding buildings furnish entrances and exits for these movements, like makeshift structures in a modern amusement park. Even far off on the horizon, activity rages as archers compete to bring down a bird being turned on a pole atop a windmill. One can only

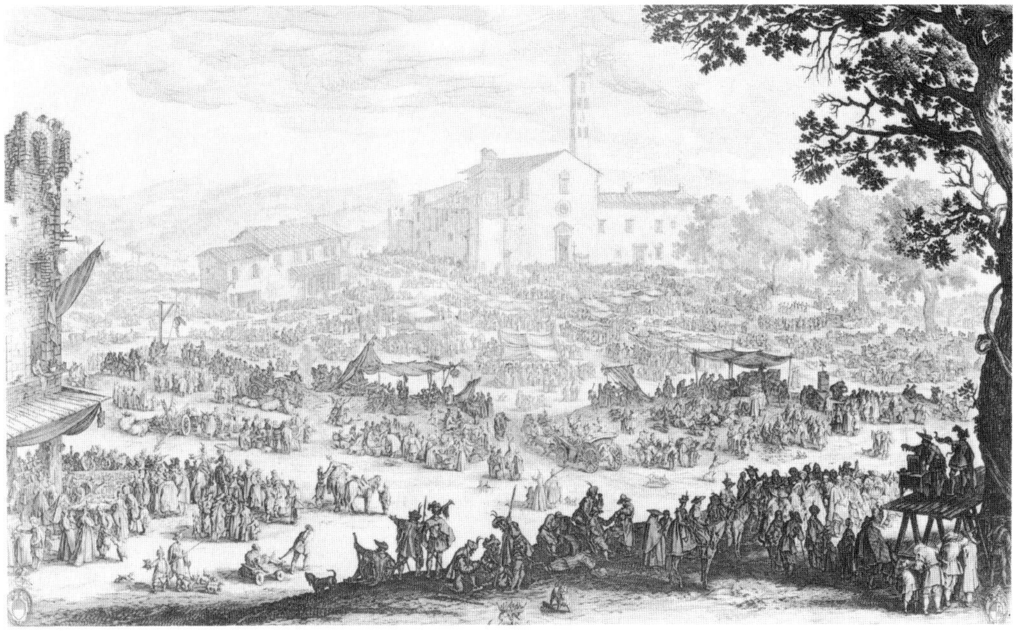

46.
Jacques Callot (1592–1635). French. *The Great Fair at Impruneta*, 1620. Etching. 43 x 66.6 cm. (17 x 26¼ in.). Metropolitan Museum of Art, New York, Harris Brisbane Dick Fund, 1917

imagine the number of separate studies the artist must have made in preparation for such an ambitious plate. This is one of the most remarkable aspects of his vision: the myriad, whirling whole is composed of many small groups of two to five figures, each individually modeled with a rich sculptural fullness but brought together to form subcompositions that have their own unity and make their own telling statements.

Jacques Callot was only twenty-eight years old and staying in Florence when he etched what is most likely the statistical tour de force of meeting-place prints, *The Great Fair at Impruneta* (plate 46): by actual count, 1138 people, 45 horses, 67 donkeys and 137 dogs are packed into one copperplate. Despite the bustling activity emanating from the huge fairground's numerous stalls, the artist directs us to a single disquieting detail. By slyly playing off light and shadow amid this vast multitude, he leads us from the courtesans in the left-center foreground along the shadow cast by the giant tree to the open-air theater below. The eye then travels right to left along a shadowy rise until we behold the familiar device of the hangman and the swaying figure doubled up in its final agony. It is a biting commentary on contemporary life: that human life is as expendable as the goods being hawked and that, in such a mass, individual compassion melts into collective indifference.

Nearly two centuries then passed before the technology of multiple-plate printing and aquatint enabled Philibert-Louis Debucourt to etch the chef d'oeuvre of printed color images of the eighteenth century, very likely the most ambitious work in color dealing with the public meeting place (colorplate 8, see page 38). Like the great Callot, Debucourt had something very specific to say on the subject. At one and the same time, he would portray the haut monde of the Paris of 1792 and indicate that its was a frivolous, skittish existence. That he succeeded superbly is apparent when one views this work. Scores of celebrities of the day are identifiable, from the Duc de Chartres (later King Louis Philippe; sprawled on four chairs) and the Duc d'Aumont (blowing a kiss, right center) to Goya's mulatto model (seated at the extreme left, in Spanish costume). The minute details of affected gesture and dress are extraordinary. No photographer of today, despite the powerful lenses and color emulsions at his disposal, could be so all-encompassing and freeze such a range of actions at the decisive, expressive moment to embody so successfully an epoch and its social strata. No witty commentary on a fashionable cocktail party of our own time has surpassed this etching in its visual analysis. The balancing act with the chairs is high theater (or cinema). In the overall composition the turbulent backdrop of chestnut trees symbolically repeats the crowded foreground and adds an ominous canopy. Does color really add to the portrayal? For this subject it works; in Goya's scathing *Caprichos* it would have been useless. The granular quality of aquatint in combination with the range of pretty pastel colors lends a subtle abrasiveness that jostles our perception.

A far cry from Debucourt's vision of impertinent high fashion in the gardens of the Palais Royal, John Sartain's view of Main Street in Midwestern America more than half a century later is full of the rowdiness and open skies of pioneer times (plate 47). In the distance can be seen a covered wagon moving out and three silhouetted horsemen galloping off to spread the results of the county election. The

47.
John Sartain (1808–1897). American. *The County Election*, 1854. Etching, engraving and mezzotint after George Caleb Bingham. 67 x 83.2 cm. (26⅜ x 32¾ in.). Private collection

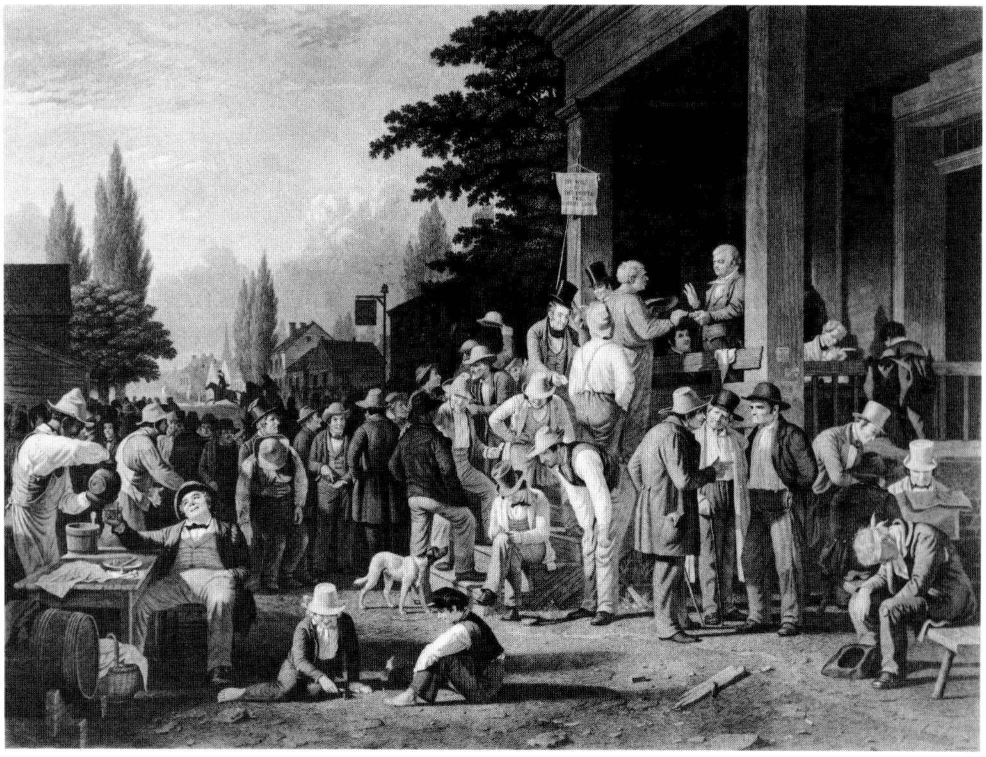

dog and the four figures flooded in light to the right of the dog lead our eyes up to the veranda where the victor is being sworn in. Higher up is a banner reading THE WILL OF THE PEOPLE THE SUPREME LAW. The swearing-in ceremony is actually placed at the apex of the long triangle that starts with the figure serving drinks at the extreme left and goes up the rise of wide-brimmed hats on the electorate, to the contrasting black high hats of two officials. The other side of the triangle descends to the slumped figure seated at the lower right. This subtly ingenious composition is given a memorable flint-rock clarity by a skillful combination of engraving, mezzotint and etching. Like the famous painting by George Caleb Bingham that it was made after, this work has earned its own renown as the most powerful example of genre printmaking in nineteenth-century America, particularly for its laconic, matter-of-fact yet solidly modeled approach to a local event. Most of the surviving impressions were hand-colored to simulate oil painting and were hung proudly in homes across the land as a symbol of the democratic process at a time when the Republic was a scant seven decades old and beginning to expand westward. But it is in the rarer uncolored black-and-white proofs that this engraving's precocious "photorealism" (there was no photography then) is most clearly in evidence.

Architecture and the Event Historical events can be inseparable from the architecture in or around which they took place. When the event was a major spectacle or fete, elaborate stage scenery—virtually architecture in its own right—was created as a setting, as with the famous Italian ballet of the seventeenth century and the *pompe* funerals of eighteenth-century France. Since such constructions and performances were short-lived, a truthful pictorial record of their existence was considered essential. By having these images engraved and etched, kings and their courts could commemorate the events by disseminating such images far and wide. No wonder, then, that Louis XV appointed one of France's ablest printmakers, Charles-Nicolas Cochin *fils*, as official illustrator of elaborate royal activities. Two such engravings (plates 48 and 49) eloquently serve their primary purpose. That the original designers of such spectacles were incomparable masters of illusion is clearly conveyed to us in the engraver's faithful renderings of their illusionistic triumphs. We can see how their presentations were immense set pieces within elaborate architectural environments. As we peer incredulously at these grandiose events of two or three centuries ago, our modern sensibilities find them bizarre and surrealistic.

The first state funeral of Marie Thérèse of Spain, Dauphine of France, was held in the Royal Abbey of Saint-Denis on September 5, 1746, and the second in Notre Dame on November 24. Cochin took this dual opportunity to commemorate the first event in side view and the

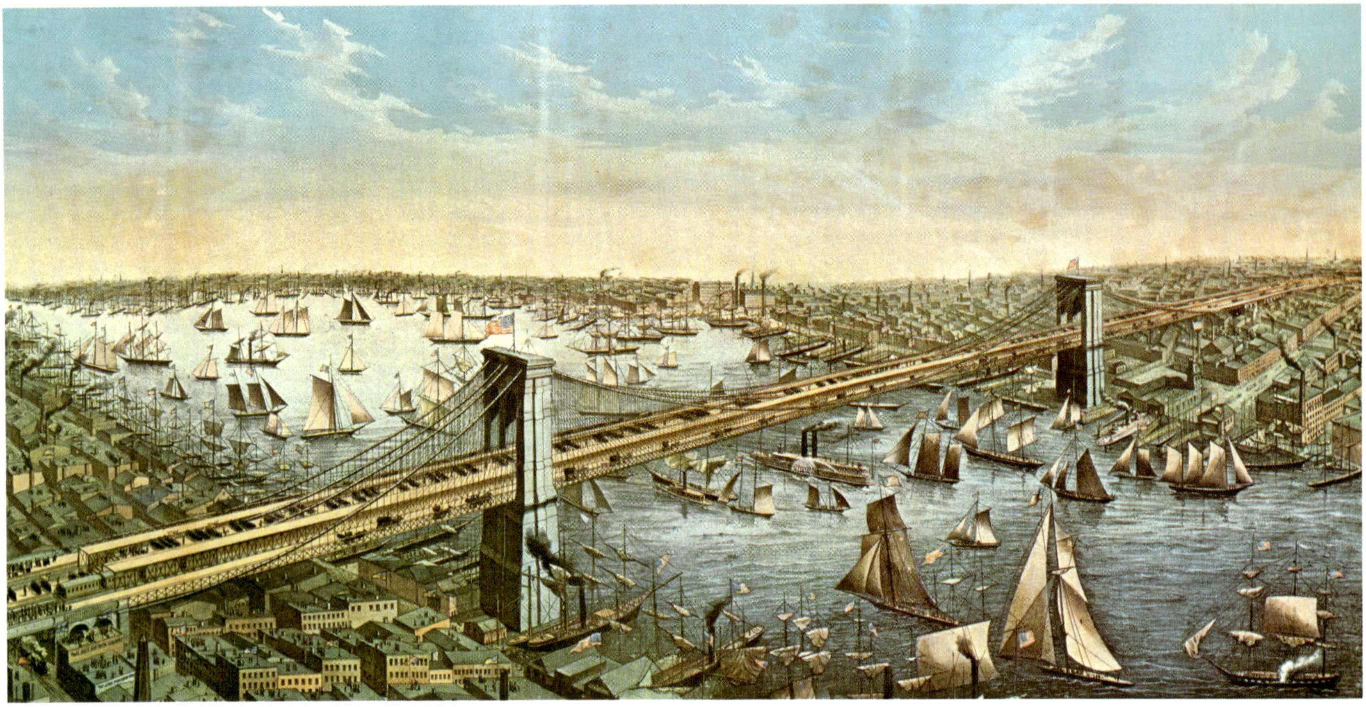

COLORPLATE 9

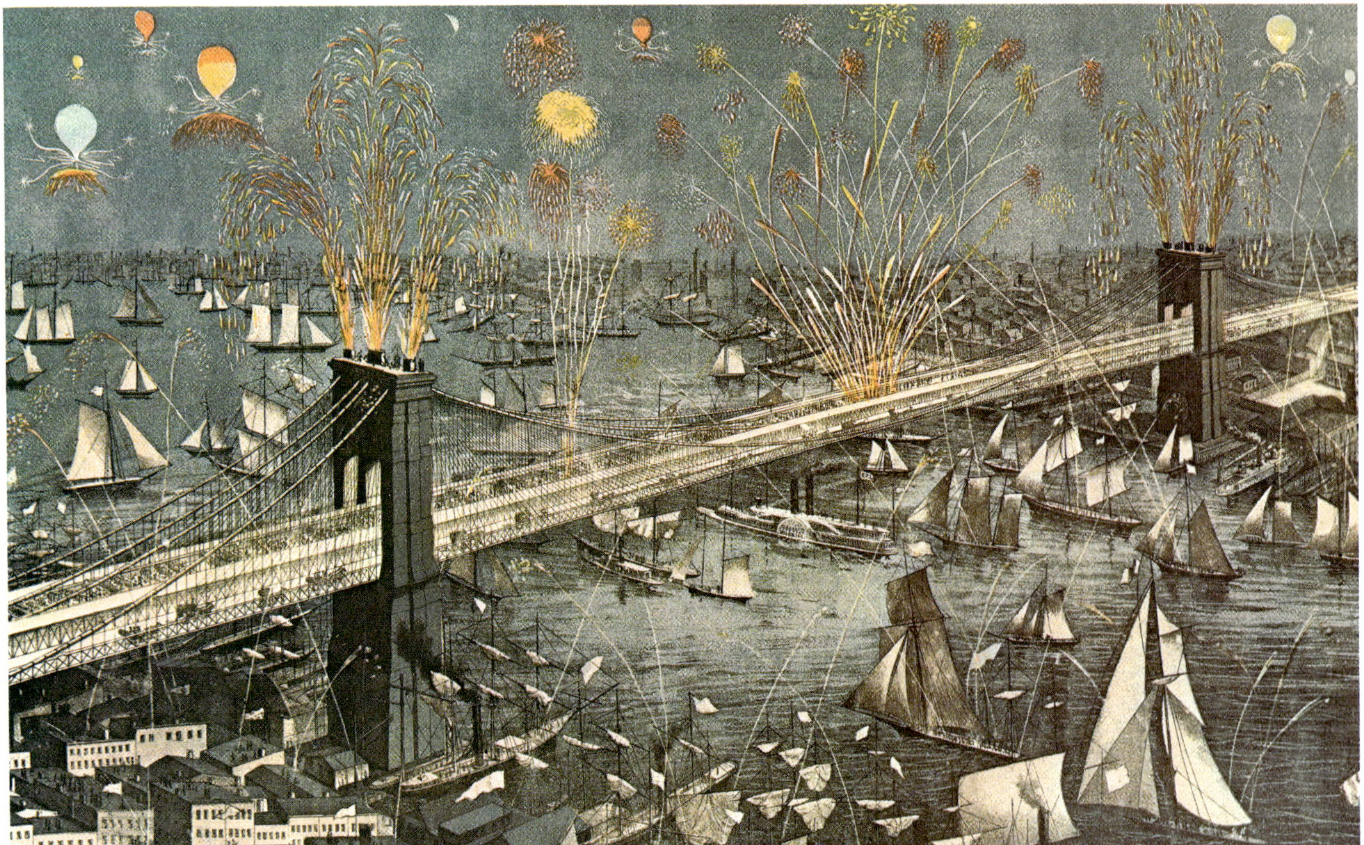

COLORPLATE 10

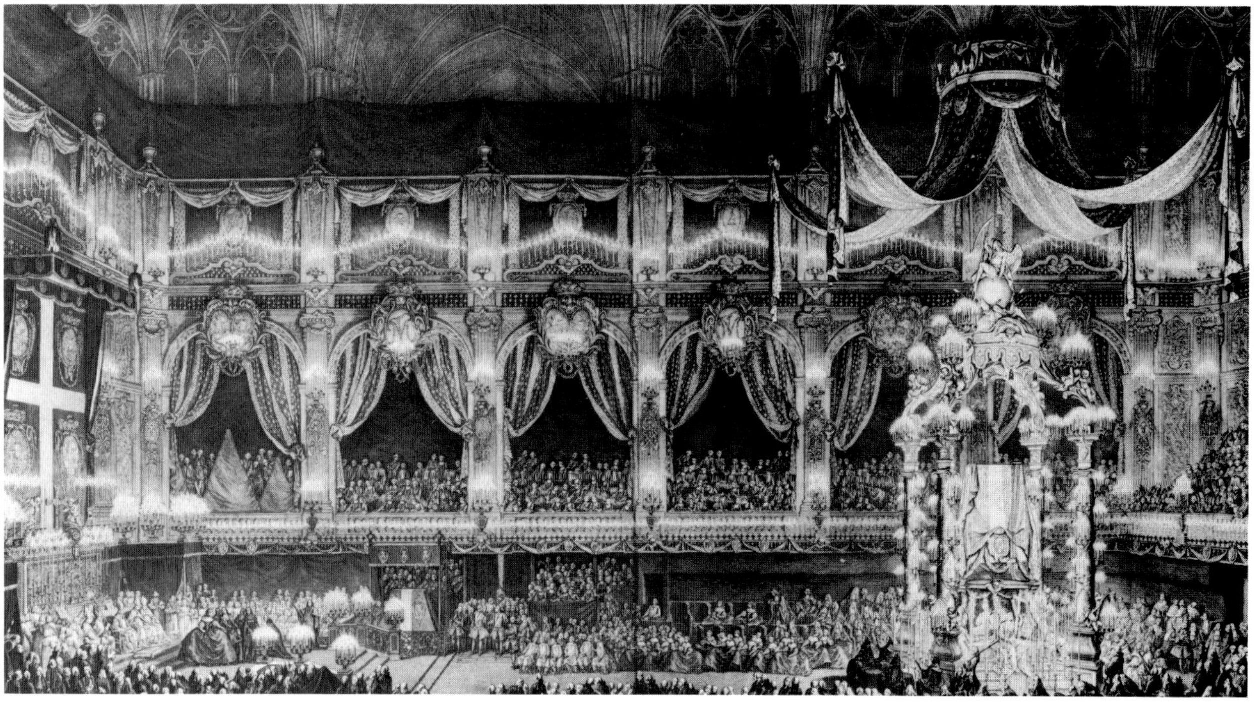

other in front view. Since the same construction was used for both occasions, we are virtually looking at the same extraordinary spectacle from two angles, as if television cameras had been placed in two locations. The chapel vaults tower above the temporary inner structures. Huge swaths of black fabric traverse the arched spaces with an airy nonchalance that belies their vast span. Our sense of scale is also upset by the inner construction, with its lavishly ornamented walls of skull motifs and tiers of seats for the assemblage. But it is the eerie lighting—thousands of candles strung like a necklace hundreds of feet long—and the mammoth festooned bier, with its shrouded forms and ominous canopy bearing skull and crossbones, that truly stagger belief. Cochin first blocked in his compositions with a light etched line as a guide for the heavier engraved line; by not engraving around the lights, he left the softly etched areas and the white of the paper to define the weird illumination. In this manner Cochin skillfully re-created the haunting pyrotechnics of these memorable events.

A pyrotechnic display of another order took place along the East River in New York in 1883. After thirteen years of construction the Brooklyn Bridge opened amid riotous acclaim, prompting two publishers of large lithographic views to memorialize the great event. We are again rewarded with a rare dual image (colorplates 9 and 10). Here the significant public event is the architecture itself and the celebration of its completion. First, one publisher issued a daytime version,

48.
Charles-Nicolas Cochin *fils* (1715–1790). French. *The State Funeral of Marie Thérèse of Spain, Dauphine of France, in the Church of the Royal Abbey of Saint-Denis, September 5, 1746.* Etching and engraving. 48.2 x 77.2 cm. (19 x 30⅜ in.). Cooper-Hewitt Museum, gift of The Council

Colorplate 9.
Bird's-eye View of the Great Suspension Bridge, published by Judge Co., 1883. Artist unknown. Lithograph. 45 x 91.5 cm. (17¾ x 36 in.). Brooklyn Museum, New York

Colorplate 10.
Bird's-eye View of the Great New York and Brooklyn Bridge, and Grand Display of Fire Works on Opening Night, published by A. Major Co., 1883. Artist unknown. Lithograph. 38.8 x 62.2 cm. (15¼ x 24½ in.). Metropolitan Museum of Art, New York, Edward W. C. Arnold Collection of New York Prints, Maps and Pictures. Bequest of Edward W. C. Arnold, 1954

49.
Charles-Nicolas Cochin *fils* (1715–1790). French. *The State Funeral of Marie Thérèse of Spain, Dauphine of France, in the Church of Notre Dame de Paris, November 24, 1746.* Etching and engraving. 49.2 x 33.2 cm. (19⅜ x 13⅛ in.). Cooper-Hewitt Museum, gift of The Council

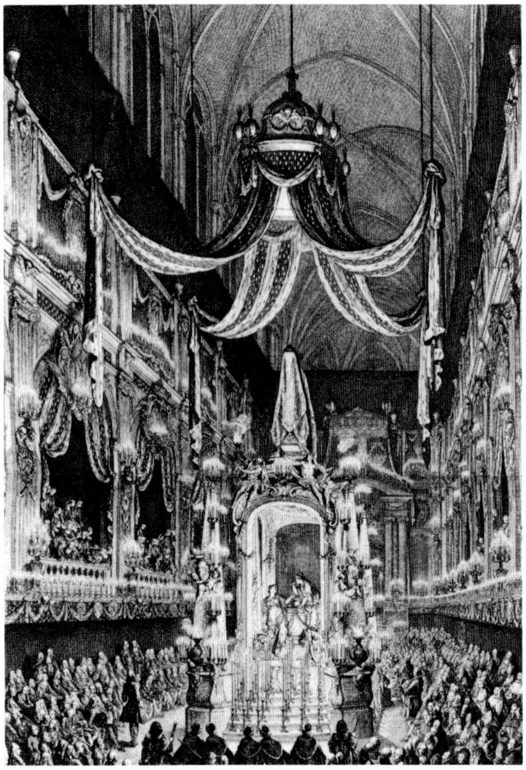

replete with a boat-clogged river. Then another enterprising firm reduced the length of the image at both ends, added a few more boats as well as the fireworks and balloons in the darkened sky, and issued a nighttime version. Although by that date a camera could have been hoisted by balloon for a daylight aerial shot, it apparently was not done, since these fine lithographs are our sole panoramic aerial views of this splendid occasion.

Thousands of "public occasion" works such as the four examples described here mark the history of the printmaker's art from the seventeenth through the nineteenth century, chronicling, for example, the history of theater, dance and architecture. Most of these prints are within the reach of collectors of all persuasions, thanks to their sizable numbers and lesser-known creators. Since public events usually involve people, there is a certain majestic relationship between man and architecture in many of these images.

Variations on Imaginary Objects: A Guide to Design In the eighteenth century, before a woodcarver began to work on a new set of ornate moldings for a client's paneled salon, he would first consult his books and albums of engravings, which presented hundreds of extremely detailed designs to choose from, some dating back generations in execution, style and motif. Such design compendiums were published for nearly every endeavor, from embroidery to stone carving, that demanded some original variation and elegant elaboration. Much of this enterprise involved the production of ornament for its own sake (for centuries surfaces almost existed only as a pretext for using decorative elements). The engraved or etched designs for this ornamentation are called *ornament prints*, but the term is not entirely accurate. Included among the so-called ornament prints are design guides that could be used in nondecorative pursuits such as architecture, science and sculpture. Four engravings of 1618 (plates 50–53), selected from a German book on perspective consisting of fifty-six plates, are examples of this type of guide. Carvers of stone and wood, metalworkers and the like may well have found ornamental applications for the four variations. But the conceptions in these engravings—works that reveal an artist with immense knowledge of perspective, modeling and architectonics and an indefatigable imagination for variants—must have helped innumerable later artists, designers and architects. One can only wonder how many students' imaginations were kindled by the engravings.

The author of the series should be hailed as an unsung hero of the aesthetic values of what seem to be merely ornament prints. Some three and a half centuries after their execution, the prints are as fresh, provocative and modern as avant-garde architecture, volumetric abstract sculpture and fantastic art. Everybody from Buckminster Fuller to Saul Steinberg seems somehow anticipated in these cunning images. Within the vast body of ornament prints are many such noteworthy opportunities for personal discovery. Elegance and wit; love of line, shadow, texture, material and illusion; fascination with the biomorphic, babies, women, beasts, digits and the alphabet—all this magnificent profusion, and more, awaits the viewer and collector.

50–53.
Jost Amman (1539–1591). Swiss. Four plates from *Perspectiva. Corporum Regularium*, Nuremberg, 1618. Engravings after Wenzel Jamnitzer. Each: 17.8 x 25.8 cm. (7 x 10⅛ in.). Cooper-Hewitt Museum, purchased in memory of David Wolfe Bishop

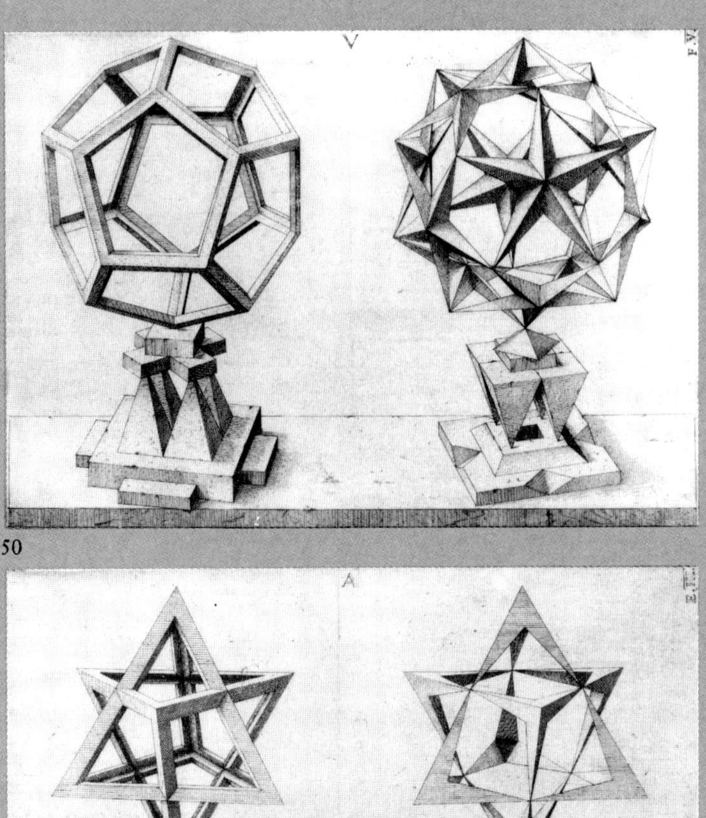

50

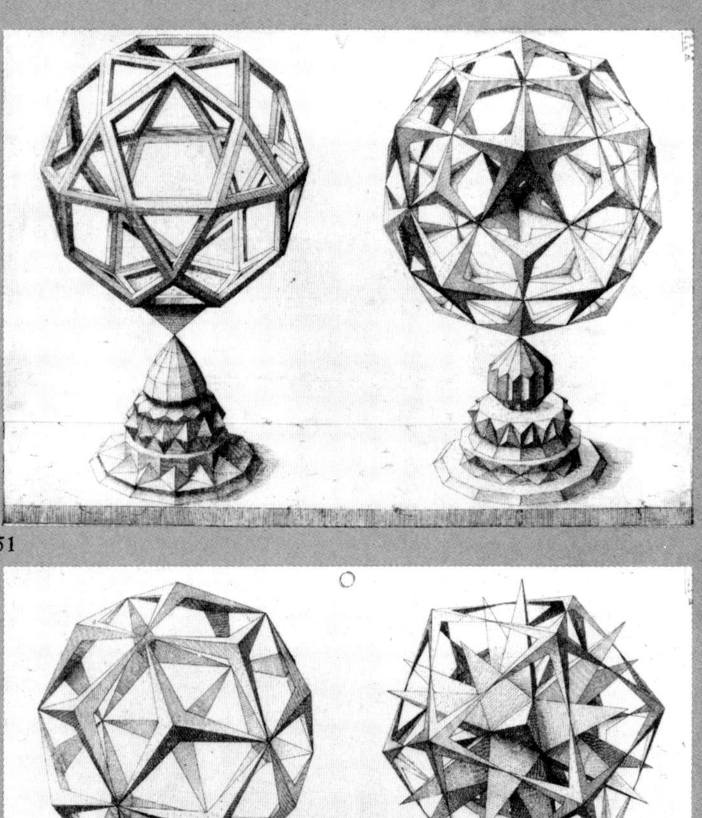

51

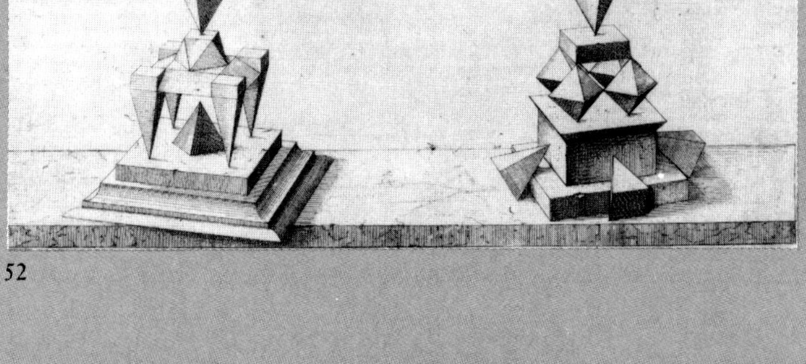

52

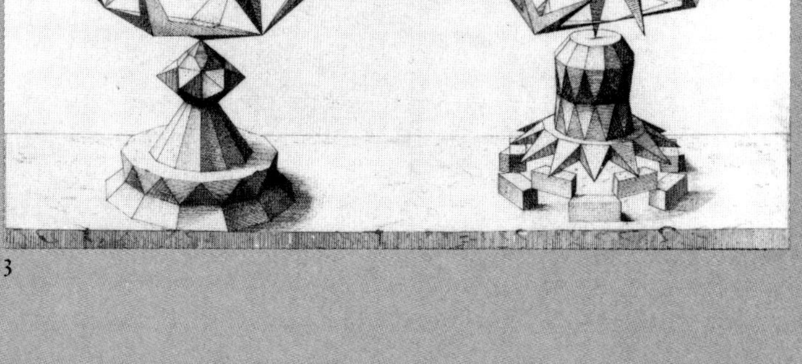

53

The Bestiary Man has continually endowed the beast with a variety of endearing or ambivalent characteristics. In the fifteenth century it was rare for artists, whose principal subject was Christianity, to portray an animal as their sole subject matter. In such early works the beast is seen mainly as a subsidiary or symbolic image, trailing subserviently behind man or perhaps taking the form of a devil-demon. Nor did myth generally provide positive or naturalistic opportunities for depiction of animals: in one oft-pictured instance, Black Forest folklore made the horse a courier of death.

The secularization of images in the sixteenth century gradually permitted artists to raise animals to a higher order of subject matter. Dürer's famed vision of a monstrous rhinoceros is the first major print to meticulously portray a lone animal (plate 54). The great German artist never saw what was then an exotic, relatively unknown creature (the rare specimen he pictured in this print had drowned while being transported from Portugal to Italy, to be examined at the Vatican). Drawn from verbal descriptions, Dürer's conception turns out—not surprisingly—to be half truth and half imaginative embellishment. The beast's massiveness is expressed by filling the picture plane almost to the bursting point. The contours of the rhinoceros touch three of the woodcut's borders, creating a strong sense of immediacy for the viewer. The protective structures of the hide are graven to look as formidable as the heavy battle armor of a medieval knight or his mount, and the reptilian scales emphasize the wild creature's prehistoric lineage. One has the impression that Dürer tried hard to be objective, to envision the rhinoceros on its own terms. Despite the beast's fearsomely aggressive image, accentuated by the huge horn on its snout, the animal somehow transcends this and in the artist's sympathetic characterization becomes an accessible creature.

The beast has also been an enduring source of satire and biting social commentary. Such an image (plate 55), extraordinary in its composition, its modeling with light and shadow and its use of the technical medium, was etched by Goya in the twilight of his life as one of the *Disparates* series (see page 63 for comment on this series). In *Other Laws for the People*, priests and lawgivers, in attitudes conveying a mixture of piousness, pomposity and fear, hold up a law code before an immense immobile elephant, as if expecting the huge beast's comprehension and obedience. The animal, symbolizing the susceptible mass of the people yet unaware of its great potential force, gapes at the learned men's gesture, its oddly staring eye expressing an unspeakable judgment. Goya has strongly contoured his etched lines along the elephant's powerful legs up through its raised, tensed back—visually heightening the strain and irony of this symbolic confrontation. The great painter of the bullfight placed the action in the blinding light of an abstract arena, whose sweeping hatched curve echoes the

54.
Albrecht Dürer (1471–1528). German. *Rhinoceros*, 1515. Woodcut. 24 x 30.3 cm. (9½ x 12 in.). Cooper-Hewitt Museum, gift of Leo Wallerstein

55.
Francisco Goya (1746–1828). Spanish. *Other Laws for the People*, c. 1816. Etching and aquatint from *Disparates*. 24.4 x 35.3 cm. (9⅝ x 13⅞ in.). Cooper-Hewitt Museum, gift of Mrs. A. W. Erickson

56.
Eugène Delacroix (1798–1863). French. *Royal Tiger*, 1829. Lithograph. 32.5 x 46 cm. (12¾ x 18⅛ in.). Metropolitan Museum of Art, New York, bequest of Mrs. H. O. Havemeyer, 1929. H. O. Havemeyer Collection

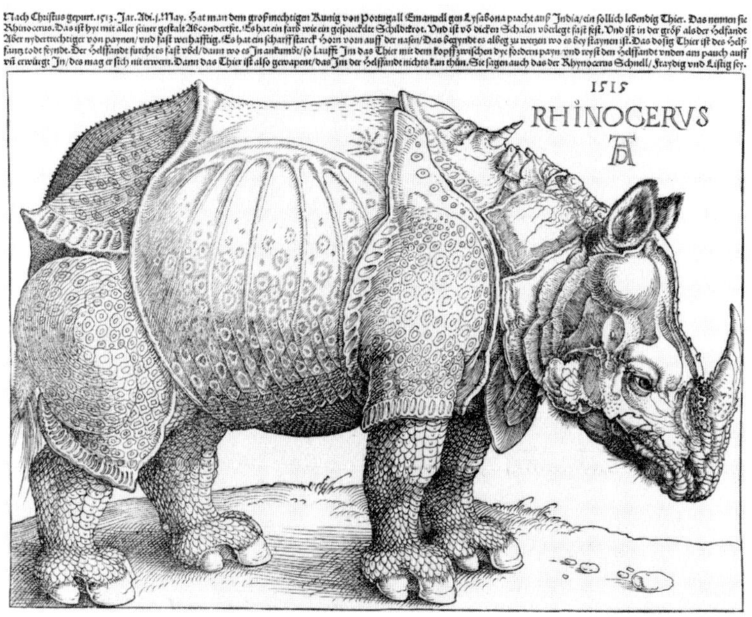

54

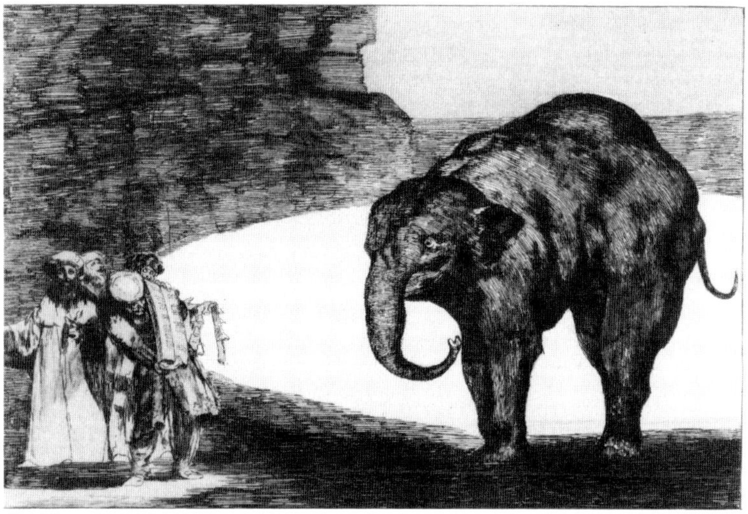

55

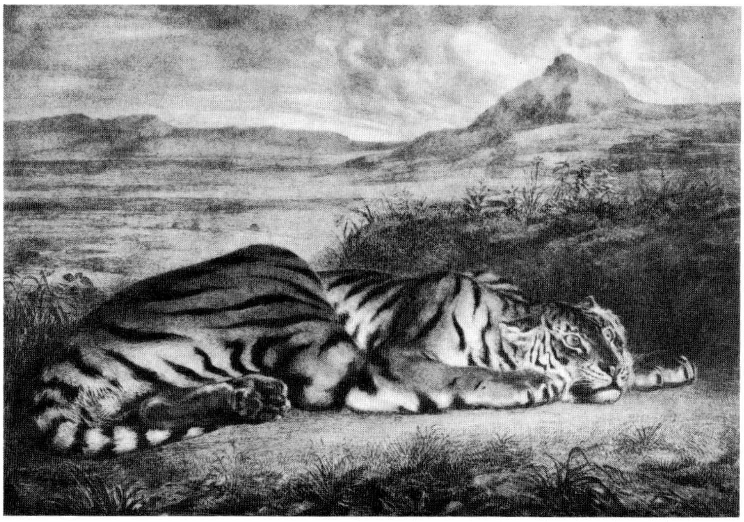

56

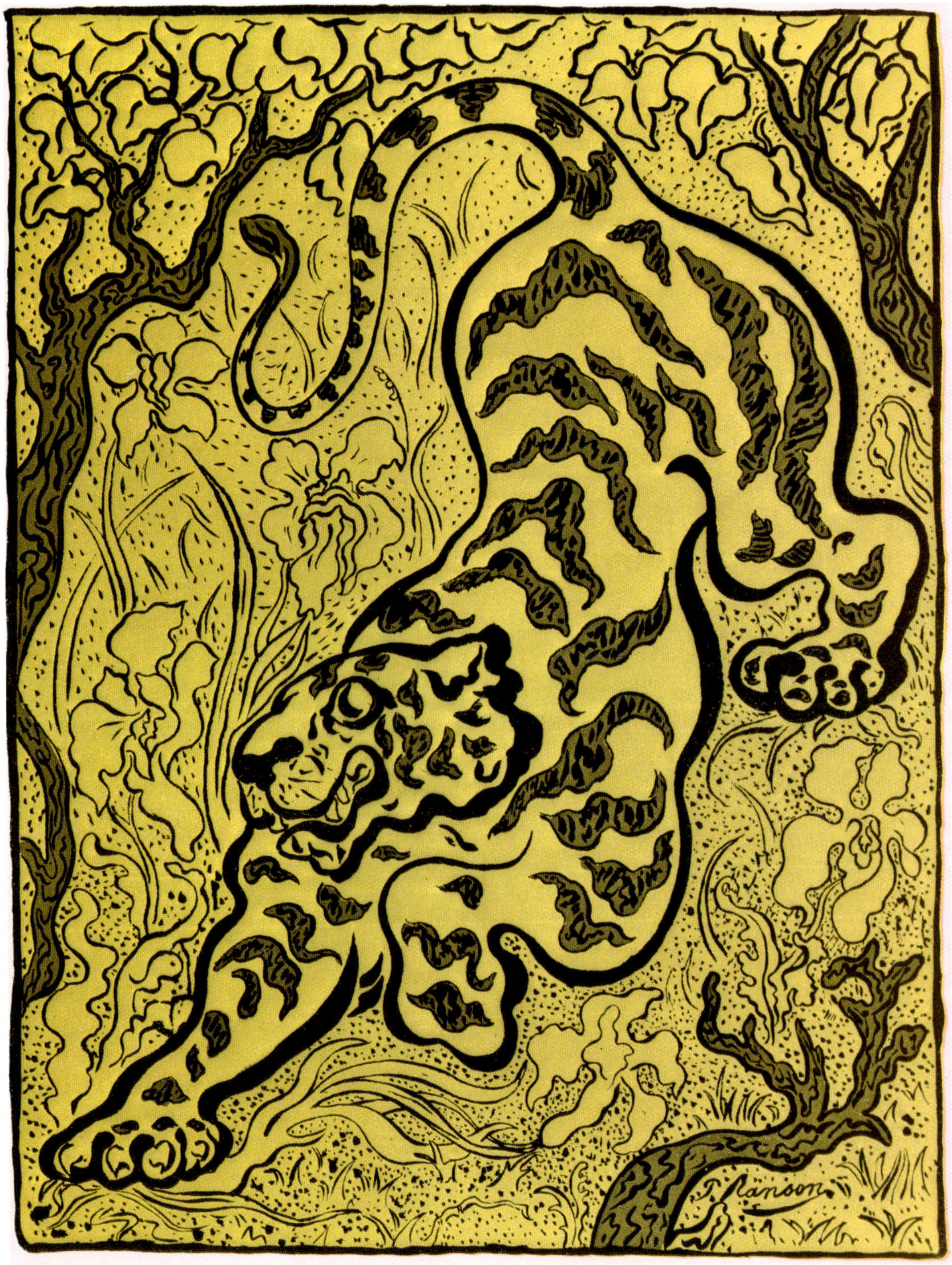

Colorplate 11

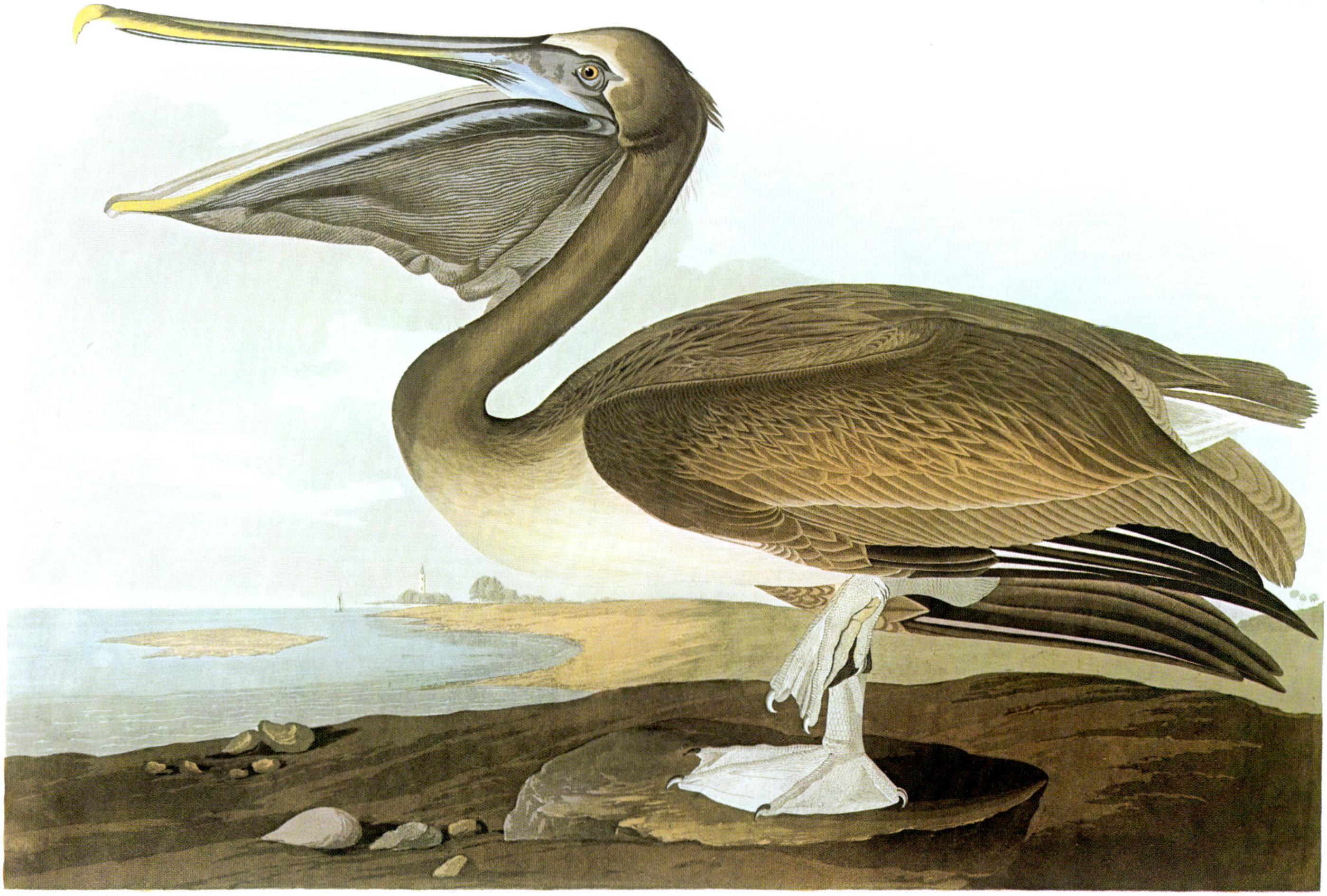

COLORPLATE 12

Colorplate 11.
Paul Ranson (1862–1909). French. *Tiger in the Jungle*. Lithograph from *L'Estampe originale*, 1893. 37 x 28.6 (14½ x 11¼ in.). Museum of Modern Art, New York, gift of Neal A. Prince

Colorplate 12.
Robert Havell, Jr. (1793–1878). American. *Brown Pelican*. Engraving and watercolor after John James Audubon from *The Birds of America*, 1827–38. 62.9 x 95 cm. (24¾ x 37⅜ in.). Private collection

linear marking used in the elephant's trunk and its overall inky mass.

The nineteenth-century romantics had far different visions of animals, typified by Eugène Delacroix's masterpiece in lithography, *Royal Tiger* (plate 56). The French painter sketched his tiger's anatomy in the Paris zoo, but then placed the graceful creature on a windswept African plain. Using a technique he helped pioneer—scratching fine lines in the inked stone to make light tones out of dark, similar to the method in wood engraving—Delacroix achieved effects that were perfectly mated with his subject. The tiger's accentuated jet-black stripes have become like forked and furrowed charges of electricity, leading toward and culminating exquisitely around the head and eyes, the cerebral zone where action is triggered. Implied in the deceptive posture of repose is all the deadly swiftness of the tiger: ever alert, the beast is ready to spring in a second. This masterful interpretation of coiled strength has never been surpassed. Delacroix has sprawled the great cat across most of the length of his composition; the viewer seems but a few feet away, can almost touch the raised whiskers. The surrounding soft grays of the landscape recede into the hazy distance, and the overall gray of the tiger's fur is warm and lustrous.

Another lithograph of a tiger, dated more than six decades later, reflects how style and attitudes had evolved (colorplate 11). Paul Ranson's highly stylized prancing tiger comes roaring at us as if the artist were paying tongue-in-cheek homage to Delacroix's earlier image. Comparisons are fascinating: one image is romantically realistic; the other is schematic, a bold flat pattern verging on the comic. Ranson brushed in the continuous serpentine contour line in a manner reminiscent of fluid Oriental brushwork, which had had significant influence on the prevailing Art Nouveau movement in Paris. Again, even though quite different from Delacroix's, the style perfectly matches the reality of the subject in its riot of vibrating stripes and spots. This stalking tiger is a caricature of burly blithesomeness. Wild orchids, repeating this vivacity, seem to quiver provocatively as they are sprung apart by the tiger's diagonal course. And the overall ground tone of bright yellow further unifies the composition, enhancing the effect of a pennant or tapestry design, its surface filled with pattern from edge to edge.

Two decades later, with Europe on the brink of World War I, Franz Marc produced his turbulent *Genesis II* (colorplate 1, see page 6). Marc's mystical expressionism was most often manifested in animals, principally horses, deer and cattle, seen as the common denominator of cosmic creation. For this woodcut, the artist cut three blocks, each for printing a different color. The velocity of the swirling, gaseous clouds is conveyed by powerful concentric cuts of the knife, organically fusing the charged primordial atmosphere with the coiled animal forms.

The artist who more than any other presented wildlife on its own terms was the American naturalist John James Audubon, whose folio *The Birds of America* is an unparalleled visual investigation. Audubon searched out birds in the remote wilderness if they were not accessible for study in captivity. Revealing a faithfulness down to the minutest detail, his renderings are actual size, so that the bird is not misrepresented by an artist's reduction or enlargement. *Brown Pelican* (colorplate 12) is a marvelous example of Audubon's scrupulous accuracy; since this species is large and streamlined, the resultant image is impressive in scale and design. The bird's habitat is also a factual rendering (Key Biscayne, Florida), and an exact time frame is identified (the subtitle reads *Young, First Winter*). The admirable balance of such a great bird on one webbed foot adds to the momentary air of expectancy, and the huge open bill suggests its fish-catching ability. The artist's role in the implied action and in the beautiful design thus seems relatively passive, as a diligent recorder of nature's reality. The natural attributes of the pelican dictated these visual innuendos; Audubon's genius was to record them with respectful awe and perseverance. He achieved a monumental objectivity, and to this day his effort remains the most authentic compendium on the subject. What makes *Brown Pelican* a work of art as well as a naturalist's document is its particular mode of execution. The American artist Robert Havell, Jr., engraved the image directly from unfinished watercolors by Audubon and supervised the subtle hand-coloring of each impression. The clarity and depth of the engraved line aided in producing the fine detail and the convincing illusion of sculptural weight and volume.

Wide-Angle Fantasy Imagination is the lifeblood of artistic creation, and fantasy is imagination's free-roving outcome. We all fantasize, and modern theory holds that we dream to relieve ourselves of daytime anxieties, of our limitations and those of the real world. In effect, our dreams drain off our fantasies. Imagine, then, what it would be like to publish such deeply personal expressions of our psyche so that the world was free to view, judge and perhaps be influenced by their imagery. Artists exercise this sort of self-exposure, of spiritual openness, when they scan their own reveries and try to convert them into images that others can understand. Since fantasy stretches the limits of the real world, its imagery is usually complex and incongruous, drawn from a divergent range of circumstances, persons and objects. To encompass such rich pictorial visions, artists have stretched their viewing frame into a kind of wide-angle spectacle not without similarity to the various wide-screen cinema processes. They have done this not simply in format but also through a distinct type of vision that has a broad sweep capable of taking in many details.

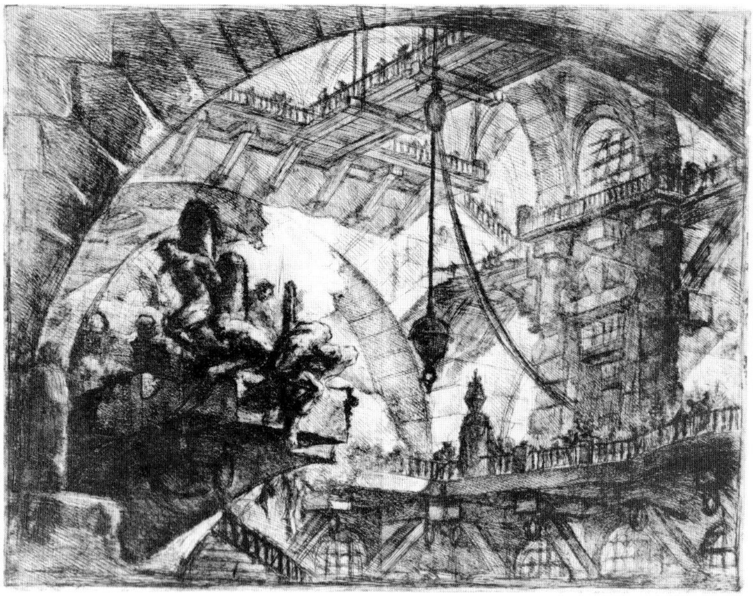

57

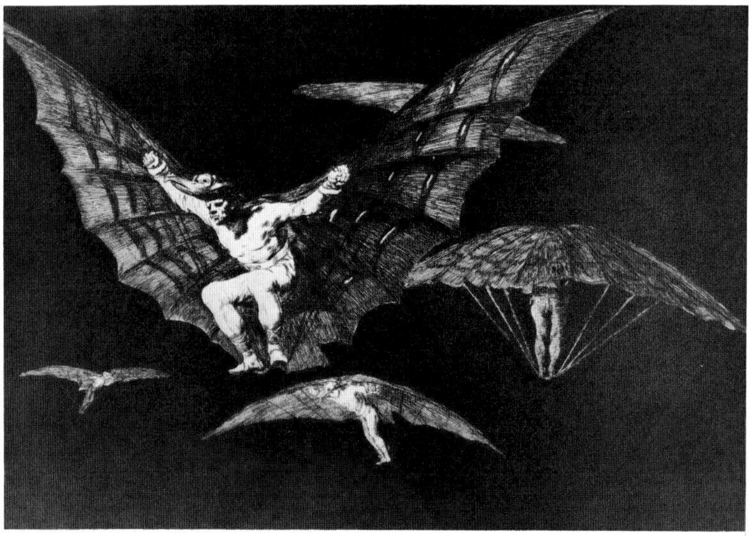

58

57.
Giovanni Battista Piranesi (1720–1778). Italian. *A Vast Gallery*, c. 1745. Etching from *Invenzioni Capric di Carceri*. 41 x 54 cm. (16⅛ x 21¼ in.). Private collection

58.
Francisco Goya (1746–1828). Spanish. *A Way of Flying*, c. 1816. Etching and aquatint from *Disparates*. 24.5 x 35.3 cm. (9⅝ x 13⅞ in.). Cooper-Hewitt Museum, gift of Mrs. A. W. Erickson

Such wide-angle images emerge with frequency beginning in the mid-eighteenth century, finally free of anecdotal ties to religion, myth and history that had inhibited a thorough, unabashed excursion into the mind. Giovanni Battista Piranesi was only in his mid-twenties when he etched his "dream prisons" series (*Invenzioni Capric di Carceri*), the first such imaginative exploration in printmaking by a major artist (plate 57). These prints may also be the most modern images, in terms of abstract freedom of composition and gestural verve, produced in the eighteenth century. Aldous Huxley, author of *Brave New World*, was so moved by Piranesi's phantasmagoria that he devoted a book to the series, in which he attempted to plumb the Kafkaesque implications of these dream visions, with their precarious ledges, spectrally populated balustrades, gangplanks that lead nowhere, and ominous networks of pulleys and cables. The son of a stonemason and engineer, Piranesi was trained as an architect. His feverish projections of vast and intricate enclosed spaces were consonant with his background.

In his early seventies Goya etched what is an equally renowned set of fantasies, *Disparates* (loosely, "incongruities"), also known as *Los Proverbios*. His largest and most ambitious aquatints, they reach into the furthest realms of his subconscious. Their only rival in his oeuvre are the great *pinturas negras* ("black paintings") he was executing on the walls of his Quinta del Sordo ("deaf man's villa") during the same period. *A Way of Flying* (plate 58) is Goya's fanciful, instinctive comment on dreams. One of the commonest phenomena in human dream activity is the sensation of flying. Goya's inky night sky —a vibrant field of aquatint—visually evokes the amorphous space-time in which dreams, and free-flying subconscious fantasy, occur. At the same time, the artist conveys irony and helplessness. The pitiful bird masks atop the heads of the flying figures and the precarious, makeshift winged supports and cables on which the bodies are suspended express a frightening predicament: human beings are captives of their own terror-filled nightmares, and even fluttering flights beyond reason offer little consolation.

James Ensor's teeming vision *The Entry of Christ Into Brussels in 1889* (plate 59) is sheer stream of consciousness. Such an amalgam of dreamlike fragments is so bizarre and outlandish that it strains any storytelling frame, let alone the conventions of Christian iconography. Ensor perches the spectator in a position similar to one a modern photographer might choose: the view is head-on as the vast parade ap-

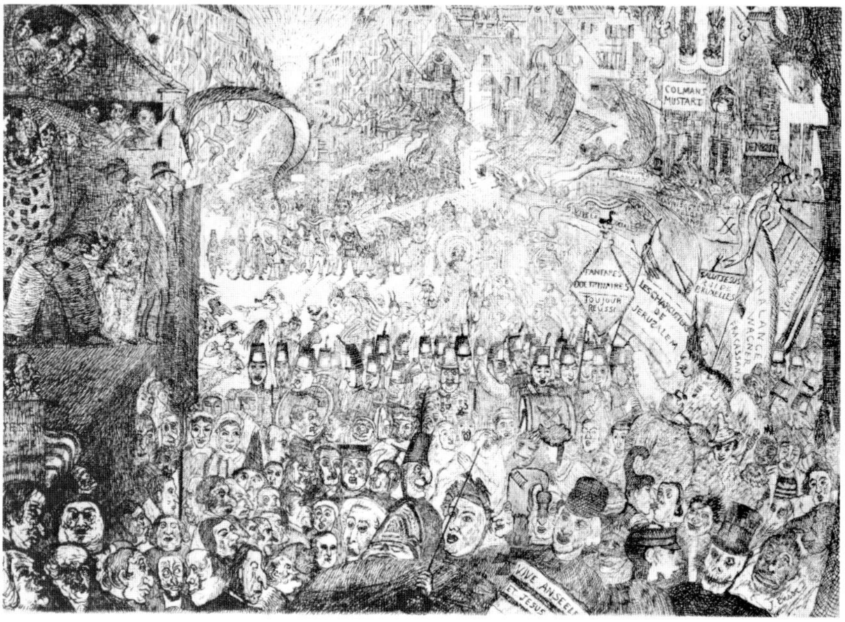

59.
James Ensor (1860–1949). Belgian. *The Entry of Christ Into Brussels in 1889*, 1898. Etching. 24.8 x 35.5 cm. (9¾ x 14 in.). Private collection

proaches. The procession stretches back to the horizon of the wide boulevard, where the sun is rising, raking its first beams over the tumultuous event. The flag-decked architecture and onlookers' dress indicate a scene contemporary with the artist: the city of Brussels at the end of the nineteenth century. Christ has returned; the giant parade is the welcome and entourage for his reentry. In the advance phalanx Christ is preceded by a military band led by a heavily bemedaled officer. In front of them are thick-necked city officials, businessmen, politicians and a skeletal Death in a high hat. Surrounding Christ, who rides a donkey and radiates four concentric halos, are rows of carnival-like, weirdly masked revelers. An enormous sickle-shaped banner coils in the air like a giant question mark.

The incongruity of the scene is mind-boggling, even before we read the many ironic or paradoxical placards and signs held by the marchers or festooned along their path. Some examples, translated into English: "The Sausage Shop of Jerusalem" (this sign, borne on a military flagstaff topped by a butcher's knife, alludes to war's carnage and the nonexistence of pork sausage in the Holy City); "Welcome, Jesus, King of Brussels" (local chauvinism); "The Flemish Movement" (the long-standing ambition of the Flemish minority in Belgium to secede). The message of "Colmans Mustard" needs no translation. Ensor painted the same panoramic subject in his largest and most ambitious canvas. But this black-and-white etched version, demonstrating again what extraordinary detail and nuance of line can be achieved by the intaglio process, does not need color to heighten its frenzied effect.

Man's Inhumanity to Man The horrors of war and civil strife remained virtually an untouchable theme in Western printmaking from the onset of the art during the late Middle Ages until well into the seventeenth century, when Jacques Callot became the first artist to portray the effects of war in any comprehensive detail. He was a frequent eyewitness to the devastating campaigns of the religious wars that seesawed across Lorraine in 1632–33. To encompass the spectrum of mass murder, torture, plunder, starvation and poverty, Callot swiftly delivered (published in Paris in 1633) his *Miseries of War*, Western art's first indictment in serial form of the horror of war.

The series opens dramatically with *Hanging*, probably the most memorable of the images (plate 60). Like all the plates, this etching is virtually a miniature. Just such a decision regarding scale reflects the particular genius of Callot, who could readily etch much larger copperplates as well (plate 46, see page 49). By working small, yet in a panoramic format, he was able to achieve a potent double effect; all the necessary details of wide-scan vision are there. The batteries of soldiers at the far left and right, the haughty commanding officers and

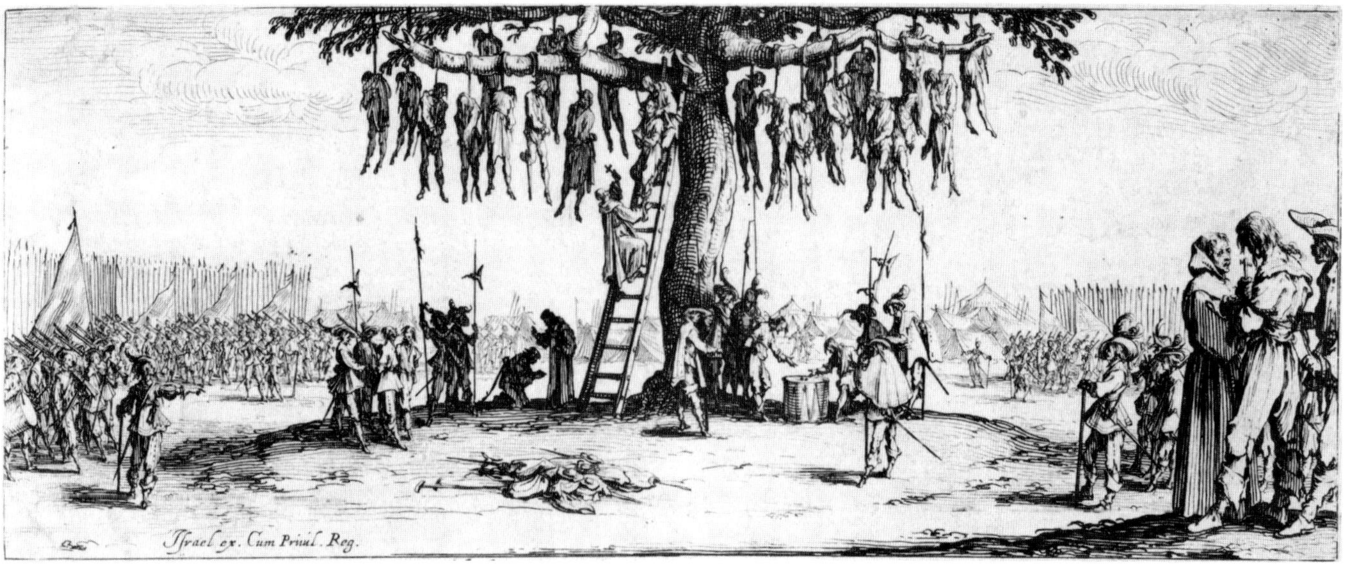

60.
Jacques Callot (1592–1635). French. *Hanging.* Etching from *Les Misères et les Mal-Heurs de la Guerre*, 1633. 8.1 x 18.8 cm. (3⅛ x 7⅜ in.). Private collection

the three priests giving final absolution are seen clearly, thanks to the distinctly sharp etched line. The clustered mortal fruit of war revealed on the giant central tree is such an electrifying sight that the work's size expands in our psyche; in its pathos and irony, the tiny etching fills us with such revulsion that it becomes mural size in its effect on our minds. The artist's sophisticated, even elegant linework and modeling, suitable to the elegant attire and weaponry of seventeenth-century warfare, serve as a stunning foil for what is actually happening: wholesale, methodical murder. It is the realization of this gentlemanly method—so pat and regulated—that sends chills through us. Callot, by brilliantly positioning the huge limbs of the gallows tree along the picture's upper border, has made the hideous mass of dead bodies appear to be dangling from the actual edge of the paper.

The world waited nearly two centuries for the next call of conscience as the result of an artist's direct contact with the carnage of war. Goya found himself in the middle of the Napoleonic invasion of Spain; six long years of attrition indelibly impressed war's imagery on the aging artist's mind. In homage to Callot's series, Goya named his own series of eighty plates *The Disasters of War. What Is the Use of One Cup?* (plate 61) is in marked contrast with Callot's effort in that Goya has brought us excruciatingly close to the sufferings of the noncombatant victims. At the same time that Goya opted for this proximity, he isolated the huddled forms in a horizonless sea of rough-graveled aquatint that smolders like ashes. The offering of sustenance to the one barely surviving figure does nothing to restore the dead children, ravaged woman and other corpses knotted in this pathetic group. The etched lines are few, and the aquatint texture is fiercely simple in its allover distribution. What we have here is an absolute masterpiece of visual terseness, of expressive understatement. What needed to be said has been said, with the same eloquent concision found in the poignant yet scathing title itself.

The third major series on the horror and tragedy of war was conceived by Otto Dix during World War I, when the artist saw action as a German soldier. He employed etching, drypoint and aquatint to produce the fifty plates on the theme that were published in 1924. The nightmarish *Bombing of Lens* is the most prophetic of the series, and

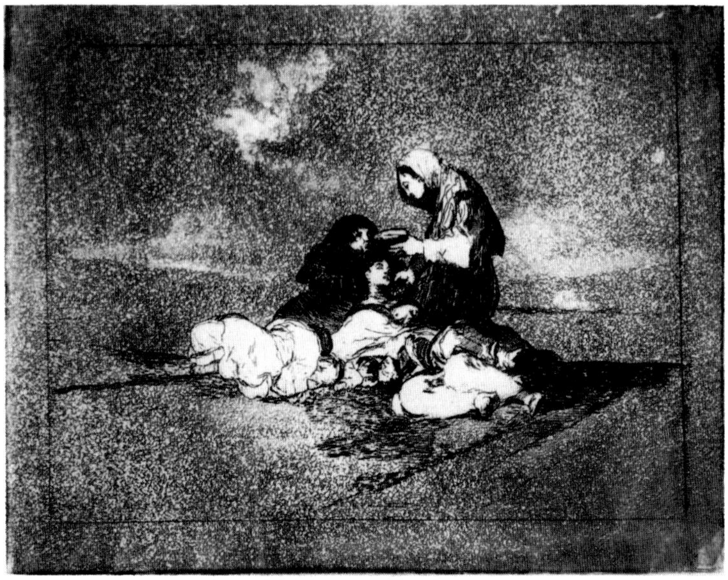

61

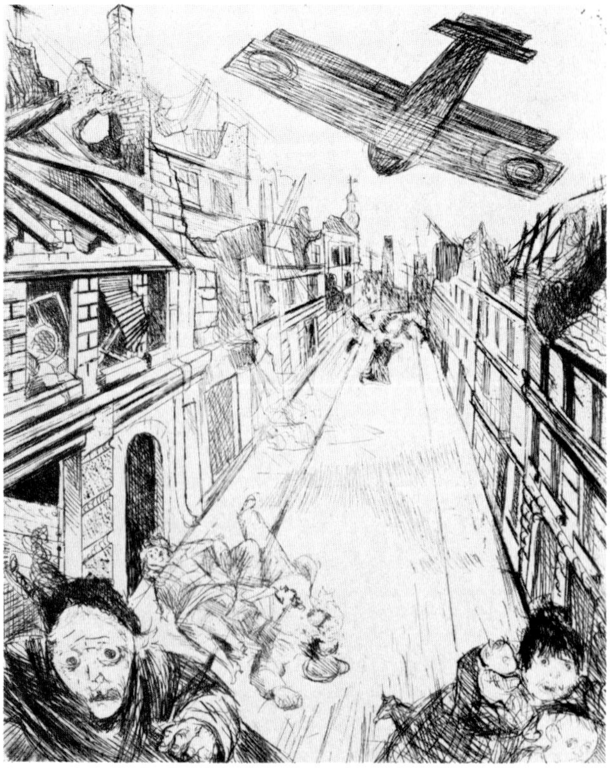

62

61.
Francisco Goya (1746–1828). Spanish. *What Is the Use of One Cup?*, c. 1810–20. Etching and aquatint from *Los Desastres de la Guerra*. Work proof before published state. 15.5 x 20.5 cm. (6⅛ x 8⅛ in.). Private collection

62.
Otto Dix (1891–1969). German. *Bombing of Lens*. Etching and drypoint from *Der Krieg*, 1924. 30 x 24.5 cm. (11¾ x 9⅝ in.). Museum of Modern Art, New York, gift of Abby Aldrich Rockefeller

for this reason perhaps the most powerful (plate 62). Drawn mainly with the drypoint needle, the composition gains a sense of immediacy and urgency through the informal, rapid manner of execution. The rushing, converging lines of one-point perspective make the street into a kind of white pathway for the merciless intruding aircraft (a blackbird of death) and its machine-gun strafing. The terrorized family in the foreground flees in the opposite direction, toward the viewer. One can almost hear the scratching of the drypoint needle; it is as if the lines are making their own shrieking sound. More than a decade before Picasso painted *Guernica*, Dix became the first major artist to describe swift death raining down from the skies on a helpless civilian population.

In 1920 Georges Rouault began work on the fifty-eight plates of his monumental *Misery and War* (later called simply *Miserere*), the fourth great series on the subject of war. Again, the artist chose a title harking back to Callot's series. *The Nobler the Heart, the Less Stiff the Collar* is a timeless portrait of self-righteousness and arrogance made dangerous by power derived from military rank (plate 63). Rather than showing us war's victims, as do Callot, Goya and Dix, Rouault brings us a close-up portrait of an individual source of inhumanity. His subject is a German officer whose stern pointing gesture embodies the lethal, yet facile, commands of war. The title of the aquatint is the converse of the reality presented; we are made to understand the

63.
Georges Rouault (1871–1958). French. *The Nobler the Heart, the Less Stiff the Collar*, 1926. Aquatint, etching and other processes from *Miserere*, 1948. 58.5 x 42.3 cm. (23 x 16⅝ in.). Museum of Modern Art, New York, gift of the artist

64.
Käthe Kollwitz (1867–1945). German. *Killed in Action*, 1921. Lithograph. 41 x 38 cm. (16⅛ x 15 in.). Cooper-Hewitt Museum, purchased in memory of Mrs. Samuel W. Bridgham

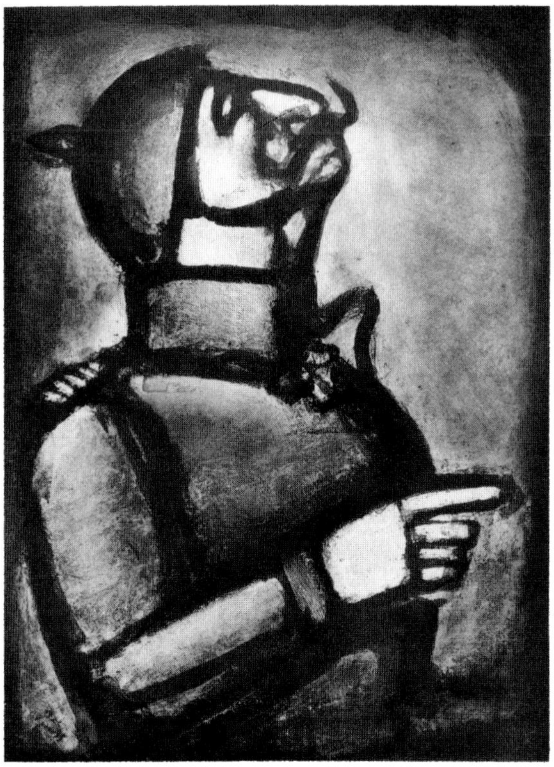
63

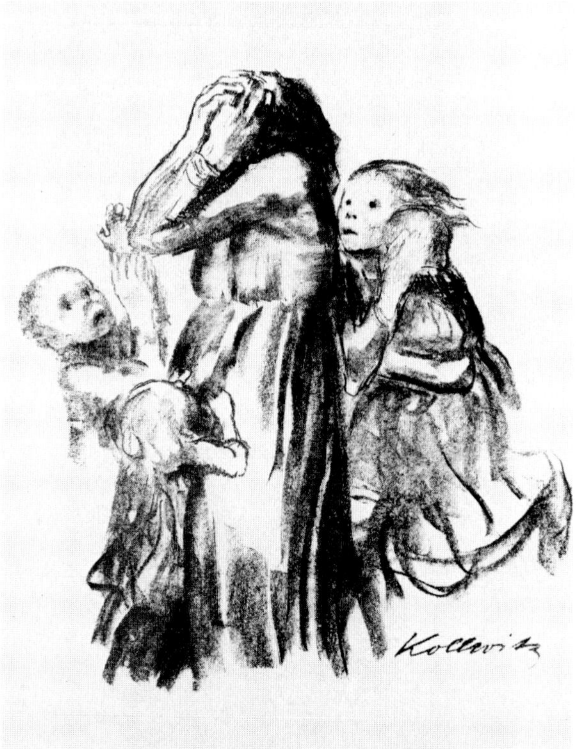

64

implications of the reverse. As a youth Rouault was an apprentice in a stained-glass workshop. His mature style reflects this early influence: the crucial elements of the composition—the officer's neck, his collar and hand—are designed as powerful, separate, accentuated segments totally bound by heavy black contours, fixed and rigid like fragments of stained glass. These areas were burnished out of the aquatint ground with the same determination that the artist showed when he wielded his palette knife to create highlights in his paintings. The light they radiate is also akin to stained glass. A brooding, ironic sense of the sacred and the profane pervades the image, reinforced by biting caricature, such as the sharply upturned military mustache that emphasizes the figure's self-promoting smugness.

Whether their prints are done in a series or made singly, as is Käthe Kollwitz's sensitive lithograph (plate 64), printmakers have, by the very act of publication, widely disseminated a condemnation of the human race's barbarous inhumanity. At the same time, however, with many of these same images they have demonstrated a humanity and empathy worthy of the best in man and woman. (Kollwitz's knowledge of the maternal predicament came firsthand.) This paradoxical message of truth lifts these artistic statements out of the realm of the merely polemic or the macabre and ennobles them for all time.

Portraits of the Famous and the Infamous Daniel Hopfer's etching (plate 65) has the distinction of being one of the earliest major examples of portraiture in the history of printmaking. Although printed portraits can be found as illustrations in books as early as 1479, the Hopfer portrait of Kunz von der Rosen, dating from about 1510, is perhaps the first outstanding example in pure etching. The artist has emphasized certain details to bring out the assertive nature of the sitter, an adviser to Maximilian I: his tense grip on the broadsword, a powerful diagonal paralleling the profile of nose and beard; the stout loop around his neck; the rakish tilt of his cap; and the sculptural depth of the massive blouse with its barblike pattern. This overall aggressivity has been masterfully tempered by the softer, almost fleecy etched lines of the gray tones and little puffs of cloud. A vibrant living presence is conveyed in the collective energy of thousands of animated etched strokes.

William Hogarth, well known for his satirical group engravings, has left us one masterpiece of individual portrait etching (plate 66). This exception derives from a fascinating concurrence of events—the kind that abounds in the history of portrait printmaking. A Scottish lord was condemned to death for high treason. Since the offending nobleman, Simon Fraser, Lord Lovat, was a particularly notorious

65.
Daniel Hopfer (c. 1470–1536). German. *Kunz von der Rosen*, c. 1510. Etching. 29.9 x 21.7 cm. (11¾ x 8½ in.). Cooper-Hewitt Museum, gift of Leo Wallerstein

66.
William Hogarth (1697–1764). English. *Simon Lord Lovat*, August 25, 1746. Etching. 36.3 x 23.8 cm. (14¼ x 9⅜ in.). Private collection

67.
Vincent van Gogh (1853–1890). Dutch. *Portrait of Dr. Gachet*, May 15, 1890. Etching. 18.2 x 13.6 cm. (7⅛ x 5⅜ in.). Museum of Modern Art, New York, gift of Abby Aldrich Rockefeller

68.
Louis Marcoussis (1883–1941). French. *Guillaume Apollinaire*, 1912–20. Etching. 49.7 x 27.9 cm. (19⅝ x 11 in.). Private collection

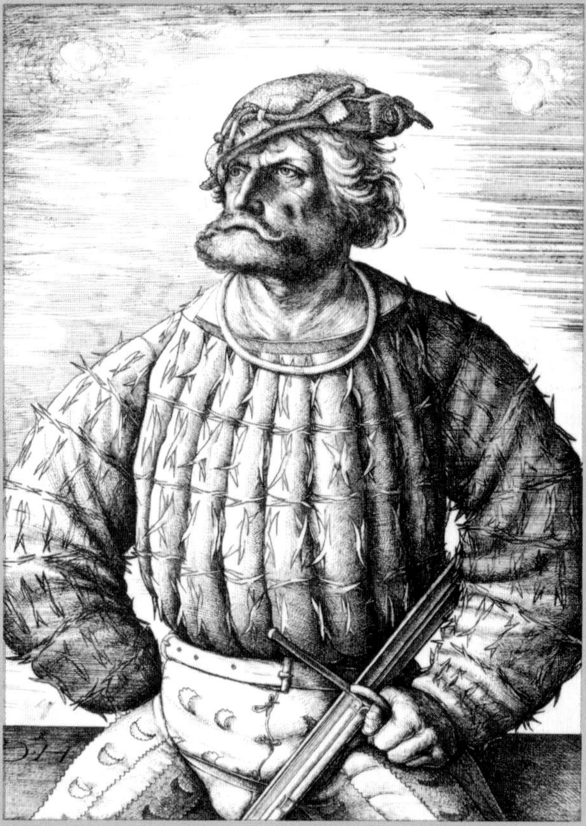

65

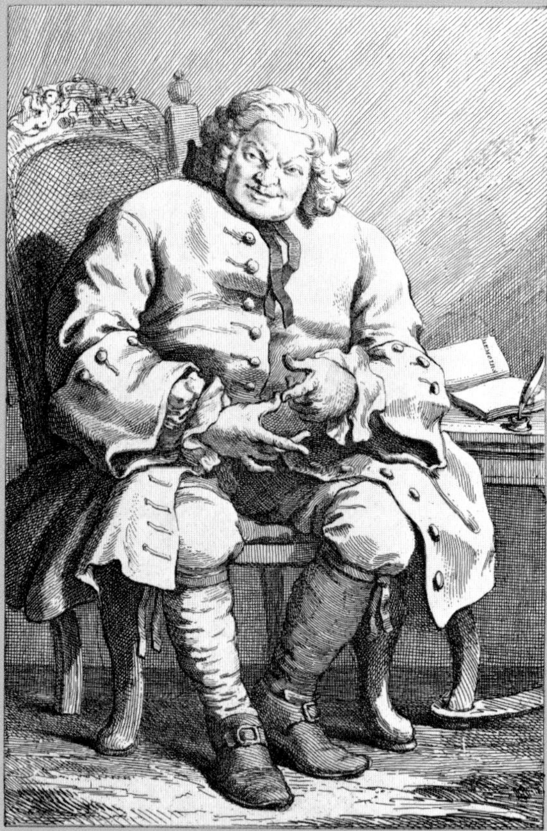

66

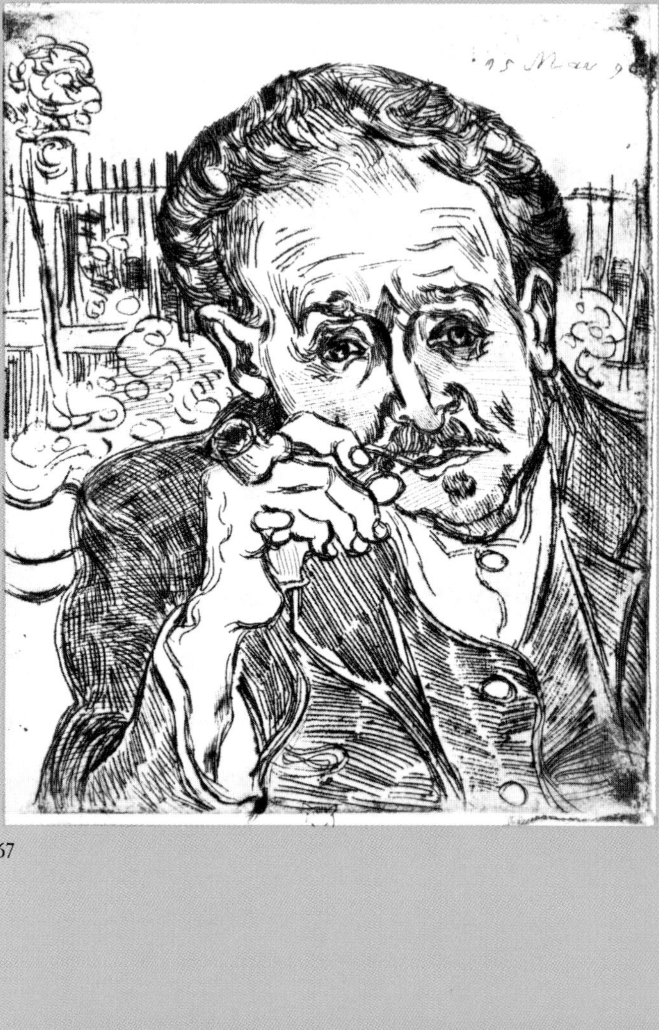

67

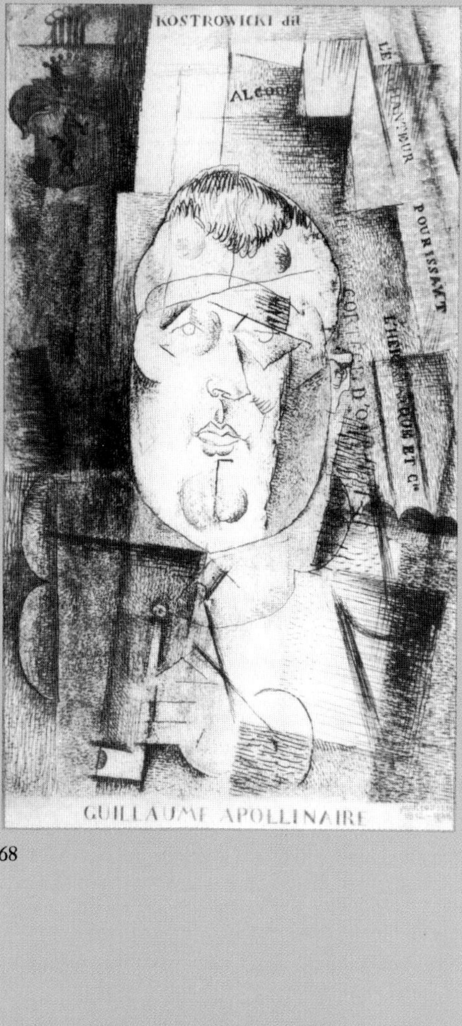

68

personality, the artist perceived a journalistic opportunity. But the beheading of the culprit was imminent. Hogarth made a rush visit to the Tower of London, where he rendered the portrait "from life" directly onto a copperplate to save time. He then sped the plate to the acid bath at his studio and proceeded to print and sell about 240 impressions a day for several weeks, at one shilling apiece. The immediacy of the public event combined with a skillful portrayal makes this etching a memorable work. As he talks to the artist, Lord Lovat is counting his clans on his fingertips to justify his action. The pages of his just-penned memoirs lie on the table nearby. The headsman awaits. (Lovat was the last British peer to be put to death for high treason.) Hogarth has drawn the chair legs so that they seem to emerge from under the sitter's waistcoat like organic extensions. The artist has subtly expressed what he felt to be Lovat's reptilian nature, focusing on the animated fingers and the sly expression of the face. Doing what he knew best, Hogarth drew his image in the manner of engraving—with strict currents of lines—even though he was wielding an etching needle. Thus we have a work in one medium done in the guise of another, perhaps obliquely echoing the guilty Lord Lovat's guise of innocence.

Another artist who, like Hogarth, produced only one major etching that is also an extraordinary portrait is Vincent van Gogh (plate 67). Dr. Paul Gachet, the painter's close friend and physician, was a printmaking enthusiast; he had his own press and encouraged van Gogh to express himself in the etching medium. The date etched so unsteadily at the upper right of the image is May 15, 1890. On that date, just two months before the painter killed himself, Gachet had finally convinced his friend to make his first etching and had sat for him. The seriousness of the painter's condition is hauntingly mirrored in the doctor's look of grave concern. Van Gogh's sad physical state and his physician's anguish are merged in the expressive, quickening etched line—a moment of high personal drama unique in art history. (The impression reproduced here was printed by Dr. Gachet on his own press.)

For his most ambitious cubist graphic work, the painter Louis Marcoussis selected as the subject of his etching cubism's most prolific and eloquent champion, the poet and art critic Guillaume Apollinaire (plate 68). Pipe in hand, the portly writer is seen fragmented and surrounded by the very same overlapping, sharp-edged shafts of light and shadow and juxtaposed lettering that he himself had analyzed and defended in the works of the cubists. In this, the most powerful printed cubist portrait by any artist, Apollinaire himself has fittingly become in perpetuity what he so strongly believed in.

The work's creation is pervaded by another fact—one of time—that endows the image with an added element of uniqueness: Marcoussis etched the portrait in 1912, made at least one proof and then put the plate aside. Two years later, World War I began, and both painter and poet left for military service. Both returned from the war, but Apollinaire had received a severe head wound and soon died, in Paris, in 1918. In sad remembrance Marcoussis in 1920 brought out the large copperplate that had rested on a shelf for eight years. He proceeded to add elements discreetly: the bandage encircling the poet's head, a deep shadow over some of the left portion of the face, the titles of Apollinaire's renowned literary works lettered at various angles, his family coat of arms barely visible in the upper-left corner and his name boldly spread across the bottom of the plate. Marcoussis then signed and dated the newly completed image: "1912–1920." He printed an edition of fifty impressions, each one an enduring icon of cubism and a stirring elegy for a great literary figure and comrade.

In his mysterious etched vision of Charles Baudelaire (plate 69), Jacques Villon has created a deceptively austere image that, when understood on its several levels of meaning, emerges as one of the most moving portraits in the history of printmaking. Villon was very close to his brother, the sculptor Raymond Duchamp-Villon, who was one year his junior. Duchamp-Villon died at age forty-two, in the same year as Apollinaire and also from war-inflicted wounds. The

69.
Jacques Villon (1875–1963). French. *Baudelaire with Pedestal*, 1920. Etching. 41.5 x 28 cm. (16⅜ x 11 in.). Museum of Modern Art, New York, gift of Victor S. Riesenfeld

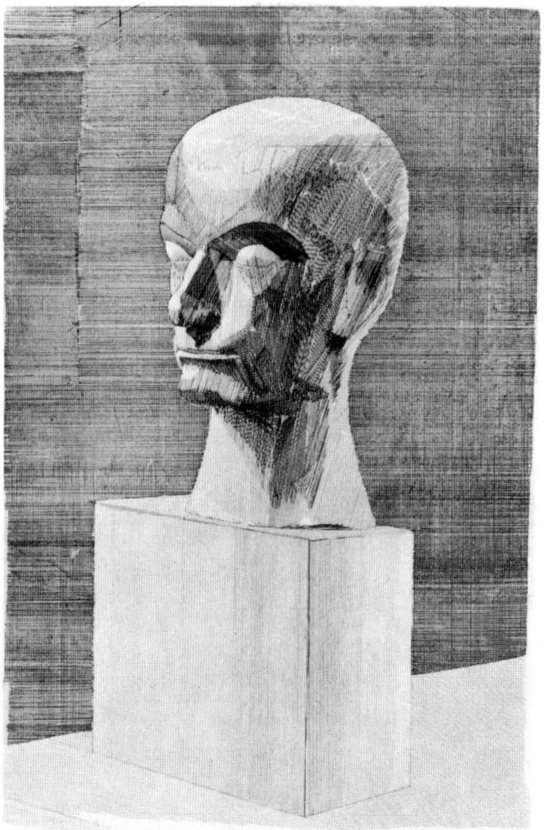

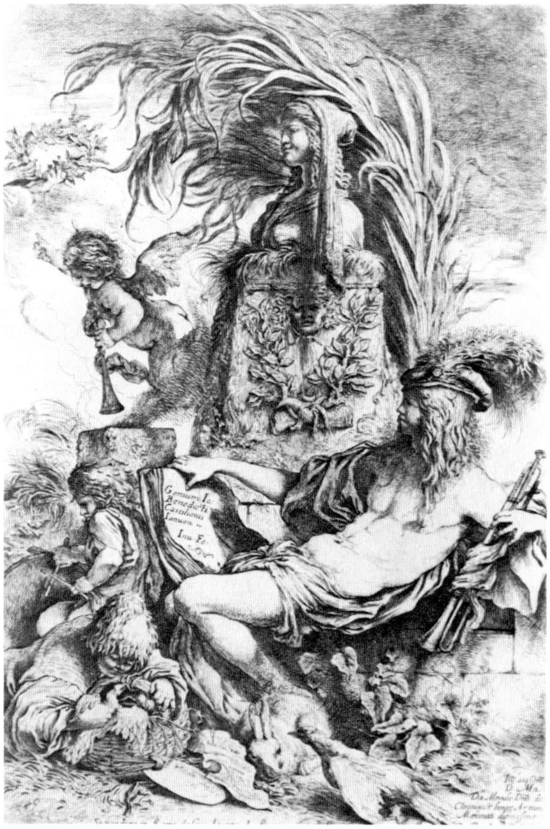

70.
Giovanni Benedetto Castiglione (1616–1670). Italian. *The Genius of G. B. Castiglione,* 1648. Etching. 37 x 24.6 cm. (14½ x 9⅝ in.). Cooper-Hewitt Museum, bequest of Erskine Hewitt

loss was incalculable not only to Villon but also to art history, since the sculptor had already produced several works that have come to be considered pivotal to modern sculpture, starting with a portrait head of Baudelaire.

In 1920, with his brother's few surviving sculptures having already become very rare works, Jacques Villon etched the Baudelaire head—a portrait of a portrait in a different medium. The sculpture had been Duchamp-Villon's homage to the deceased writer. The pronounced domed forehead, exaggerated staring eyes and determined lips of the sculpture, retained in the etching, seem to underscore the cerebral tension, the dynamism of Baudelaire's thoughts, which ultimately made him immortal. Villon has set the head on an unusually high pedestal; the precision and surface quality of this slab, composed of the finest vertical lines in contrast with the unremitting horizontals of the dark background, make it appear like a block of ice. This remarkable etching is therefore many things. It is an elegy for Duchamp-Villon based on Duchamp-Villon's elegy for Baudelaire. It is a testimony to Duchamp-Villon's potential immortality through a rendering of his sculpture, an homage to his first major work as well as a perceptive analysis of what constitutes its true greatness. And it is probably the all-time tour de force of opposing rigorous straight lines used to express an austere ideal, the near absolute, the pure.

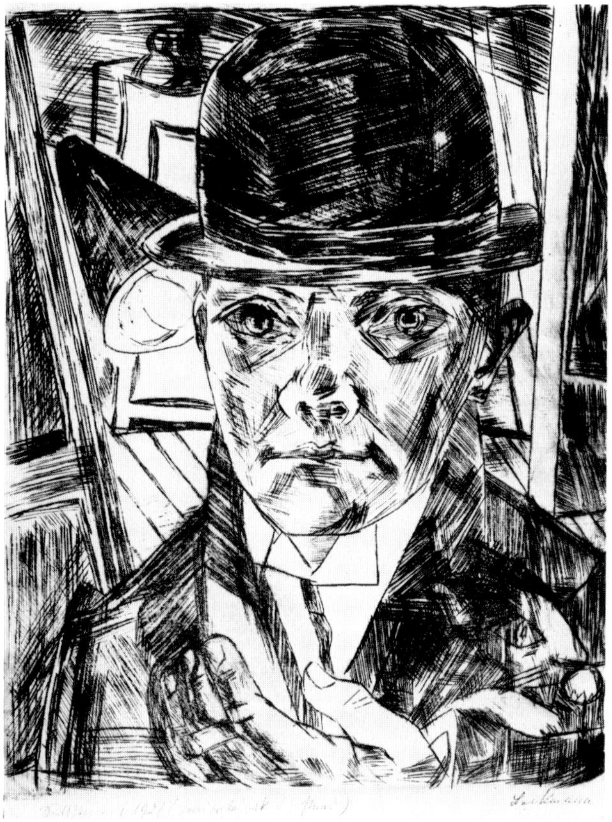

71

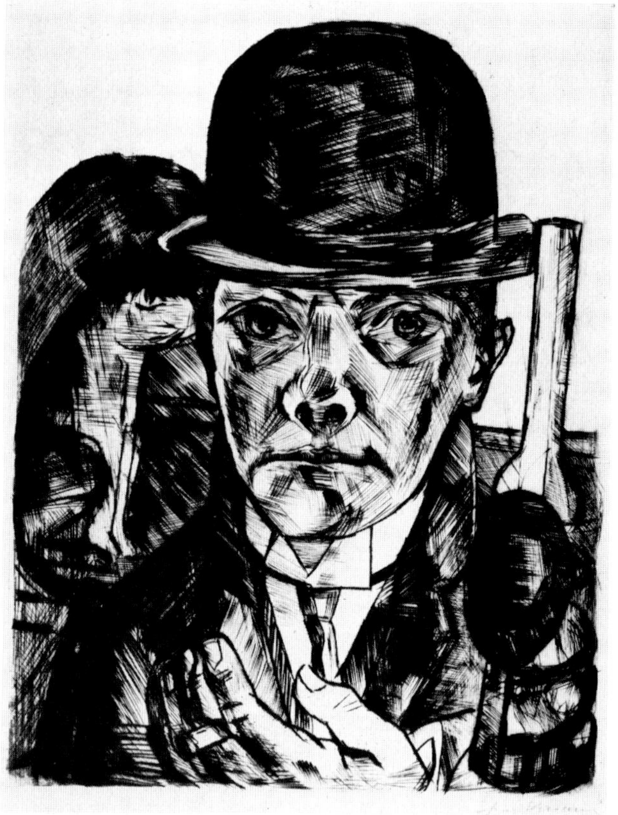

72

71.
Max Beckmann (1884–1950). German. *Self-Portrait with Bowler Hat*, 1921. Drypoint. Work proof. 31.3 x 24.5 cm. (12⅜ x 9⅝ in.). Museum of Modern Art, New York, anonymous gift

72.
Max Beckmann (1884–1950). German. *Self-Portrait with Bowler Hat*, 1921. Drypoint. Final state. 32.3 x 24.8 cm. (12¾ x 9¾ in.). Museum of Modern Art, New York, gift of Edward M. M. Warburg

Self-Portraits The range of imagery of the self-portrait—in style, spirit and historical and social import—is as varied as the artist-subjects themselves. There is perhaps no better way to get close to artists than to view, and if possible collect, their revealing self-portraits.

Artists have made self-portraits either to express how they saw themselves or, for convenience' sake, to express ideas, emotions or effects that ordinarily would be obtained by using another model. This utilization of the self-image reflected in the mirror, though practiced in graphic art since the late fifteenth century, only achieved momentum in the late seventeenth century.

Giovanni Benedetto Castiglione, a contemporary of Rembrandt, went so far as to transform himself into a classical symbol of artistic inspiration and audaciously titled his etched image *The Genius of G. B. Castiglione* (plate 70), thus illuminating a significantly changed posture for artists, from generally subservient in earlier centuries to vain and self-important. Castiglione was thirty-two years old when he conceived this flamboyant, undulating composition; hardly an area within it is not caught up in some wave of motion. We see the artist represented as perhaps the god Apollo, in whom all the arts were united. He is nearly nude, sprawled out in an arc that, continuing into the fluttering foliage behind him, becomes a dominant, sweeping semicircle. In one hand he holds a trumpet; in the other, what may be a large sketchbook, bearing the title of the etching in classical Latin. One of the *putti* blows a horn while another beats a drum and the third, with a fruit basket, plays with domestic animals, symbols of fecundity. Inscribed in the lower-right corner is a dedication to a Dutch nobleman and collector who befriended the artist in Rome.

From baroque splendor and extravagant gesture to the depersonalized isolation of modern man is another vast spiritual leap, as typified by Max Beckmann's self-portrait. Two states of this drypoint are reproduced (plates 71 and 72): the first is a work proof pulled midway in the creation of the image in order to judge its development; the second is the completed, published image (*final state*). Printmaking's early proof states are indelible records of creation-in-process and its crucial decision making. No other art medium can leave such a revealing residue.

As we examine these different states of the Beckmann self-portrait, several important design decisions become apparent. To intensify the artist's stare of bewildered alienation, the cat has been moved from lower right to left center; Beckmann has aligned the cat's stare with his own. The curve of the animal's spine and head meets the brim of the bowler and, together with the shadow behind, repeats the hat's curve. The importance of the bowler has been heightened as an ironic symbol of the predicament of the bourgeoisie in the crisis-wracked Berlin of the time. With more space to work with on the left, the artist could now show the tensed hind leg of the cat, which repeats the taut curve of the artist's grip on his cigarette. The cat has emerged as a substantial party to the frozen, disoriented feeling. In the right-hand area freed of the animal, Beckmann has drawn an ominous oval for counterbalance. The black band of the cravat and sharpened contour for the collar have been added to introduce stiffness and contraction.

Before making these changes, Beckmann had polished out the entire background, with its angular interior details, to create a white field. He retained this field in the upper segment, so that the image of himself and the newly installed lamp, cat and shadow are starkly silhouetted. Finally, he attacked the copperplate with a new vehemence, strengthening the overall crosscurrents of line by cutting deeply into the plate to create overlapping swaths of black burr that add dramatic impact to this masterpiece of German expressionism.

When, almost contemporarily, Marc Chagall employed the mirror in his Parisian studio to contemplate himself, he reflected an entirely different temperament and circumstance (plate 73). Though just returned to France from the Berlin of Beckmann's anxieties, Chagall instead chose to distort his face not in the pain of a neurosis-ridden victim but as a kind of cheerfully defiant survivor. Chagall's grimace is an act of incorrigible buffoonery, his eyes full of mischief and dare and his unruly hair enhancing the mood of youthful rebellion. As

Beckmann had wisely opted for drypoint, Chagall selected the technique most appropriate to his statement: aquatint's loose highlights against a soft gray field, combined with etching's deep-biting lines to render a minimum of facial accents.

Yet a third temperament inhabits a moving self-portrait by Georges Rouault, drawn in Paris about the same time as Chagall's (plate 74). Deeply religious, Rouault modeled himself in a haunting, meditative mood, as if he had just received a benediction. As opposed to the usual first-person presence of the self-portrait, a kind of third-person humility pervades this image. The painter's eyes are virtually closed, and an almost imperceptible smile is on his lips. These features have been subtly chiseled by a superbly modulated light, and lithography's velvety cloak is soothing and consoling.

73.
Marc Chagall (b. 1887). French. *Self-Portrait with Grimace*, c. 1924. Etching and aquatint. 37.2 x 27.3 cm. (14⅝ x 10¾ in.). Museum of Modern Art, New York, gift of the artist

74.
Georges Rouault (1871–1958). French. *Self-Portrait with Cap*, 1926. Lithograph. 23.2 x 17.4 cm. (9⅛ x 6⅞ in.). Museum of Modern Art, New York, gift of Samuel A. Berger

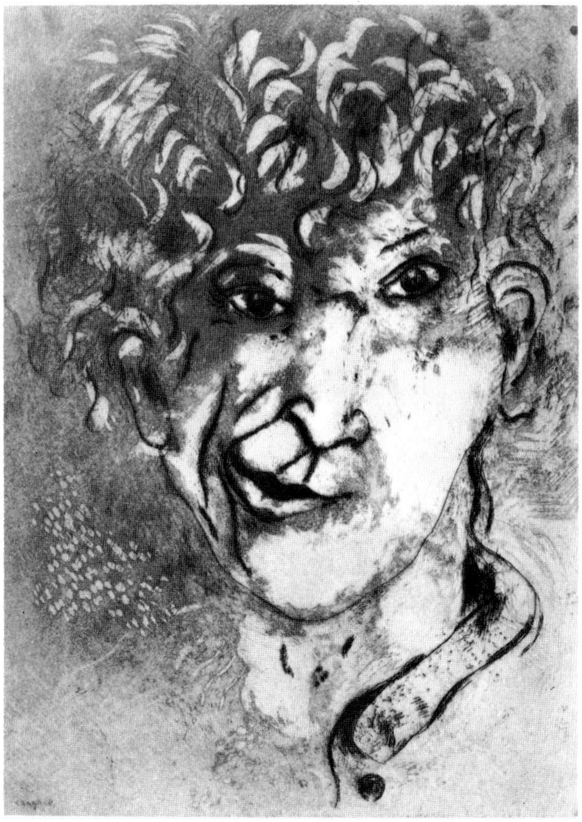

73

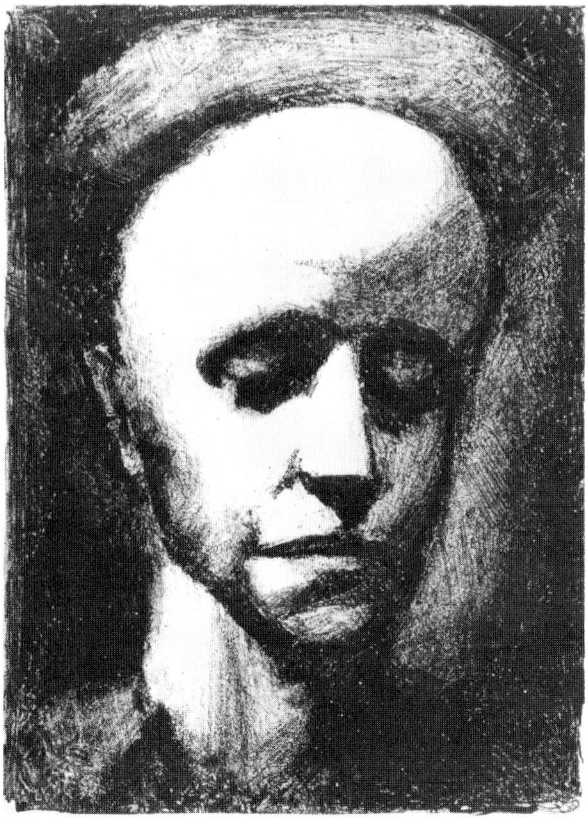

74

City Views in Series A great city is the single most profound and concentrated amalgam of a civilization's aspirations and achievements. As such, it generally defies comparison with any other metropolis. Uniqueness stems from its particular mix of topography, architecture, activities, people, costumes, language, climate and history—to name just a few determinants. To encompass some of these features, a few ambitious printmakers have created sequences of views of a particular city. Before photography and film could be employed to document and pay homage to cities, such graphic portfolios were the only visual means of recording, widely disseminating and propagandizing these characteristics. Printmakers did not begin in earnest to create sets of views until the mid-eighteenth century, with the first emergence of widespread tourism (which these portfolios in turn helped expand) and the popular collecting of etchings, which justified, for example, publishing Canaletto's views of Venice (plate 75) and Piranesi's views of Rome. Another great city that has been much blessed by such efforts is, of course, Paris. Four major series devoted to its beauty and life, and indebted to the earlier Italian images, were etched and lithographed during the nineteenth century: two by Frenchmen and two by Englishmen.

Thomas Girtin's twenty printed views of Paris have almost the same 180-degree horizontal span as our own eyes; that may be why they have such an impact of reality. The view down the crowded Rue St.-Denis has all the convincing density and sparkle of a bustling Parisian street (plate 76). Masterfully handled, the granular aquatint and the deeply etched lines seem at one with the actuality of rough-textured building facades, shutters, balcony metalwork and street paraphernalia. A thrusting perspective adds to their dramatic concentration and disheveled charm. Girtin died at age twenty-seven, in 1802, just after etching the lines and adding the tones in watercolor as a guide to laying in the aquatint. (A Mr. F. C. Lewis was duly credited in the lower-right margin for his subsequent collaboration.) Published in London the same year, the series was fetching to English tourists, both as an encouragement to make the voyage abroad and as an extraordinary souvenir of what had been experienced.

The Paris set of Thomas Shotter Boys is the first important city print series in color, an incunabulum of color lithography (colorplate 13). When the portfolio was published in London in 1839, its fifteen plates were highly praised for their exceptional chromatic subtleties, and this judgment has endured. The delicacy of composition and line dictated such hues, which in this lithograph reach a sublime level in the sky with a barely discernible wisp of cloud. The calming openness, the softly diffused Paris light, the faded earthen colors of the Pavillon de Flore (part of the Louvre) and the accents of red that lead the eye into the picture like depth markers are all master-

Colorplate 13.
Thomas Shotter Boys (1803–1874). English. *Pavillon de Flore, Tuileries.* Lithograph from *Picturesque Architecture in Paris, Ghent, Antwerp, Rouen,* 1839. 34.1 x 29 cm. (13⅜ x 11⅜ in.). Cooper-Hewitt Museum, gift of Susan Dwight Bliss

Colorplate 14.
Pierre Bonnard (1867–1947). French. *Street Corner Viewed from Above.* Lithograph from *Quelques aspects de la vie de Paris,* 1895. 36.8 x 21 cm. (14½ x 8¼ in.). Brooklyn Museum, New York

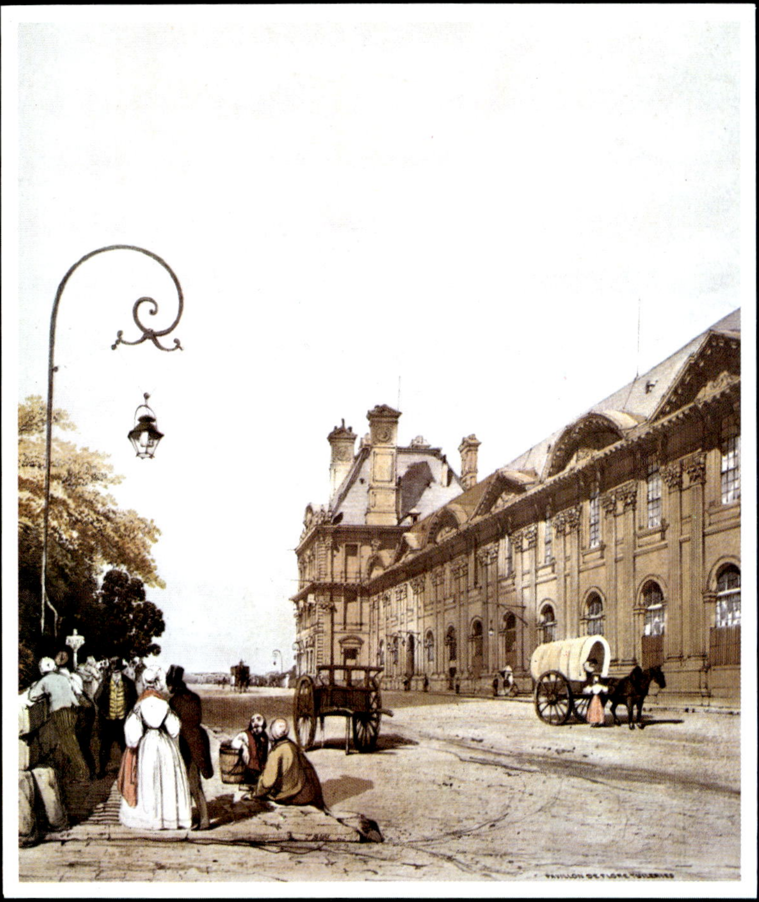

COLORPLATE 13

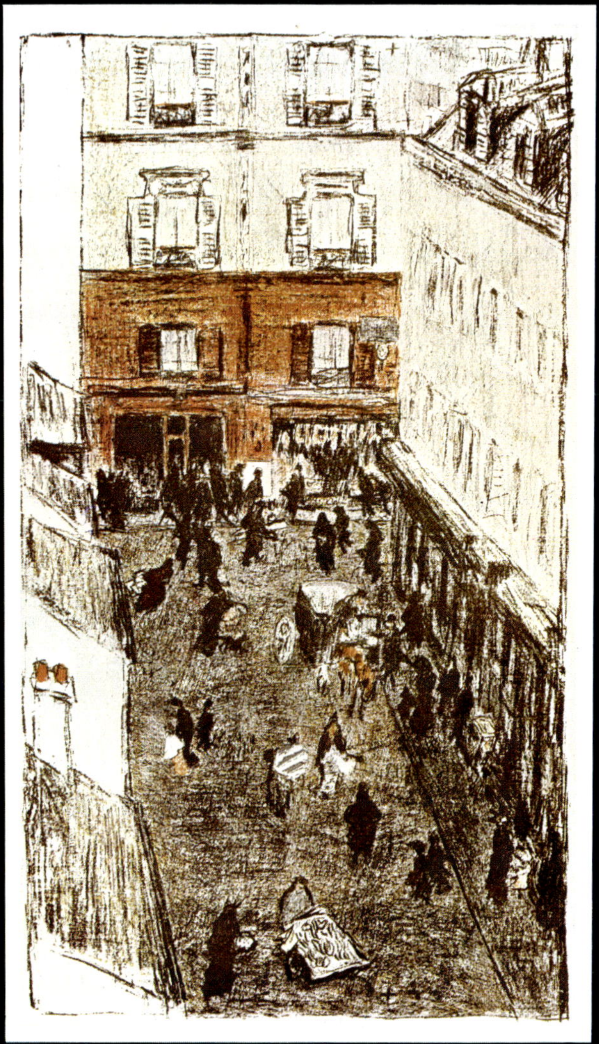

COLORPLATE 14

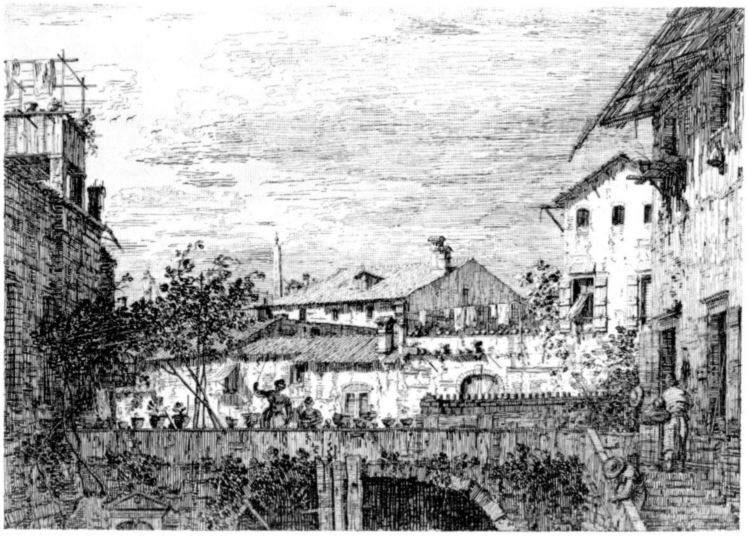

75

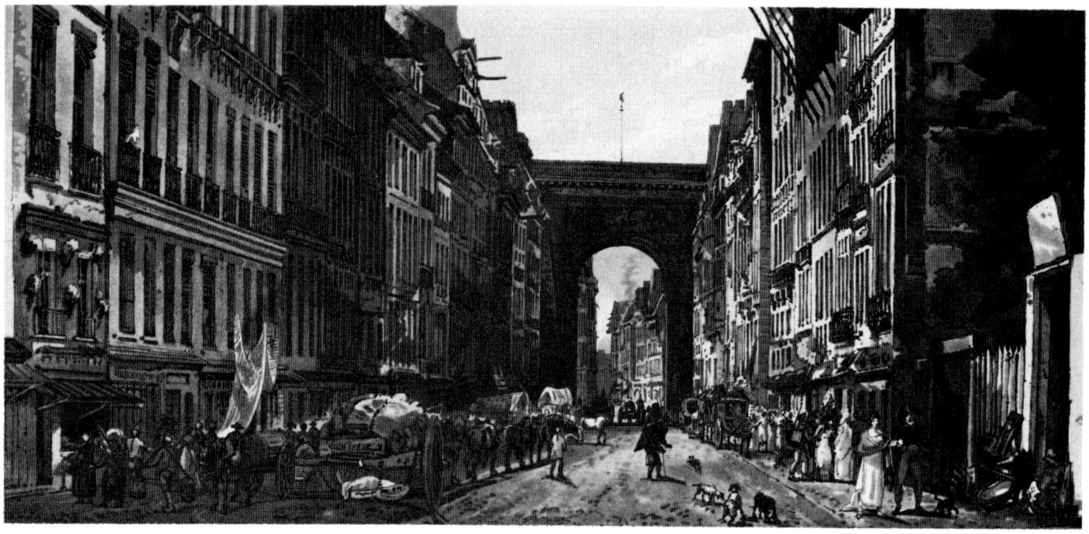

76

fully conceived. Rarely in art has a prosaic lamppost served as such an elegant, reassuring foreground object.

Charles Meryon's discovery of his color blindness led him to quit painting and turn to etching at the age of twenty-seven. Two years later, at the midpoint of the nineteenth century and about the same time that Baudelaire began writing about Paris, Meryon began etching Paris with a vision so intense that its obsessive imagery already betrays his eventual madness. No city views ever combined such faithfulness to architectural detail with such bizarre and sinister minutiae of the life it harbored. So haunting were these etchings, which by 1854 had accumulated to twenty-two plates, that Baudelaire—a sort of kindred soul—proposed to write poetry for them, to be added at the bottom of each etching.

Although Meryon's aggregate view of Paris consists of imposing buildings, ramparts, towers, churches and even a morgue, it is the many bridges spanning the Seine that appear most frequently in his

75.
Antonio Canal, called Canaletto (1697–1768). Italian. *The Terrace*, 1740–43. Etching. 14.2 x 20.9 cm. (5⅝ x 8¼ in.). Private collection

76.
Thomas Girtin (1775–1802). English. *View of the Gate of St. Denis.* Etching and aquatint from *A Selection of Twenty of the Most Picturesque Views of Paris*, 1802. 30 x 55.8 cm. (11¾ x 22 in.). Cooper-Hewitt Museum, gift of Museum of Graphic Art

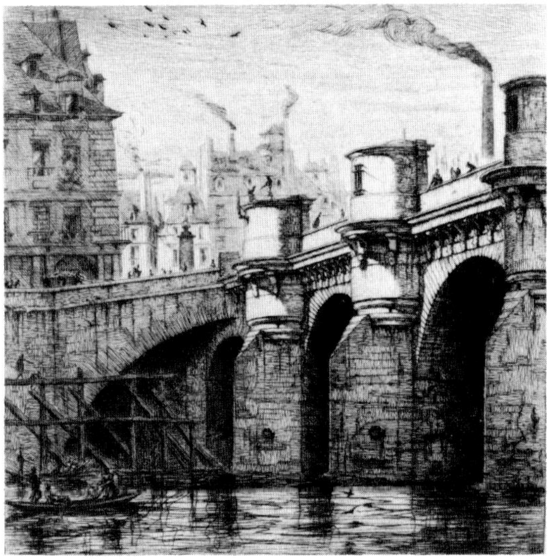

77

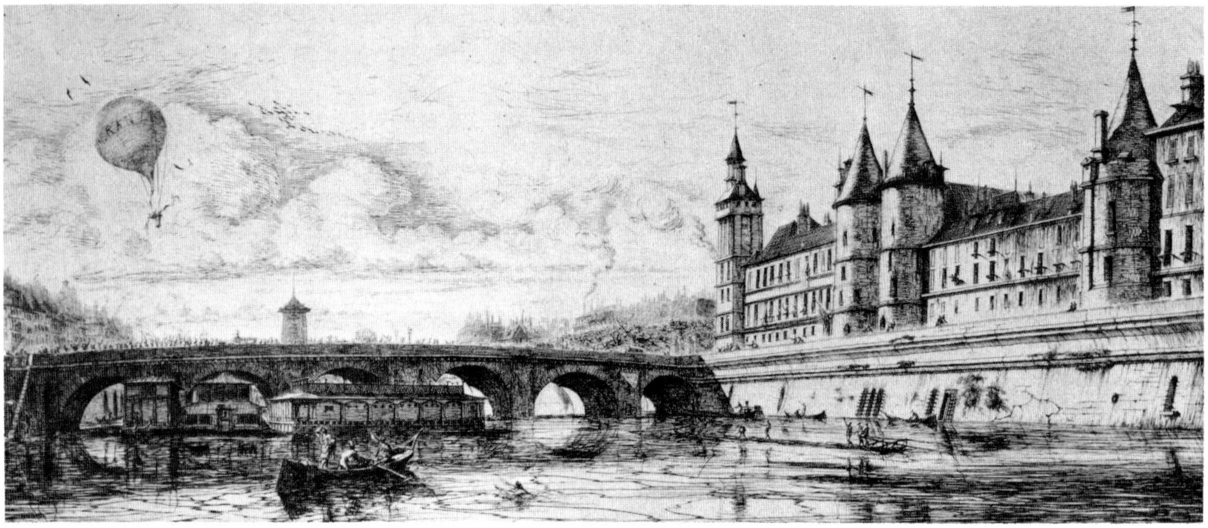

78

plates, both close up and at a distance. In *Pont Neuf* (plate 77) the artist has bathed the convex turrets of the bridge in bright light while shadowing the concave openings below in ominous inkiness. As do the darting birds and swirls of smoke, the eerie, specklike creatures that animate this view emphasize by contrast the stony implacability of the architecture. From farther away Meryon could encompass the entire span of the Pont au Change (plate 78) and include the broad sweep of the river's stone embankment and the spire-festooned Palais de Justice. A funeral cortege moves across the bridge, the hearse an open wagon. The surreal balloon surrounded by soaring birds of prey is like an inflated punctuation mark, a lampoon of the dead person's spirit rising to heaven—Meryon's morbid whimsy. Again there are the tiny strange creatures on the bank and in the long boats on the murky, turbid waters. The artist has added another incongruous, disquieting note by etching a woman half-submerged in the river, pleading for help. The vertical forms lined up along the river

77.
Charles Meryon (1821–1868). French. *Pont Neuf*, 1853. Drypoint and etching from *Eaux-Fortes sur Paris*, 1852–54. 18.4 x 18.2 cm. (7¼ x 7⅛ in.). Private collection

78.
Charles Meryon (1821–1868). French. *Pont au Change*, 1854. Etching and drypoint from *Eaux-Fortes sur Paris*, 1852–54. 15.6 x 33.3 cm. (6⅛ x 13⅛ in.). Cooper-Hewitt Museum, bequest of George Campbell Cooper

wall at right are only windows; yet by accentuating the separations of the enframing stones, the sharp strokes of the etcher's needle have transformed these architectural elements into menacing, insectlike presences.

The remarkable feat of Meryon's series is that, despite these gloomy grace notes, the imposing architecture somehow endures—becoming so memorable, so etched into our minds, that the odd images have helped to monumentalize the grandeur and reality that are Paris. Meryon's genius, dark as it was, has gripped the city's configuration with a bittersweet passion. Perhaps the implied element of danger is the foil, the adversary, that was needed to lend an awesome fortresslike permanence to his beloved structures—as well as a cutting edge to our perceptions.

Pierre Bonnard was only twenty-eight years old when he began the twelve lithographs that constitute the set *Some Aspects of the Life of Paris*, published by Ambroise Vollard at the close of the century. Their titles tell much of the artist's approach: *Street Corner; Street Corner Viewed from Above* (colorplate 14); and *Street Viewed from Above*. Influenced by the flat tones, foreshortened perspective and simple geometry of Japanese prints, this visual orientation serves as a stage for the characteristic wriggling contours Bonnard used to capture the restless tempo of *fin-de-siècle* Parisian life. The artist has left us permanent witness to the throbbing heart of a city that is its intersections, where shoppers, workmen, peddlers, mothers, children and dogs all converge and crisscross in marvelous chance choreography. Like the three other sets of cityscapes, Bonnard's should ideally be viewed and collected in its entirety, the total effect being greater than the sum of its parts.

The Sensuous and the Exotic Although sensually provocative images occasionally appeared in prints of the sixteenth and seventeenth centuries, these were usually exceptional cases reserved for the private appreciation of a few collectors and artists. It was not until the eighteenth century in France, during the reigns of Louis XV and Louis XVI, that a virtual art movement of mildly lascivious or titillating imagery arose, catering to a widespread demand among the aristocracy for the visual delights of refined naughtiness. Clearly reflecting the heedless frivolity of a dissolute, doomed society, this aesthetic boom in amorous paintings, watercolors, pastels and engravings ceased abruptly with the onset of the French Revolution. The printmaking sector of this output is described as *l'estampe galante* ("tasteful print"), since the impropriety involved was always portrayed with a typical politesse, chivalry and brittle elegance. This touch of fashionableness toned down the roughness of the subject matter while raising its intrigue to a tongue-in-cheek theatrical level.

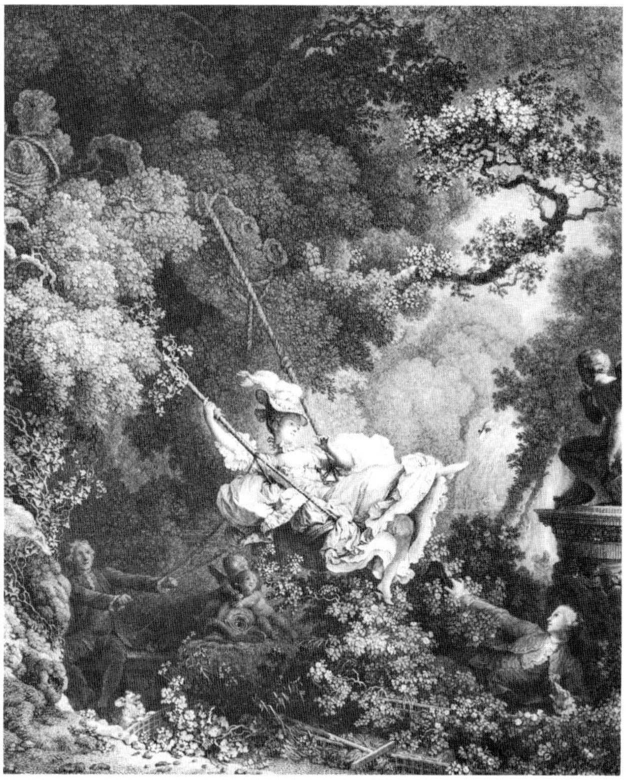

79.
Nicolas de Launay (1739–1792). French. *The Happy Accidents of the Swing*, 1782. Engraving after Jean-Honoré Fragonard. 62.5 x 45.7 cm. (24⅝ x 18 in.). Private collection

Probably the most renowned of these engravings is Nicolas de Launay's cunningly titled *The Happy Accidents of the Swing* (plate 79), a tour de force of engraving that translates an ethereal oil by Jean-Honoré Fragonard into the lush detail and monochromy of the graphic medium. The clergyman's hat on the bench is the only evidence that it is a bishop who swings the dainty lady. (This telltale clue was eventually censored with heavier shadow.) Unknown to him, the prying nobleman on the right feasts his eyes on his own mistress, who has just kicked off a slipper in an indecorous gesture that visually puns the expression "throwing caution to the winds." Three other onlookers—an admonishing statue on the right, a pair of worried *putti* in the center and a growling terrier at the lower left—share in this sylvan peekaboo. A more subtle device, high amid the rich foliage on the left, is an apelike gnarled limb bound in rope, symbolizing bridled primitive passion.

The huge plate for de Launay's engraving started to wear down from the corners (as such plates did on old-style wooden presses), because of the enormous print runs needed to fill the ceaseless orders for this scene. Well after the Revolution, impressions were still being pulled from the battered plate, by then reduced to an oval to eliminate its worn portions. It is said that the popular nineteenth-century cancan traced its origins to the abandoned kick of this amply clad swinging damsel.

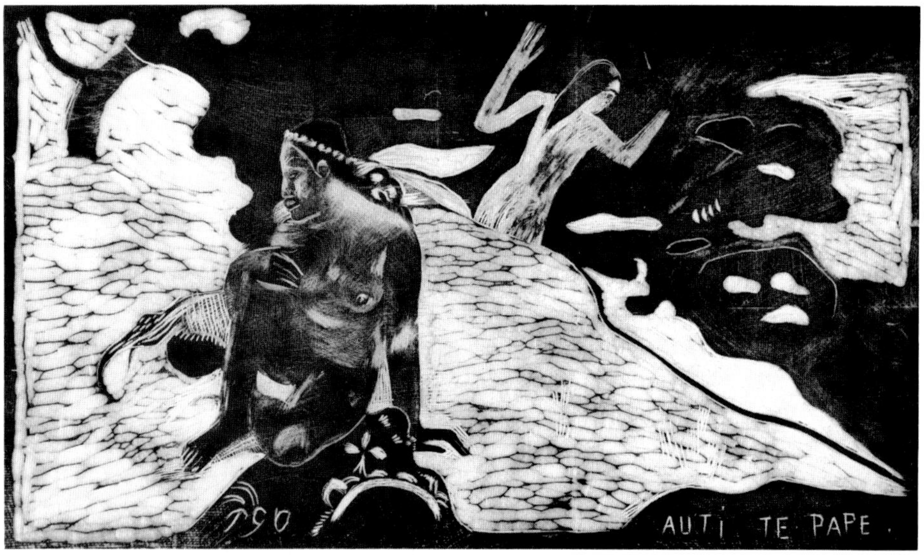

80

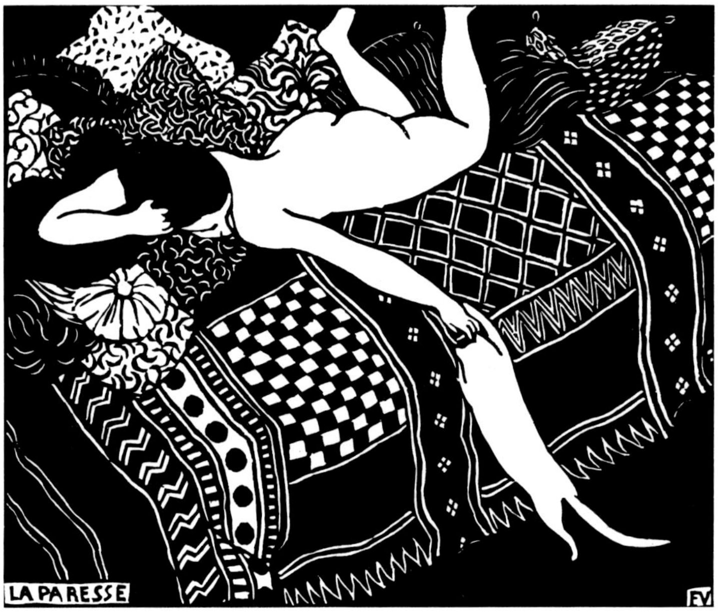

81

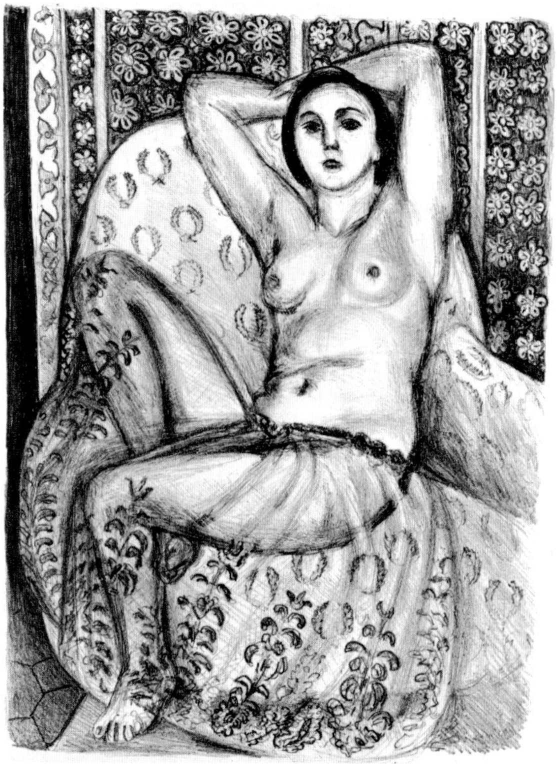

82

80.
Paul Gauguin (1848–1903). French. *Women at the River*, 1891–93. Woodcut and wood engraving, printed in black. 20.5 x 35.5 cm. (8⅛ x 14 in.). Museum of Modern Art, New York, Lillie P. Bliss Collection

81.
Félix Vallotton (1865–1925). Swiss. *Laziness*, 1896. Woodcut. 17.8 x 22 cm. (7 x 8⅝ in.). Private collection

82.
Henri Matisse (1869–1954). French. *Odalisque with Lace Skirt*, 1923–24. Lithograph. 35.8 x 27 cm. (14⅛ x 10⅝ in.). Private collection

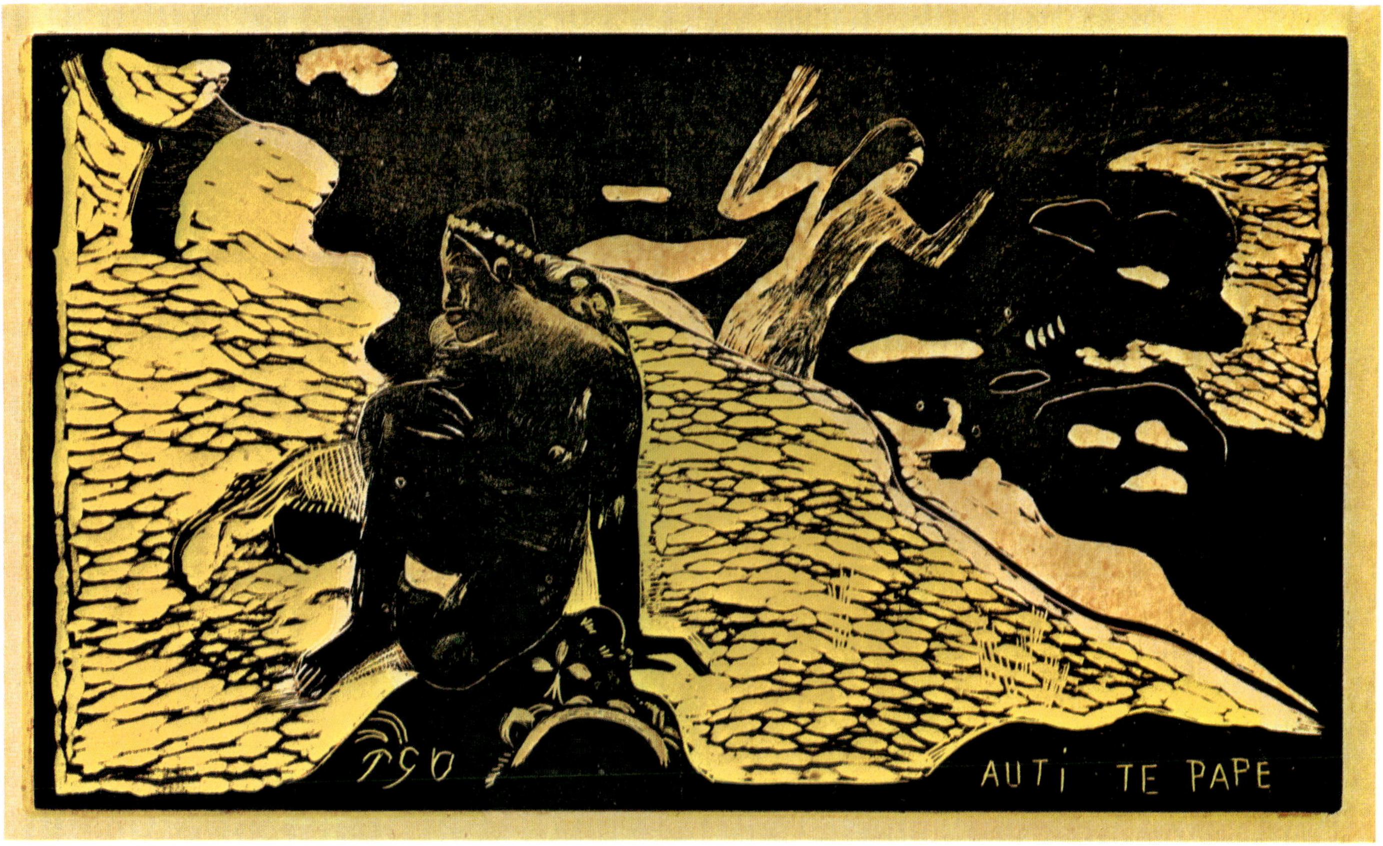

Colorplate 15.
Paul Gauguin (1848–1903). French. *Women at the River*, 1891–93. Woodcut and wood engraving, printed in color with the aid of stencils. 20.5 x 35.5 cm. (8⅛ x 14 in.). Museum of Modern Art, New York, gift of Abby Aldrich Rockefeller

The nineteenth century saw sensuousness in art reach beyond the local variety of boudoir exotica to the allurements of distant lands as restless European and, later, American artists traveled to North Africa, the Near East and even Oceania. Such a breakaway from the familiar doldrums of middle-class life in a search for primordial roots culminated in the odyssey of Paul Gauguin, who went off to Tahiti at the close of the century. In his *Women at the River* (the Tahitian title is engraved at the lower right) the colors, yellow and orange, were laid in with the aid of stencils (colorplate 15) after the basic printing of the block in black ink (plate 80). In this combined woodcut and wood engraving the artist brought together elements from two of his paintings and divided a horizontal rectangle in half with a sinuous diagonal of shoreline. A timeless dichotomy has been constructed: repose on land and action in the water; the seated figure dark against a sunlit beach, the diving figure glistening against dark waters. The spare areas of luminous color in juxtaposition with so much black ink, the schematic shorthand of design and the work's small scale endow this image with touching innocence, a kind of sensuous privacy. As the unrestrained lushness of de Launay's engraving typifies rococo indulgence, so the rawness of the bare gouge marks and the childlike simplification of the woodcut mirror an unspoiled, naturally harmonious vision of life. Both works, seemingly so disparate, are fine examples of the medium's being (a generous part of) the message.

In his woodcut *Laziness* (plate 81) Félix Vallotton pays homage to two aesthetic and sociological extremes: to court painter François Boucher's notorious portrayal of the mistress of Louis XV and to Gauguin's quest and his liberating woodcut style with its image cut out in the negative. Less adventuresome than his contemporary Gauguin, Vallotton was content with finding the exotic in an anonymous Parisian interior, made splendidly seductive by a richly patterned spread and a mound of decorative pillows. Vallotton's animated white diagonal is completed by the frisky cat, which nearly fuses with the beckoning arm of its mistress.

Henri Matisse, edging closer to North Africa by moving from Paris to the shores of the Mediterranean, adorned his images with Moorish designs, filling the entire background with their repeated floral arabesques; moreover, he arranged his models in the exotic pose of the odalisque and clothed them in the diaphanous skirt of the Casbah. Such lush decoration emphasized by contrast the soft, languid attributes of the sitter (plate 82). In a side-by-side comparison, the differences in technique and style between Vallotton's hard-edge staccato woodcut and Matisse's velvety lithograph, with their similar subject matter, become abundantly clear.

Mother and Child Probably no other subject is so endearing to a family that collects or appreciates prints as the expressive theme of mother and child. The portrayal of this closest of all human relationships by major artists has resulted in exquisite images of great binding force, emotional warmth and hushed eloquence.

When Rembrandt etched the Holy Family in 1654, he conceived an image of warm embrace so frank and natural in its emotion that his little masterpiece (plate 83) exists as a universal standard for all intimate views of maternity graven in subsequent centuries. Though many genre images of the seventeenth, eighteenth and nineteenth centuries include this aspect of daily life, rarely has it been treated with such unabashed central focus. Significantly, it was a woman artist who, in 1891, would etch the first major graphic work on the subject since Rembrandt, inspired by a recent influx into Paris of Japanese woodcuts that treated the maternal theme in close-up (colorplate 16). Choosing the delicacy of drypoint and the subtle hues of aquatint, Mary Cassatt began her unprecedented color series dealing with women's daily occupations and introduced what was to become a prime subject for several important painters-turned-printmakers in the closing decade of the century. With touching sensitivity, Cassatt shows the mother testing the temperature of the bath before immersing her child, an act performed by countless mothers around the world. Not surprisingly, the baby here looks more Oriental than Occidental—in homage to the artist's source.

In the lithograph *Family Scene* Pierre Bonnard divided his rectangle into a series of looping, almost abstract curves and flattened color patterns (colorplate 17). Mother, father and baby merge in a cuddling intimacy, and the viewer, placed only inches away in this candid-camera view, shares in the warm familial proximity. As in Rembrandt's

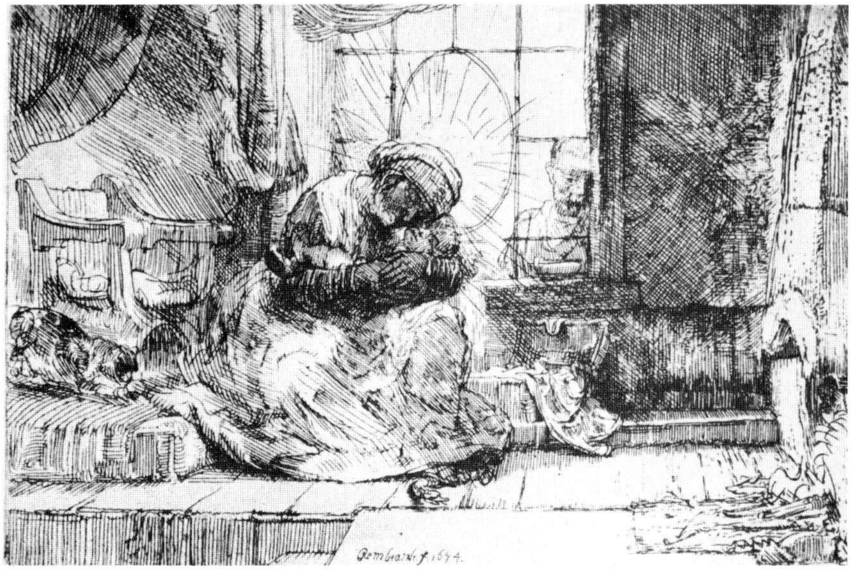

83.
Rembrandt Harmensz. van Rijn (1606–1669). Dutch. *The Virgin and Child with the Cat: And Joseph at the Window*, 1654. Etching. 9.4 x 14.3 cm. (3¾ x 5⅝ in.). Cooper-Hewitt Museum, gift of Leo Wallerstein

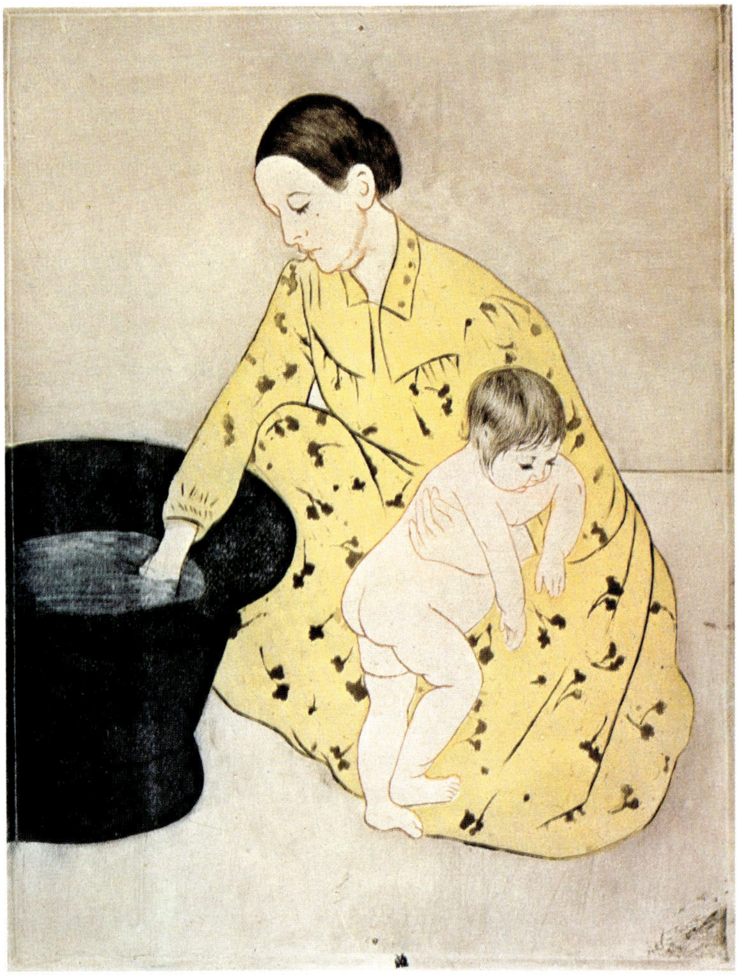

Colorplate 16

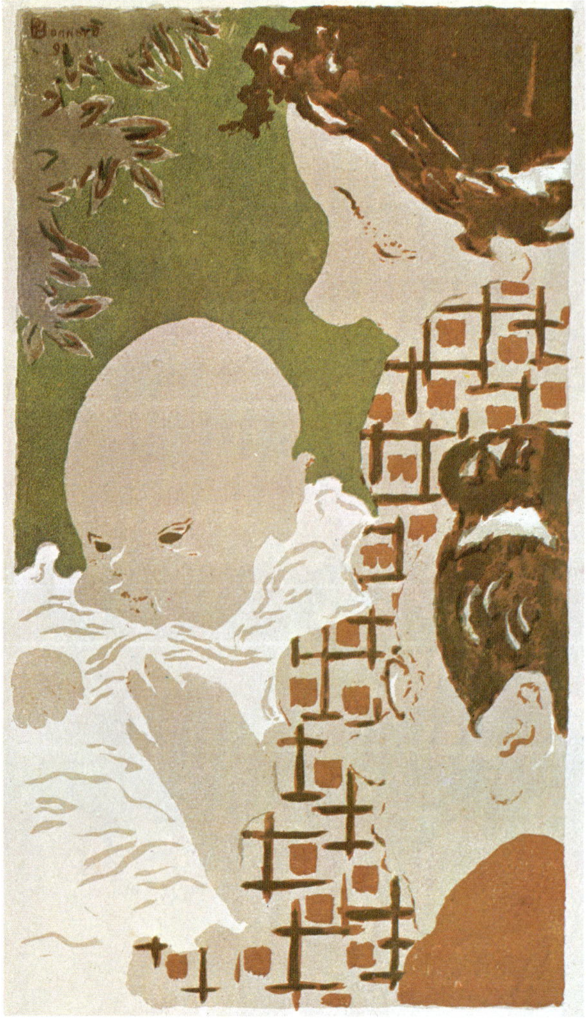

Colorplate 17

Colorplate 16.
Mary Cassatt (1845–1926). American. *The Bath*, 1891. Drypoint, etching and aquatint. 31.5 x 24.8 cm. (12⅜ x 9¾ in.). Private collection

Colorplate 17.
Pierre Bonnard (1867–1947). French. *Family Scene*. Lithograph from *L'Estampe originale*, 1893. 31.3 x 18 cm. (12⅜ x 7⅛ in.). Museum of Modern Art, New York, Purchase Fund

Colorplate 18.
Maurice Denis (1870–1943). French. *Our Souls in Languid Motions*. Lithograph from *L'Amour*, 1898. 28 x 40 cm. (11 x 15¾ in.). Brooklyn Museum, New York

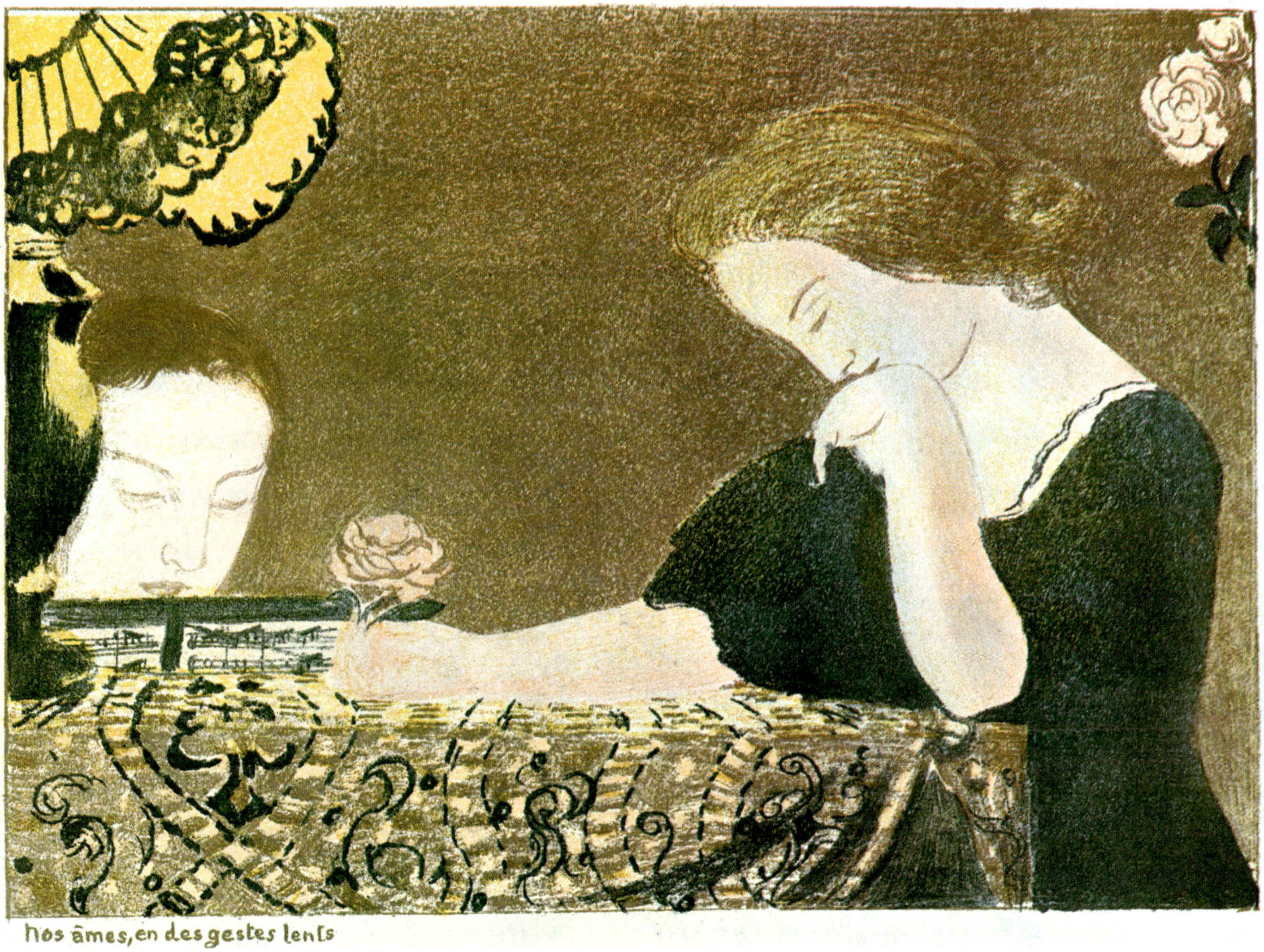

COLORPLATE 18

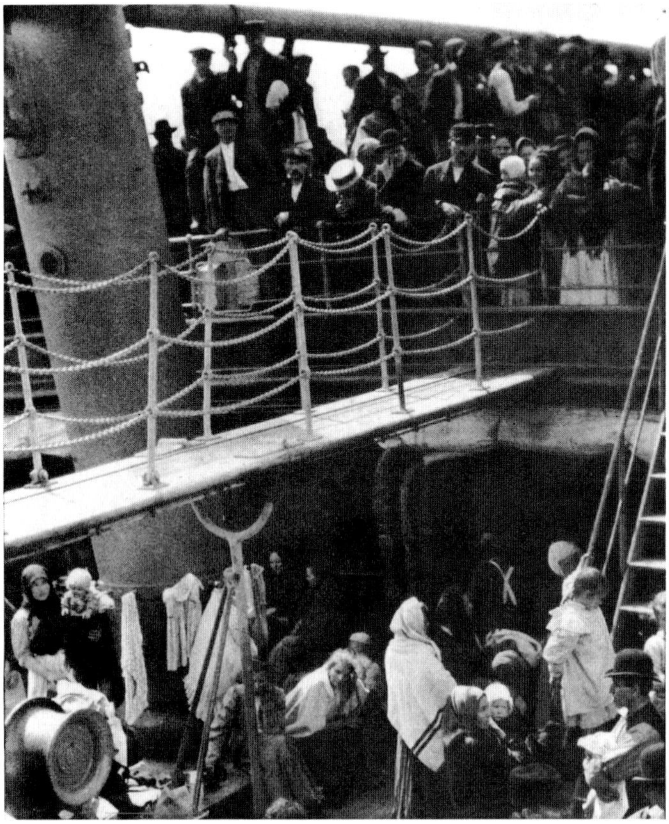

84.
Alfred Stieglitz (1864–1946). American. *The Steerage*, 1907. Photogravure in *291*, 1915. 33.3 x 26.7 cm. (13⅛ x 10½ in.). Private collection

vision, the male experience during this happy interlude is less a direct physical contact than an appreciative awe.

In a remarkable suite on the theme of love, Maurice Denis selected a horizontal frame (colorplate 18) to form a meditative bond between mother and child, implied in the mother's relaxed, outstretched arm, as both share the music the child plays. (Note the music score emerging out of the design of the piano cover that in itself adds a colorful accent to the domestic scene.) Instead of using the solid ink tones and bold contours of Bonnard's image, Denis wielded his litho crayon in a looser manner reminiscent of the fresh, informal effects of children's wax crayon drawings. The poetic title lettered in by the artist in the lower-left corner underscores the tranquil, easy mood of the composition.

When Alfred Stieglitz beheld the scene we view in *The Steerage* (plate 84), it was a complex, moving multitude; but the famed photographer perceived and captured what Henri Cartier-Bresson was later to describe as "the decisive moment." Stieglitz's keen vision immediately fathomed the rich fabric of humanity that was amazingly stratified before him. His through-the-lens focus was courageous for the time (only nine years after Denis's gentle lithograph, for instance), since this teeming image had none of the familiar formalities of composition rendered by artists till then. The massive angled mast, the plunging stairway and the onrushing perspective of gangplank and boom are mechanical elements that dismember the picture with a counterdiagonal ferocity anticipating the angular fragmentation of cubism. The two tiers of people framed by these flying structures seem also to be locked into their own time frames; their distinct separation is further defined by a differing scheme of action, density and lighting.

Within the overall dynamics, our eyes dwell on dramatic human details as if they had been staged by a film director. Above, a straw hat is bathed in light as its wearer peers down; to the right, a man in a black derby looks pensively outward with a completely different posture. Farther right, a woman in a large dark shawl aligns her gaze with the seemingly unsteady gangplank before her. Below, the seated woman in the center appears as if cast for a stage role, her tunic and head aglow in an ethereal light. At the extreme right, a young man in shirtsleeves and bowler hat stands in full profile, gazing laconically into the picture. The most arresting subjects, however, are three pairs of mothers and children; the white bonnets of the babies seem to glow with a miraculous reflected light. It is this spiritual triangular constellation within the crowded, affecting portrait that has made the work a major crossroads in the history of photography—even perhaps its most renowned statement.

Stieglitz himself understood the importance of his photograph, for a few years later he transferred its image onto a copperplate by the photogravure process. Each impression was lovingly hand-pulled like a fine-grained aquatint etching (to which photogravure is similar) and placed in a limited edition of his art journal *291* as a manifesto of photography as fine art. It is these warm-toned prints that represent *The Steerage* in the world's museums.

The Landscape of Impressionism The impressionist approach inspired printmakers to conceive a diffuse landscape where ephemeral light and texture could interweave through the entire image. Theirs was an enchantment with and celebration of the power of sunlight to shimmer over and dissolve the very substance of landscape into a resplendent pattern of tone and color. The printmakers' romance with impressionism, although foreshadowed in Canaletto's tremulous, sun-drenched Venetian etchings of a century and a half earlier, actually spans a short period of only about fifty years in all. But their contribution to the impressionist movement is a stunning corpus of like-inspired imagery, superbly rendered in infinite gradations of black, white and gray.

Six years before Claude Monet exhibited *Impression: Sunrise*, the painting that would inspire the new term "impressionism," his teacher, Johan Barthold Jongkind, actually etched the first impressionist masterpiece (plate 85). The Dutch painter's nervous scrawls create a

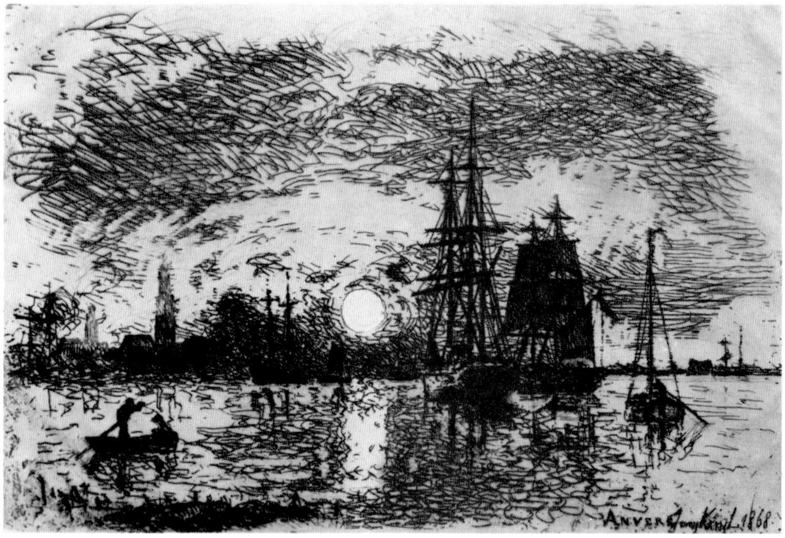

85

85.
Johan Barthold Jongkind (1819–1891). Dutch. *Sunset at Antwerp Harbor*, 1868. Etching. 16 x 23.5 cm. (6¼ x 9¼ in.). Private collection

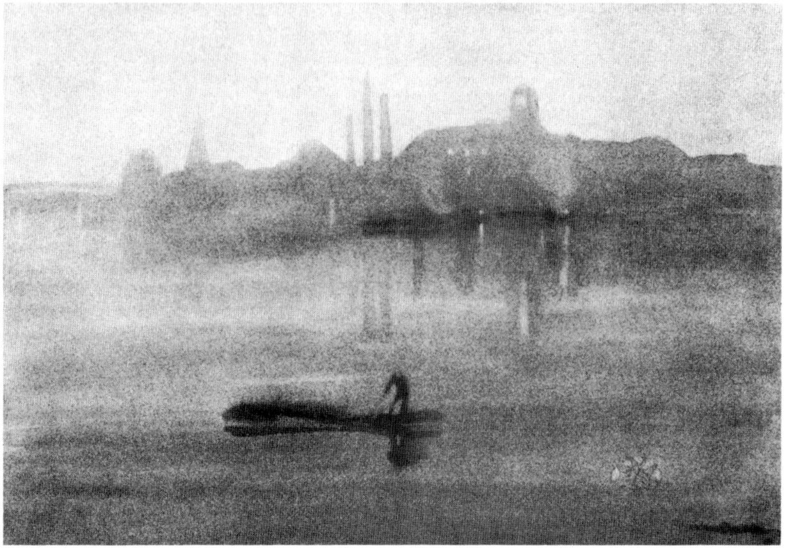

86

86.
James McNeill Whistler (1834–1903). American. *Nocturne (The Thames at Battersea)*, 1878. Lithotint. 17 x 25.7 cm. (6⅝ x 10⅛ in.). Private collection

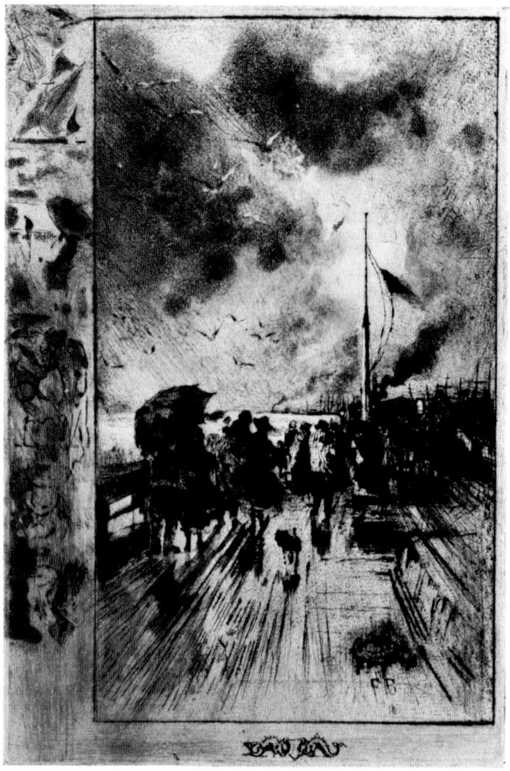

87

87.
Félix Buhot (1847–1898). French. *A Pier in England*, 1879. Etching, aquatint, drypoint and engraving. 29.9 x 19.8 cm. (11¾ x 7¾ in.). Private collection

labyrinth through which the light of the setting sun appears to tunnel. This effect has been heightened by a technique peculiar to the intaglio process. In this technique (*retroussage*) the plate is not wiped thoroughly clean after the incised lines have been inked; instead, an ever-so-thin layer of ink is retained on most of the plate's surface. In the Jongkind plate only the areas of the sun and its reflection were wiped to a glistening polish. The visual result is apparent in the printed image: spots of profound luminosity contrast with the overall hazy tone of the rest of the plate. Monet, who never took up printmaking, was influenced by Jongkind's work, as is evident in his famous *Impression: Sunrise*, exhibited in 1874.

Four years later, across the North Sea, James McNeill Whistler devised a new lithographic technique for his impressionist vision and created his chef d'oeuvre with the process, a heavily etched, stipple-brushed tonal effect he called *lithotint* (plate 86). He was a master at brushing in broad swaths of subtly varied gray in his paintings and invented the lithotint to realize this effect graphically. The juxtaposition of the Jongkind and Whistler images, with their similar subject matter, vividly underscores the totally different aesthetic of each artist and his chosen printmaking technique. Note Whistler's distinctive signature—the stylized butterfly at the lower right.

Félix Buhot left a significant graphic oeuvre, employing every intaglio method—etching, drypoint, engraving (with the roulette) and aquatint—to produce smoky, mottled effects, as in the blustery *A Pier in England* of 1879 (plate 87). As seen in this example, Buhot's etchings are distinctive for the practice of ruling a frame for the main composition well within the plate margins so that tiny impressionistic vignettes could be added within the inner border thus created. This simultaneity of views underlines the impressionists' involvement with capturing the fleeting moment, as change takes place through movement and light.

The leading figures among American impressionists working mainly on American themes were Maurice Prendergast, who found his compatible process in the delicate brushings of remarkable color monotypes (colorplate 4, see page 24); and Childe Hassam, whose airy and crisp etchings of sun-splashed rural Long Island are unsurpassed masterpieces of their kind (plate 88). The printmaker Joseph Pennell, a disciple of Whistler, in 1915 lithographed—of all things—an impressionist vision of a vast oil refinery in Indiana (plate 89). The subject was well chosen for the technique: the roiling smoke, belching flames and light-filtered haze of this reality translated effectively into lithography's granular and luminous properties. Pennell might have recalled Whistler's smokestacks of Battersea (see plate 86) and decided to outdo him with a stirring visual anthem to industrial might.

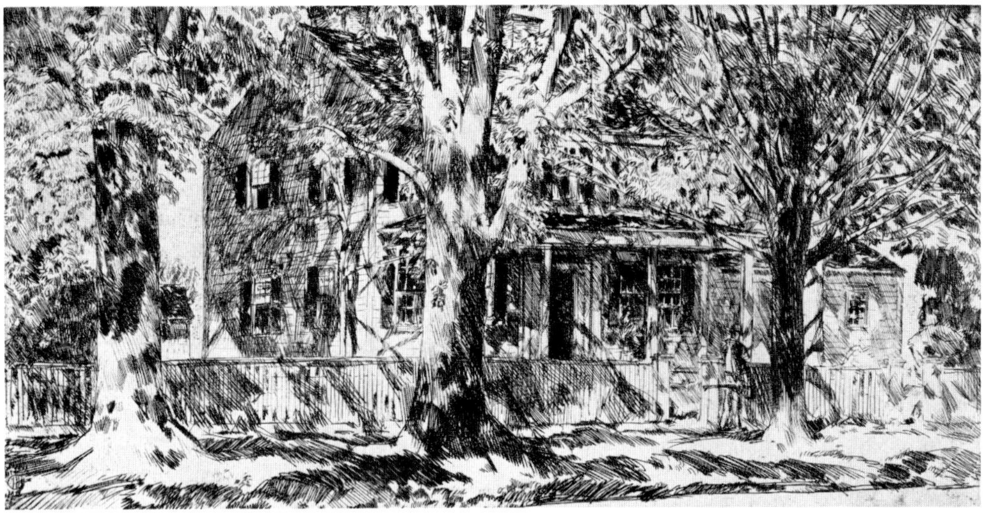

88.
Childe Hassam (1859–1935). American. *House on Main Street, East Hampton*, 1922. Etching. 15.5 x 30.7 cm. (6⅛ x 12⅛ in.). Museum of Modern Art, New York, Abby Aldrich Rockefeller Fund

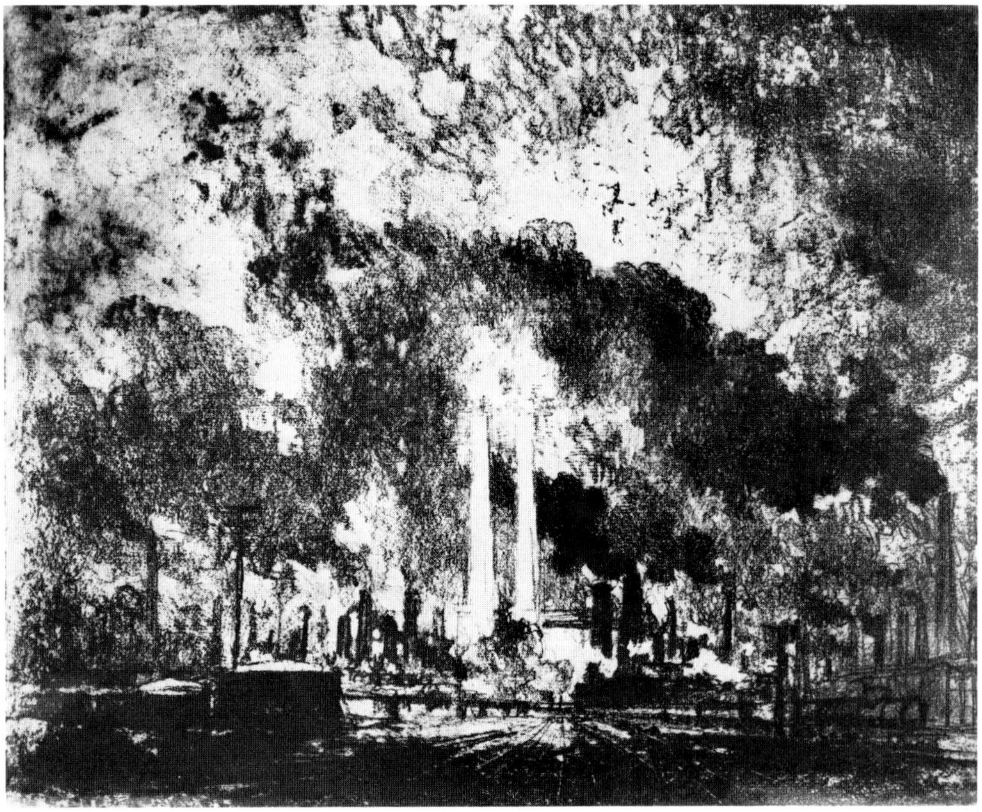

89.
Joseph Pennell (1857–1926). American. *Oil Refining, Whiting, Indiana*, 1915. Lithograph. 42 x 54.2 cm. (16½ x 21⅜ in.). Museum of Modern Art, New York, gift of Donald Karshan

The Direct Message of the Poster The utilization of major artists to design posters, starting in the mid-nineteenth century, was a fortunate circumstance for advertisers, artists, the public and the history of printmaking. It was soon realized that artists could skillfully manipulate words and images to catch the attention of preoccupied pedestrians and thus achieve lasting visual impact for the advertised product. For artists the poster became a popular form of commissioned work in which they could find great scope to express themselves even though ordinarily they did not originate the subject matter or text. Because posters were often large-scale and lavishly colored to satisfy the demand for nearly instant recognition, they presented unique aesthetic challenges and opportunities; and their substantial numbers and wide exposure added notably to an artist's fame. So successful was this new practice that manufacturers, theaters, cabarets and galleries, among others, all vied for wall space along the boulevards of Paris, where the first poster boom occurred. This popular phenomenon was soon rightfully dubbed the art of the streets; not surprisingly, the street posters most admired by discerning collectors often disappeared during the night.

Despite having initially been circulated in large quantities, some posters subsequently became quite rare. This rarity is not entirely puzzling. The very profusion of the posters would seem to have discouraged a proper evaluation of their aesthetic worth, so that little effort was made to preserve them. (It is noteworthy that many of the rarest works in the printmaking catalogue are among those that were most abundant when issued.) Other factors may also have contributed to the rarity of these graphics: large-format posters could not be moved or stored easily, and many posters were mass-produced on an inexpensive paper that was not designed to last.

Originally published in France, Scotland, Germany, Russia and America, the six examples reproduced in color here indicate the international scope of poster activity and identify as well some of the major contributors who turned this commercial vehicle into an impressive art form. Viewing the vibrant lithographic colors and dynamic imagery of these works, we are reminded that no other form of graphic art is so striking in scale and chromatic brilliance. Such aesthetic qualities are ideal for collectors who wish to adorn their walls with bold, colorful art that can be enjoyed even from some distance.

Pierre Bonnard's *France-Champagne* (colorplate 19) boasts at least four historical distinctions: since Bonnard was the first major painter to create multicolor posters, this example, his first such effort, is a milestone; the young Toulouse-Lautrec was so impressed with the poster that he asked Bonnard for an introduction to his printer and soon began his own extraordinary lithographic oeuvre; the highly stylized lettering of the poster's title, eminently suiting the lyrical, bubbly charm of the overall image and the product, is one of the

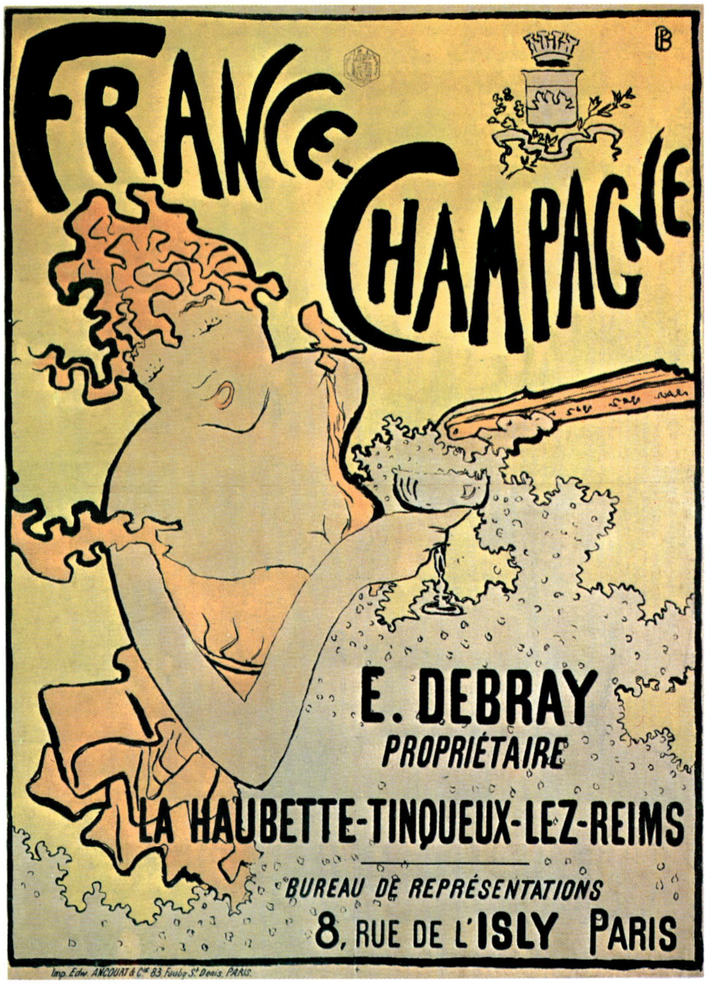

COLORPLATE 19

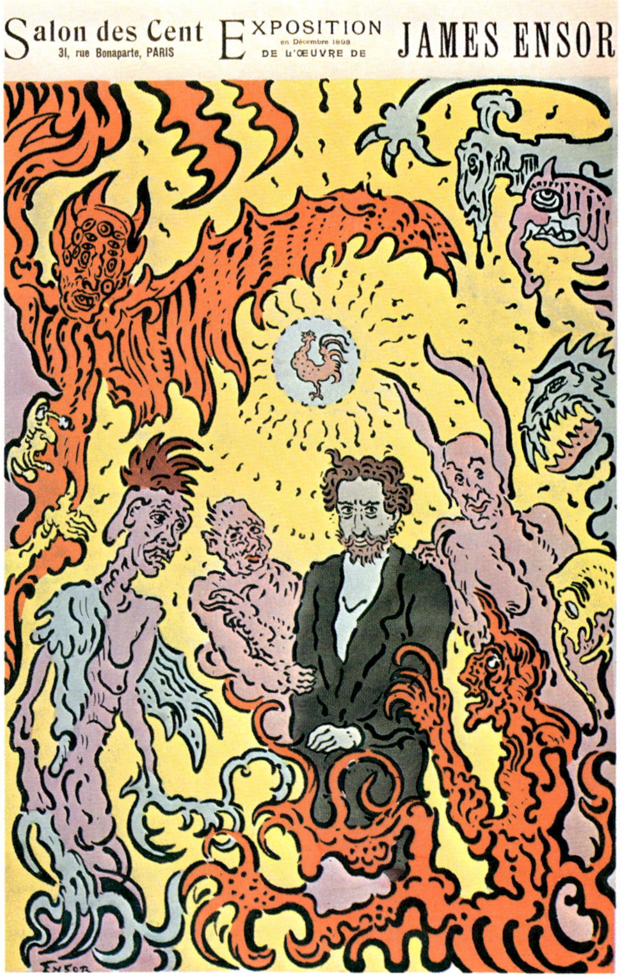

COLORPLATE 20

earliest examples of a device that became an integral feature of modern poster art; *France-Champagne* arrived at the outset of the decade that was to be called the golden age of the poster in France and America.

One of the weirdest posters of all appeared like an apparition in the streets of Paris in 1898 (colorplate 20). Inspired by Schongauer's engraving of the tormented Saint Anthony, done more than four hundred years earlier (plate 33, see page 41), the Belgian painter James Ensor brushed onto the litho stone a startling self-portrait. The lurid red, lavender and gray-green of the taunting demons lend an unearthly aura to the artist's predicament, which he perhaps equated sardonically with the event being announced by the poster—his first exhibition in Paris. The earliest poster in which an artist is known to have represented himself, this is Ensor's most ambitious printed self-portrait, his most important graphic work in color and his only major poster. For these reasons the surviving twenty-odd impressions, most with the lettering carelessly cut off, are highly prized collector's items.

A truly extraordinary poster for a music periodical was conceived around the turn of the century by Charles Rennie Mackintosh of Glasgow, a pioneer modernist architect and designer (colorplate 21). Within the poster's soaring eight-foot height a huge stylized woman seems transported by music, lifted by a chorus of birds within a pattern of rising repeated verticals. For lithographs of this scale, several sheets of printed paper were joined, because no litho stones or presses were large enough to print the image on a single sheet. Few paintings by any artist of the time reveal such abstract modernity as this brilliantly architectonic image, shaped to some degree by the purposes of poster art.

Another kind of spirituality is expressed in Wassily Kandinsky's poster done in 1901 for the opening exhibition of the rebellious art group Phalanx, which he helped found in Munich that same year (colorplate 22). Inspired by a style of fairy-tale illustration from his Russian homeland and by Bavarian folk paintings on glass, Kandinsky ingeniously changed ordinarily benign imagery into vigorous militant symbolism by using heavily outlined repeated forms. The crusading knights (the artist and his colleagues), their sainthood implied by the suggestion of halos, advance against a common adversary, represented by classical columns joining the lettering below with that above—an effective architectural device for both separating and connecting the areas of text. What is so singular about this poster is that it served as the artist's own aesthetic manifesto, through its very style and visual content no less than by way of the event it advertised.

As Kandinsky used war as a make-believe metaphor for artistic combat, his countryman Kazimir Malevich executed a series of war posters dealing with the real combat of World War I (colorplate 23). Like the old popular broadsheets, these posters were fashioned with peasant simplicity and bright colors, and their texts, relegated to a

Colorplate 19.
Pierre Bonnard (1867–1947). French. *France-Champagne*, 1889. Lithograph. 77.5 x 57.8 cm. (30½ x 22¾ in.). Private collection

Colorplate 20.
James Ensor (1860–1949). Belgian. *James Ensor, Salon des Cent Exposition*, 1898. Lithograph. 56.5 x 37.2 (22¼ x 14⅝ in.). Private collection

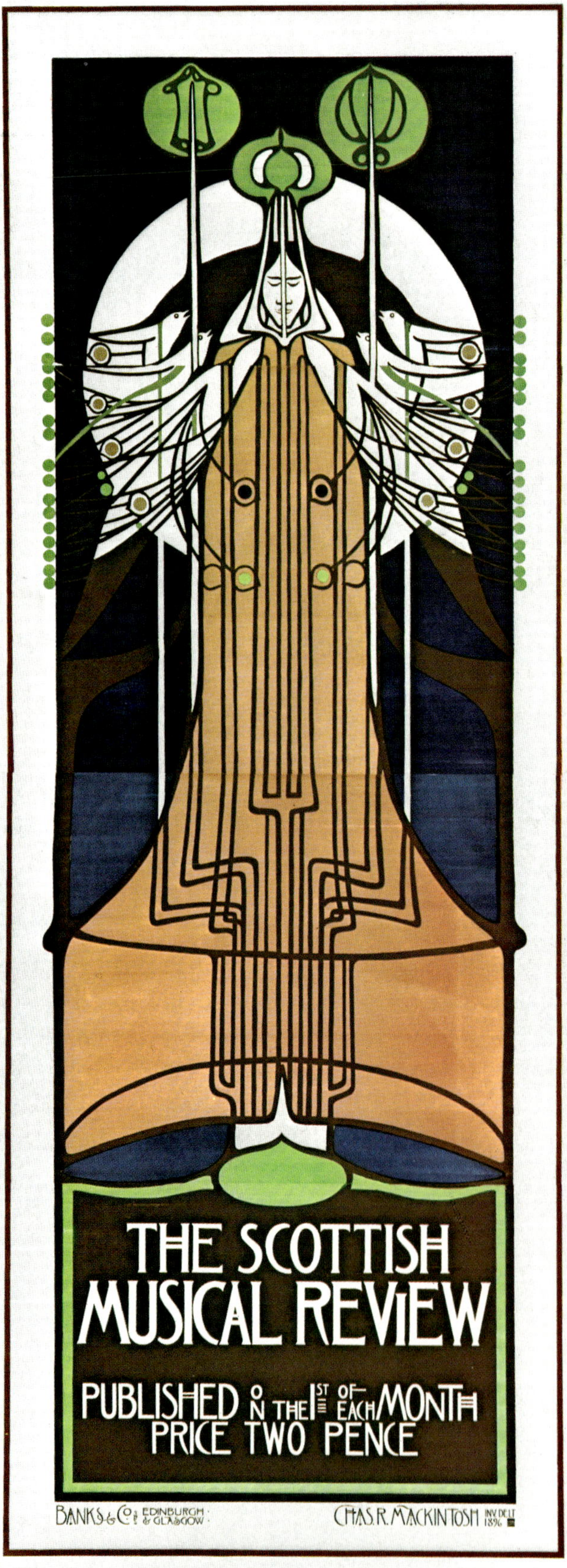

Colorplate 21

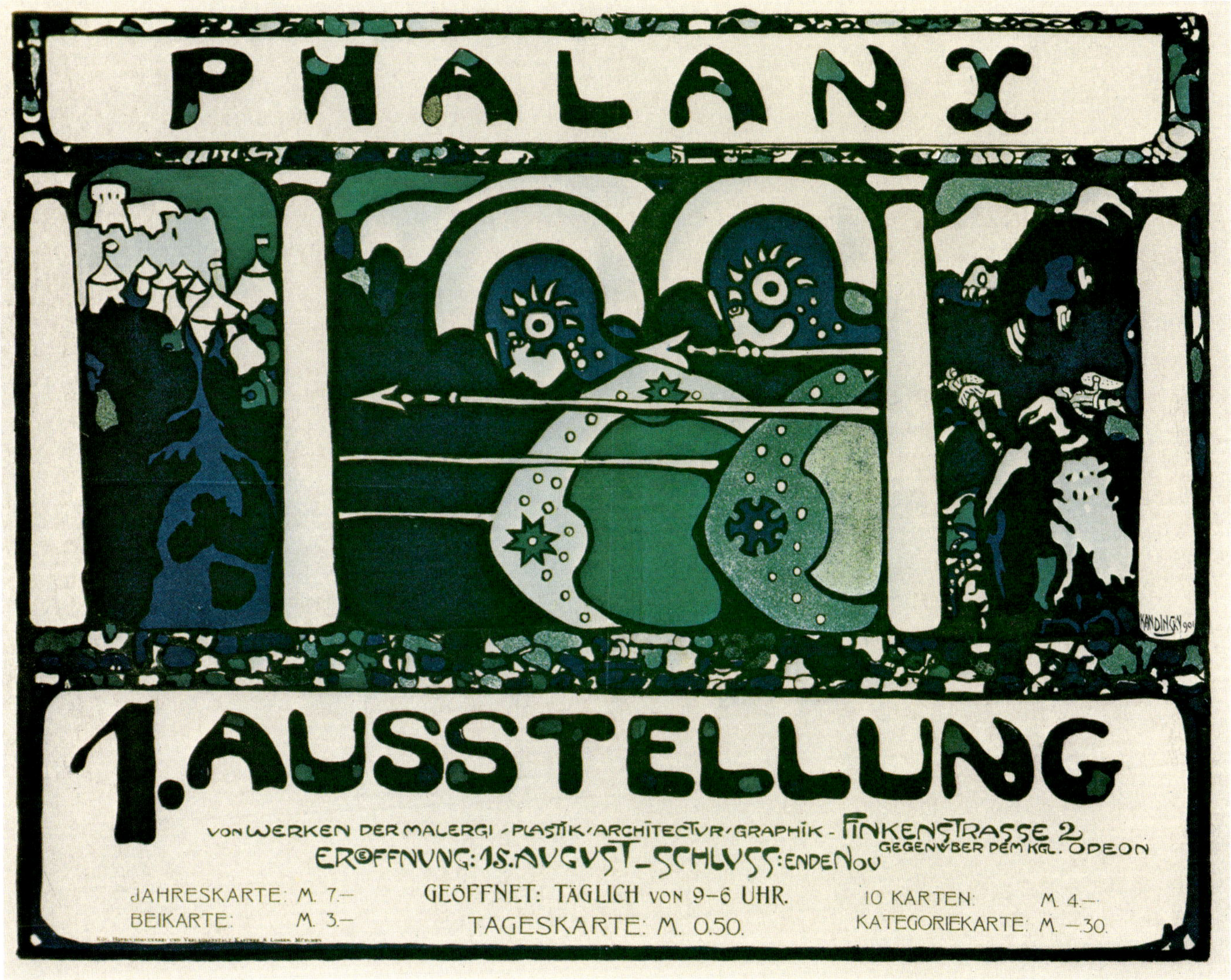

COLORPLATE 22

Colorplate 21.
Charles Rennie Mackintosh (1868–1928). Scottish. *The Scottish Musical Review*, 1896. Lithograph. 246.5 x 99 cm. (97 x 39 in.). Museum of Modern Art, New York, Purchase

Colorplate 22.
Wassily Kandinsky (1866–1944). Russian. *Phalanx: First Exhibition*, 1901. Lithograph. 45.7 x 59 cm. (18 x 23¼ in.). Museum of Modern Art, New York, gift of Mme. Wassily Kandinsky

space beneath the forceful images, were full of candid sarcasm. The poet Vladimir Mayakovsky wrote these bristling lines, and Malevich employed the neoprimitive style of his prewar paintings to create powerful graphic propaganda. Here a peasant cuts down German soldiers with a giant sickle as if they were sheaves of yellow wheat. Their bayonets twisted like broken stems, the corpses lie in files within the folds of rolling land, its form echoing the deadly arc of the farm tool turned weapon.

Although influenced by the sensuous lithographs published in Paris, American graphic artists developed their own inimitable style. One of the most inventive of these designers was Will Carqueville, who like many fellow artists was hired to produce a poster for every issue of a popular monthly magazine, each meant to be striking and different enough to catch the attention of the casual passerby (colorplate 24). With the Fourth of July in mind, Carqueville chose red, white (the paper itself) and blue, plus a delicate green, and made a prankish explosion his subject. The result seems to anticipate pop art's hard-edge, comic-strip pyrotechnics of many decades later (or, indeed, even comic strips themselves). The mischievous little boy who has made the lady drop her magazine and cover her ears is cleverly merged with the billowing smoke; the flying copy of *Lippincott's* is realistically detailed, appearing like the collages of cubism. A Chinese lantern hangs whimsically from the letter *S* in the title. This masterpiece of schematic brevity and riveting appeal certainly fulfills all the requirements for an effective poster.

Colorplate 23.
Kazimir Malevich (1878–1935). Russian. *What a Boom! What a Blast!* . . . , 1914–15. Lithograph. 33.3 x 51.7 cm. (13 1/8 x 20 3/8 in.). Private collection

Colorplate 24.
Will Carqueville (1871–1946). American. *Lippincott's July*, c. 1895. Lithograph. 47 x 30.5 cm. (18 1/2 x 12 in.). Private collection

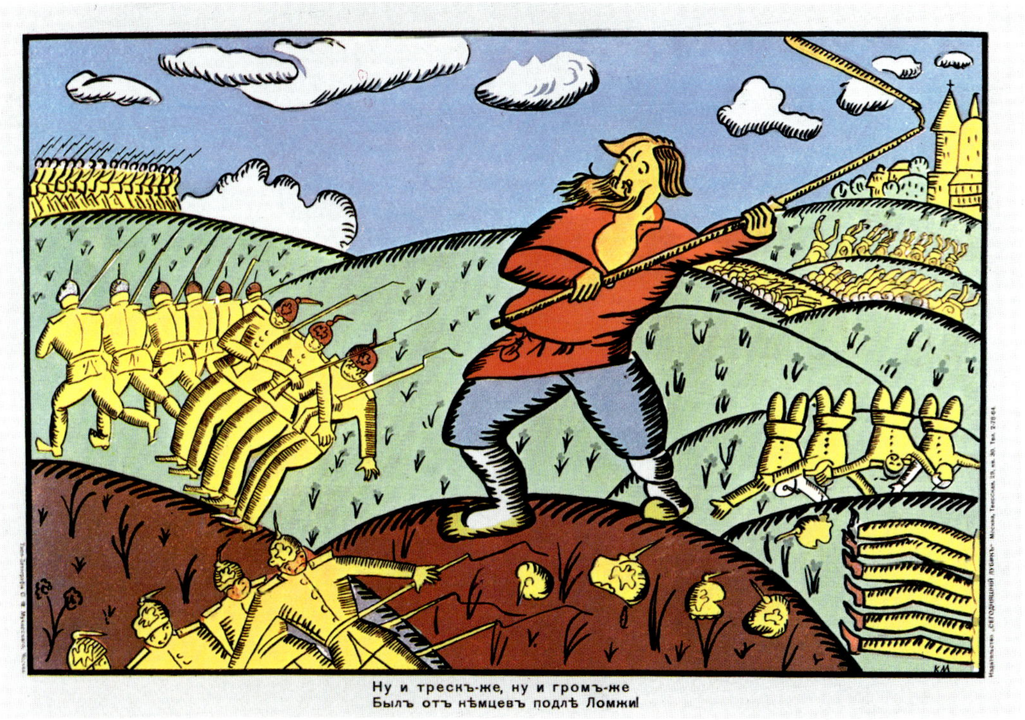

COLORPLATE 23

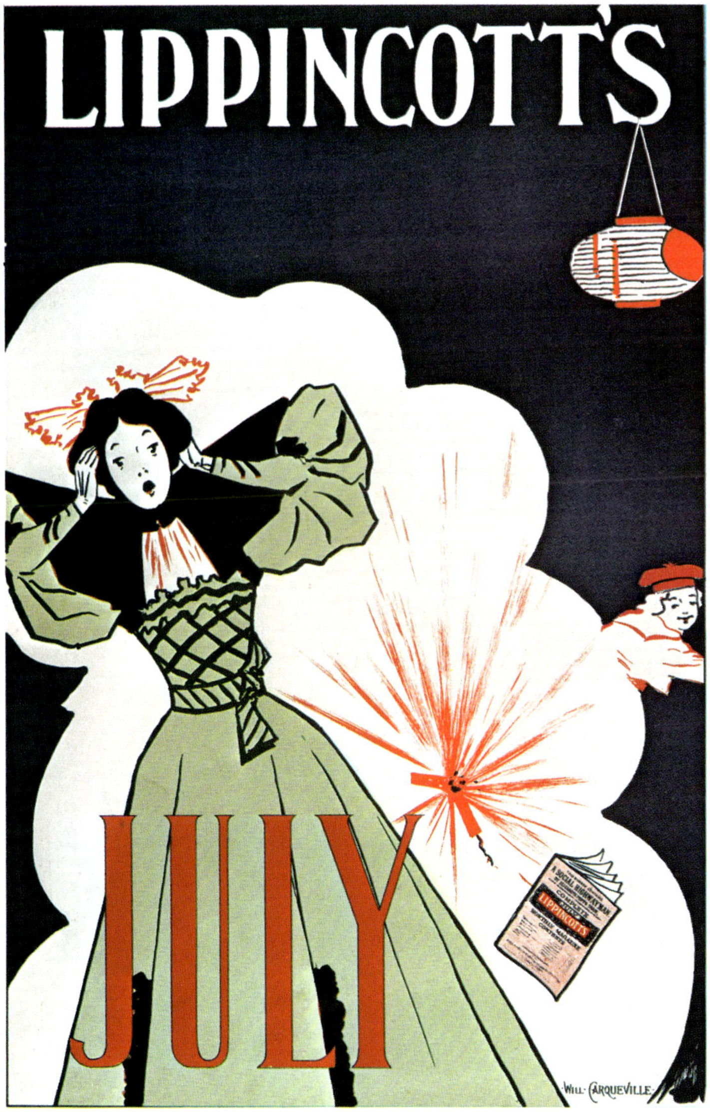

COLORPLATE 24

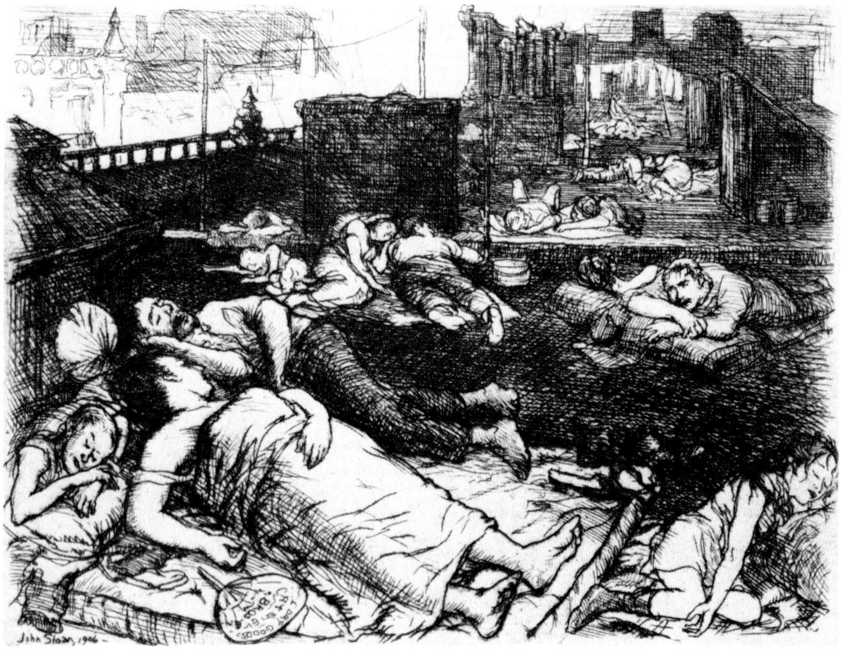

90.
John Sloan (1871–1951). American. *Roofs, Summer Night*, 1906. Etching. 13.4 x 17.8 cm. (5¼ x 7 in.). Museum of Modern Art, New York, gift of Abby Aldrich Rockefeller

Life in the City In etching varied scenes of daily life in New York early in this century, the American painters John Sloan, Reginald Marsh and Edward Hopper testified to their fascination with the city's myriad activities. Each artist searched out his own personal viewpoint, as revealed in the four images reproduced here.

For John Sloan, a crowded nighttime perspective of tenement rooftops meant neighbors brought together by a common aim, to cool off on a sultry summer evening (plate 90). Sloan places us close to an entire family in the foreground, among whom the girl asleep at the right is positioned so that she forms one side of a V completed by the bulky form of her mother. This repeated compositional device leads the eye deep into the picture plane, ending at a limp washline three roofs beyond. We are thus given an overview of several sleeping family groups and of one pensive man (perhaps a stand-in for the artist) who, as the sole wakeful witness, looks out toward the viewer. Sloan has separated this intimate vignette of city life from the glaringly illuminated bustle and heat of the streets below, adroitly using the heavily etched, inky divider of a silhouetted parapet.

In another curious personal choice of ambience, Reginald Marsh places us in an all-male audience at the famous Gaiety Burlesk (plate 91). Rather than being the object of a single person's scrutiny, the unclad performer is stared at by some sixty well-individualized men intent on her every move. Slyly, Marsh placed his friend John Sloan in the front balcony box (the leaning figure with the glasses) and himself in the orchestra (with cigar, at the far right). While Sloan had played off shadowy depth and sharp contrast in his etching, Marsh

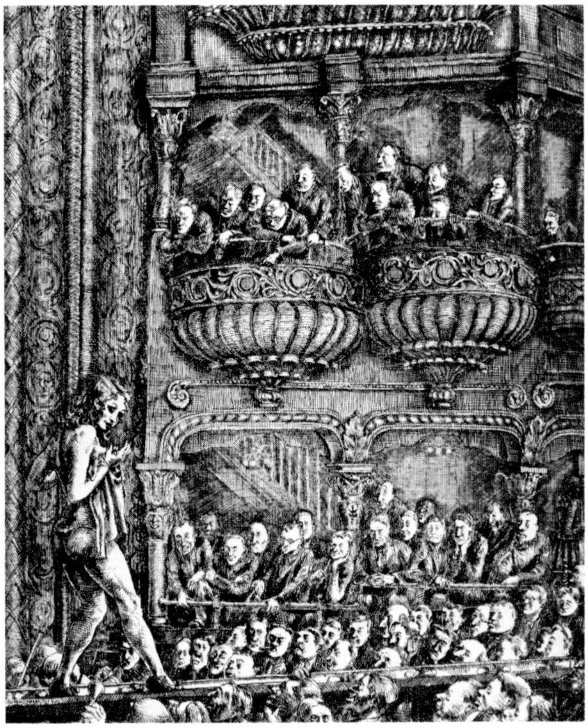

91

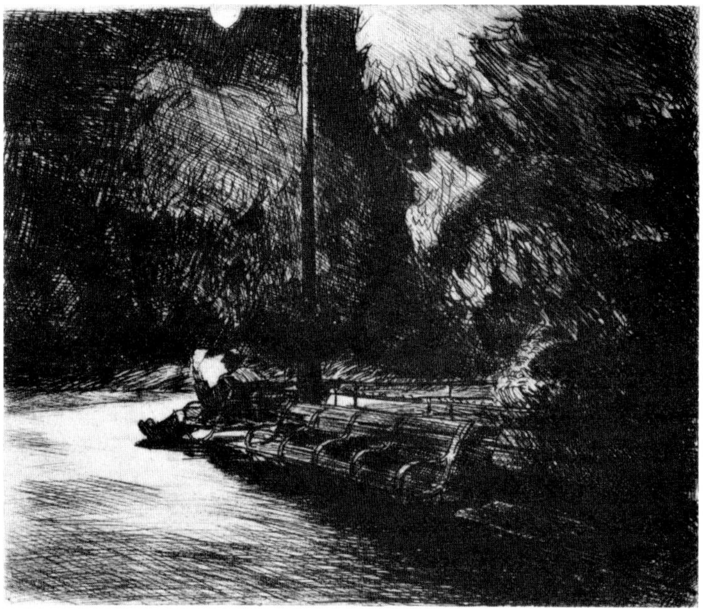

92

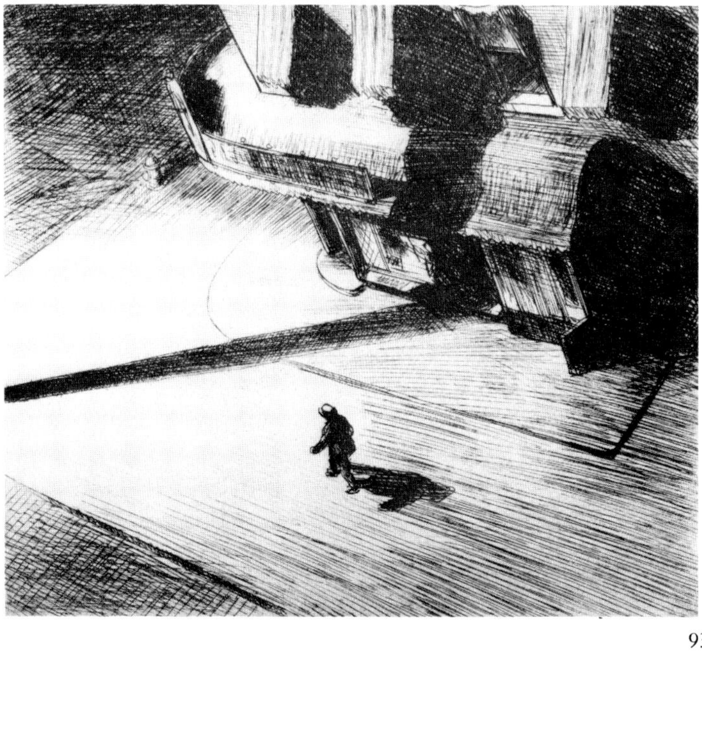

93

91.
Reginald Marsh (1898–1954). American. *Gaiety Burlesk*, 1930. Etching. 30.3 x 24.9 cm. (11⅞ x 9¾ in.). Private collection

92.
Edward Hopper (1882–1967). American. *Night in the Park*, 1921. Etching. 17.8 x 22.2 cm. (7 x 8¾ in.). Private collection

93.
Edward Hopper (1882–1967). American. *Night Shadows*, 1921. Etching. 17.5 x 20.9 cm. (6⅞ x 8¼ in.). Private collection

instead made a shallow sculptural frieze in fairly uniform middle tone, filled from corner to corner with faces and figures and the theater's intricate architecture and decoration. The artist's characteristic cross-hatching throughout generates an overall surface excitement perfectly suited to his subject.

As Sloan and Marsh were superb interpreters of collective life, Hopper was the supreme poet of the isolated figure immersed in the impersonal vastness of the modern city. Two of his most memorable etchings on this theme focus on the lone male as seen from different angles (plates 92 and 93). A streetlamp, so high that it appears to hang from the beveled top edge of the plate, illuminates a man sitting in Gramercy Park. The onrushing lines of empty benches and the strong vertical of the lamppost converge on this anonymous city dweller. What could have been a trite expression of loneliness in the hands of a lesser artist is given a more complex tension: the isolated figure seems deep in thought as he reads his newspaper bathed in lamplight. Hopper's image is a statement of individual resourcefulness and resilience amid the verdant mystery of a city park at night.

Similar isolation imbues an aerial view of a solitary figure in dark suit and fedora striding along a bleak nighttime street. From such a steep downward vantage point Hopper could strikingly present the topography of his drama. The deliberate direction of the striding figure and the strongly etched parallel strokes of the pavement lead to some situation outside the picture. The heavy diagonal shadow is that of a lamppost just out of sight on the corner. The strong light that could produce such shadow and flood the sidewalk might be from an open bar or diner on the opposite corner—perhaps the destination of the determined pedestrian. Again Hopper breathes life into the individual in an even more alienating urban environment: the closed shops are menacing hulks cleaved by massive shadows. Conceived years before filmmakers employed similar dramatic techniques, this masterpiece of twentieth-century graphic art, like all Hopper's etchings, required no assistance from embellishing color. Selecting the whitest paper and the deepest black inks, Hopper pursued the extremes of monochrome with singular concentration and devotion.

Personal Confrontations A dramatic visual dialogue between two powerful presences has made for provocative subject matter throughout the history of printmaking. Hans Holbein the Younger's tiny sixteenth-century woodcut of Death surprising a monk as he begs for alms is an early example of such an encounter (plate 94). Against the billowing fumes in the background, the unrelenting grasp of Death's fateful reach drives the point across, and the monk's gasp of recognition almost becomes audible. The scrawny dog has luckily escaped—literally half out of the picture.

By the late nineteenth century these confrontation images were of a more intense and ambiguous emotional nature, influenced by the literary currents of symbolism. Winslow Homer's 1889 etching of an unconscious woman being rescued on a lifeline by a mysterious, faceless male figure is charged with all sorts of implications (plate 96). One interpretation suggests anonymous aggression with total submission on the part of the woman.

Edvard Munch's brooding woodcut of seven years later carries the dialogue into even closer psychological quarters with the fixed, motionless head of a man (the artist?) enshrouded in the faint, sensuous tentacles of a woman's hair (colorplate 25). The man's white face, the only uninked portion of the image, is surrounded oppressively by deep blue, sienna and overprinted dark gray.

Paul Klee's acerbic 1903 etching of diplomatic behavior is less a humorous satire than a merciless investigation of clawing, aging male vanity (plate 95). The bilateral symmetry of this pair of naked reptilian creatures adds to the futility of the implied stalemate. Compare their emaciated arms with those of Holbein's Death, and also compare the horizontal alignments of the eyes of the two pairs of figures. Klee knew well the early German woodcuts and engravings.

Well into the era of Freudian perception, Emil Nolde's famous lithograph of 1913 depicts gripping parlor combat (colorplates 26 and 27). The sophisticated intimidations of personal contact, stare and pointed conversation are all theatrically embodied in this vivid expressonist statement. Nolde, taking advantage of the versatility of the graphic process to search out new psychological effects, printed the image in several different color combinations. We compare two examples here: one of them is overlaid in blood reds and black, the other in light green and light blue—which mixes into a strange off-key chartreuse—together with charcoal gray. The artist has handled the inking so that the colors appear like boldly splashed paint rather than carefully laid-down ink, a device that heightens the undercurrent of emotional violence.

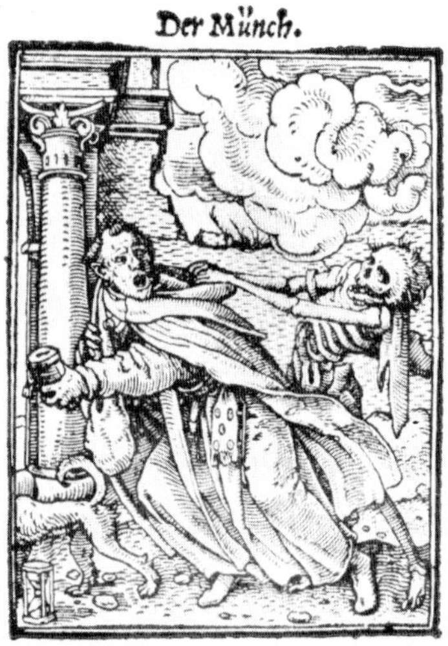

94

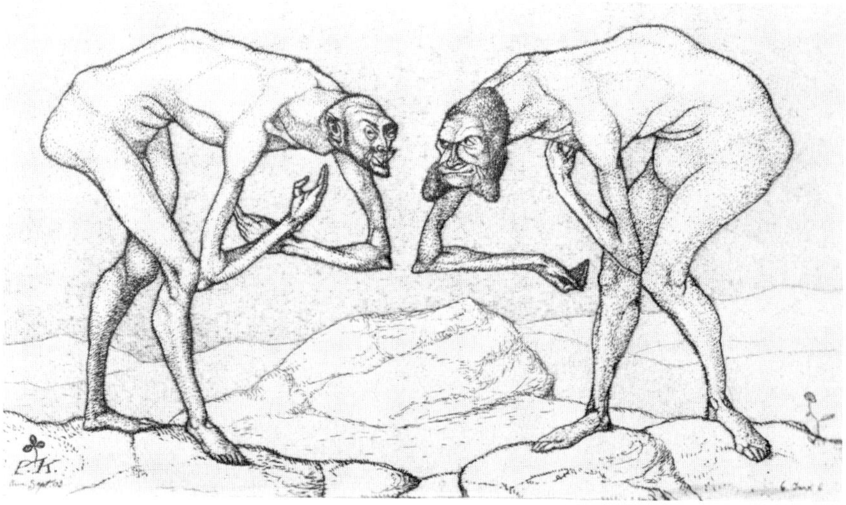

95

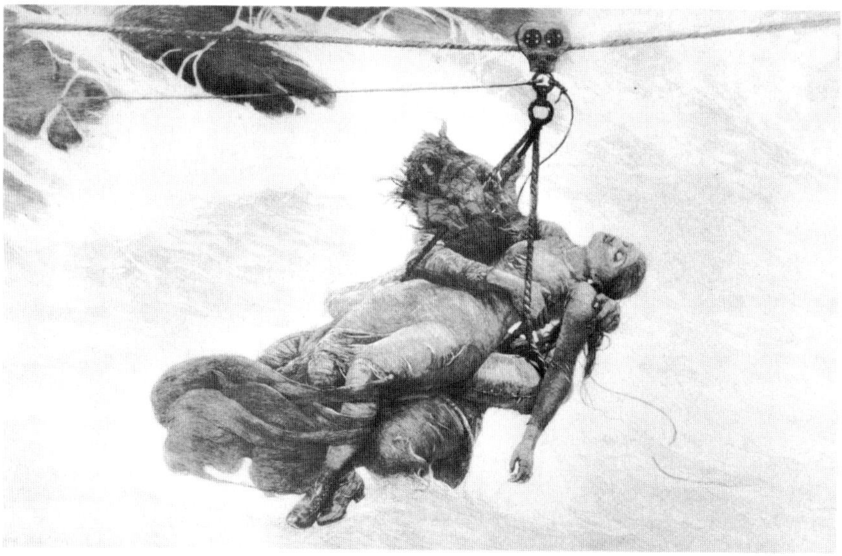

96

94.
Hans Holbein the Younger (c. 1497–1543). German. *The Monk*. Woodcut from *The Dance of Death*, 1538. 6.7 x 4.8 cm. (2⅝ x 1⅞ in.). Private collection

95.
Paul Klee (1874–1940). Swiss. *Two Men Meet, Each Believing the Other of Higher Rank*, 1903. Etching. 11.8 x 22.6 cm. (4⅝ x 8⅞ in.). Museum of Modern Art, New York, gift of Mme. Paul Klee

96.
Winslow Homer (1836–1910). American. *Saved*, 1889. Etching. 57.7 x 83 cm. (22¾ x 32⅝ in.). Cooper-Hewitt Museum, purchased in memory of Erskine Hewitt

Colorplate 25.
Edvard Munch (1863–1944). Norwegian. *Man's Head in Woman's Hair*, 1896. Woodcut. 54.6 x 38.1 cm. (21½ x 15 in.). Museum of Modern Art, New York, William B. Jaffe and Evelyn A. J. Hall Collection

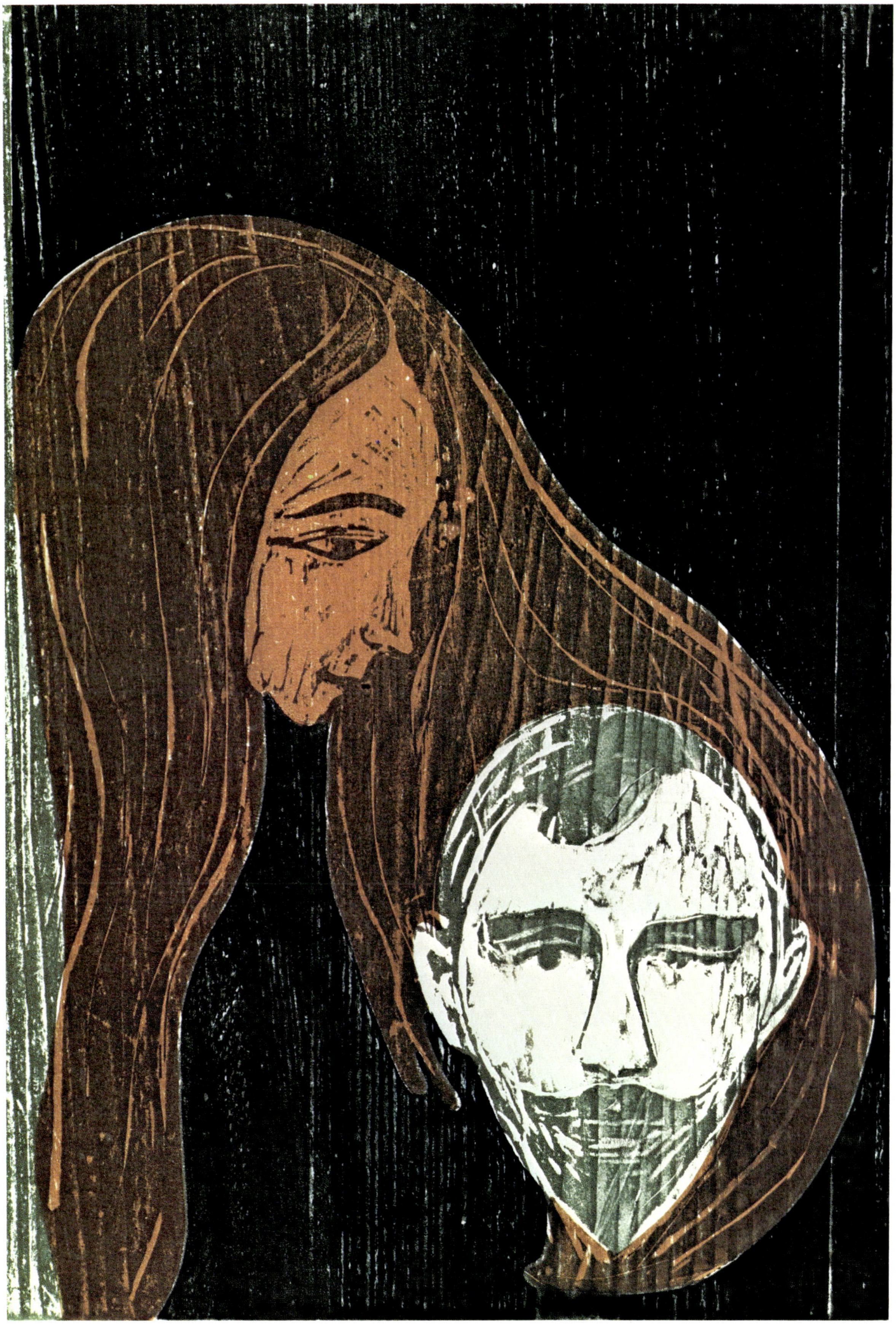

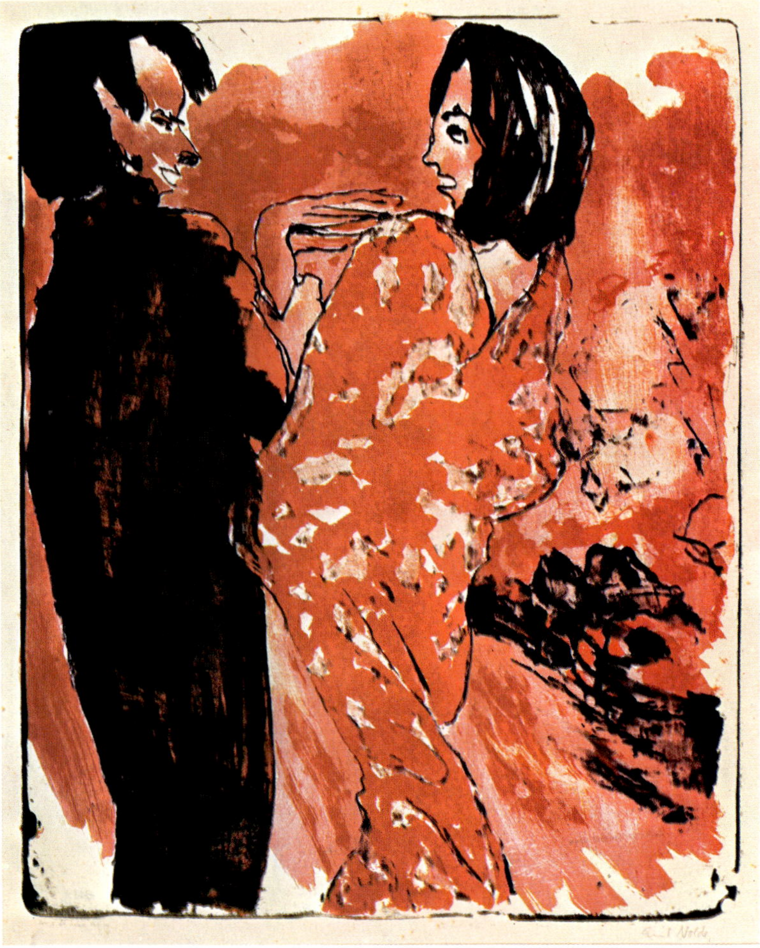

Colorplate 26

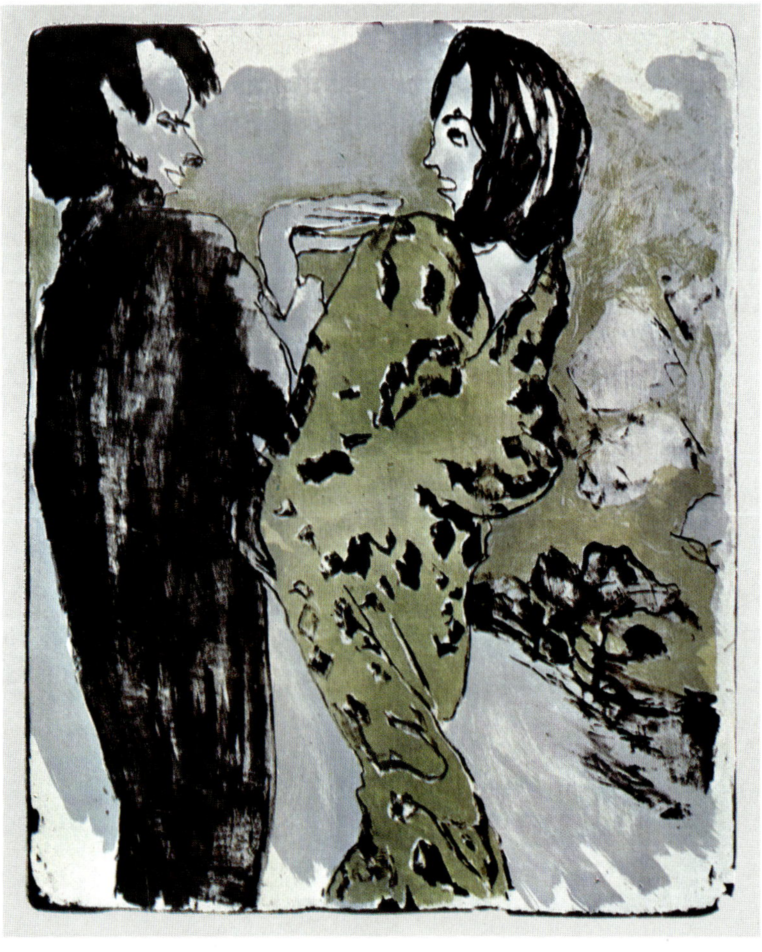

Colorplate 27

Towers The prevailing direction of modern civilization is upward, and since the early years of this century, particularly, the tower has been one of its principal symbols. It is probably no coincidence that the graphic masterpieces of four major twentieth-century painters are forceful images of towers. Regardless of whether the artists' excursions were by way of cubism, futurism or precisionism, the one underlying ingredient in these images is a sense of exultation, of glorying in a soaring man-made structure.

John Marin's two etchings with drypoint of the Woolworth Building in New York City are fascinating to compare (plates 97 and 98). As they were executed and published one right after the other, their conception and development can be traced as if the first print were a progressive state in evolving the final composition. The simpler earlier work only hints at the explosive dynamism of the artist's subsequent effort. In the former, the tersest strokes of the etching needle indicate low foreground buildings, the schematic suggested curves of trees and the looming skyscraper itself. Although a certain sense of relative height is achieved in the first print, Marin opted for a far more emphatic imagery in the later plate, which he subtitled *The Dance*. Foreground structures are now in more convincing perspective as they approach the viewer on the right and curve into the picture, their arc concentric with the curves of the prickly, writhing trees. Strong drypoint accenting of low rooflines, shadowy windows and pedestrians gives the street level weight and tone, establishing a definite groundrow from behind which springs the giant skyscraper, here a visionary white in contrast with the bustling foreground and heavily worked sky. The tower's tilt is now more pronounced, and streaks of windows enhance its majestic, cathedral-like ascent, culminating in the rich burr of the columns and steeple high in the sky.

Lyonel Feininger's prismatic tower (plate 99) is actually a rustic church steeple in the Bavarian Alps, translated with cubist fragmentation into a formidable modernistic obelisk looking as if finely tooled out of black marble. In what is probably the most powerful of all cubist woodcuts, this piercing needle is set against massive overlapping planes of ice. In light of the tranquil alpine subject that nominally inspired this surging work, the overwhelming personal vision of its creator cannot be overestimated in judging the result.

When the Eiffel Tower first rose over the Paris skyline toward the end of the nineteenth century, it made a great avant-garde statement in itself; it was a virtual manifesto of the new century's irresistible upward strivings. One would think, then, that such nearly instantaneous credentials would discourage an artist from using the Eiffel Tower as ready-made subject matter for his own manifesto. But that is precisely what Robert Delaunay did. With an audacious use of cubist vocabulary, he dismantled the complex metal scaffolding of this imposing tower and reassembled it his own way (plate 100). Newborn in front

Colorplate 26.
Emil Nolde (1867–1956). German. *Young Couple*, 1913. Lithograph. 62.2 x 51 cm. (24½ x 20⅛ in.). Museum of Modern Art, New York, Purchase Fund

Colorplate 27.
Emil Nolde (1867–1956). German. *Young Couple*, 1913. Lithograph. 62.2 x 51 cm. (24½ x 20⅛ in.). Museum of Modern Art, New York, Purchase Fund

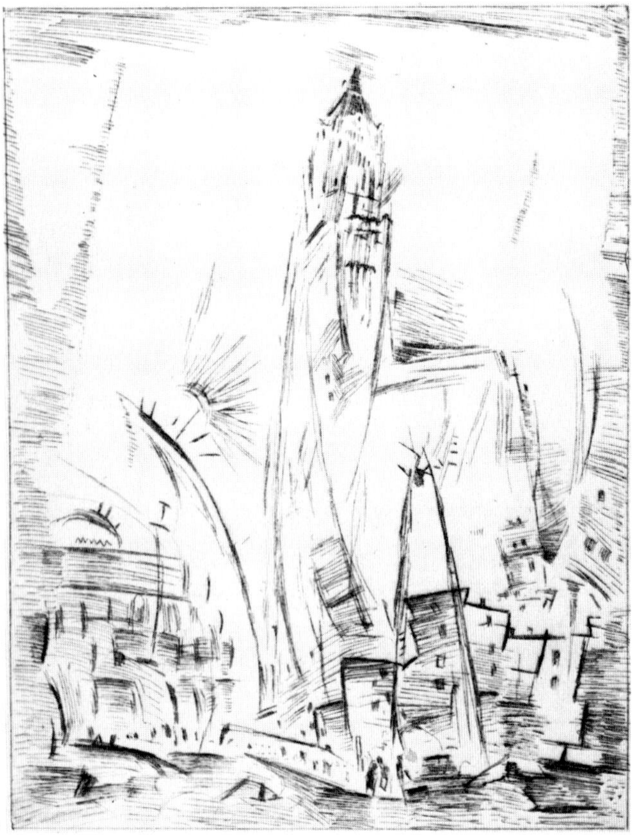

97

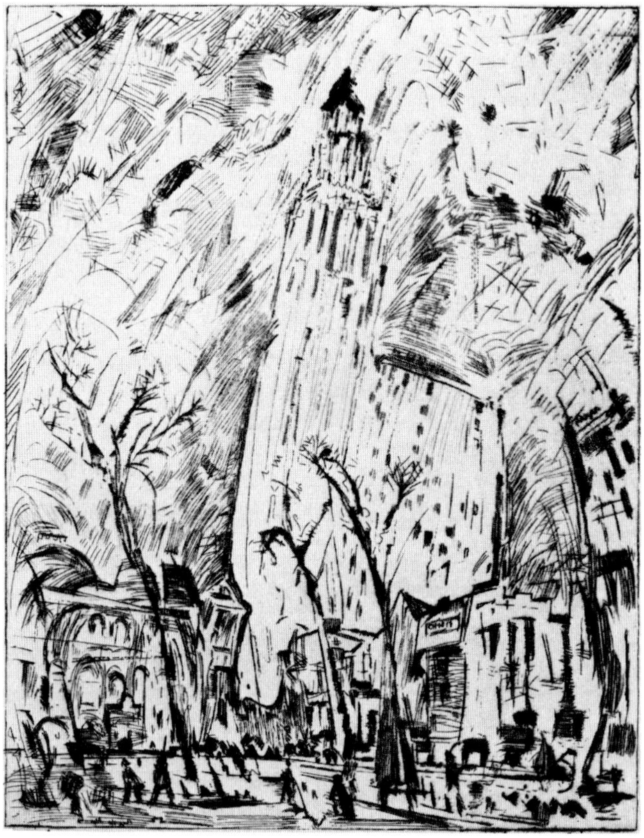

98

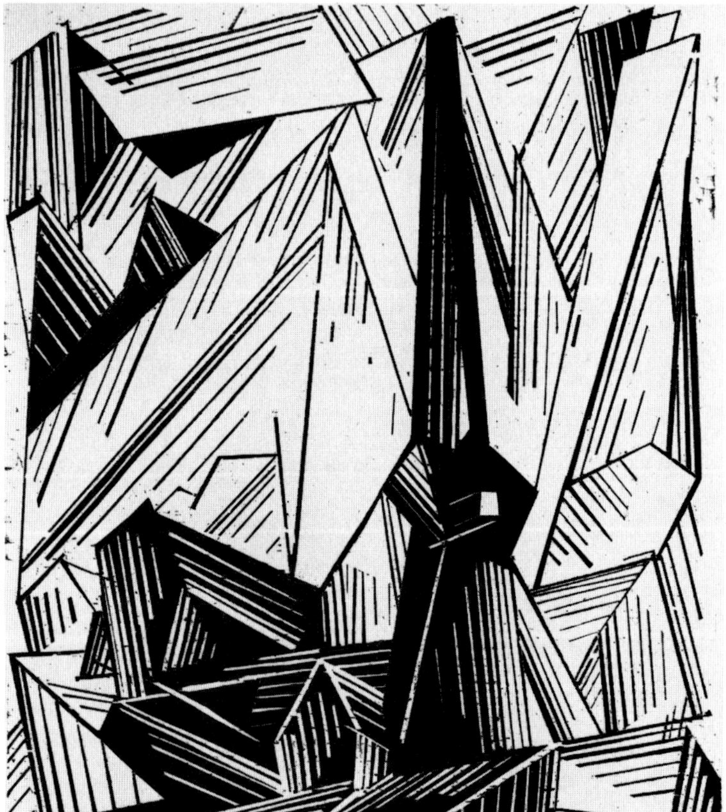

99

97.
John Marin (1870–1953). American. *Woolworth Building No. 2*, 1913. Etching and drypoint. 32.5 x 26.5 cm. (12¾ x 10⅜ in.). Museum of Modern Art, New York, gift of Abby Aldrich Rockefeller

98.
John Marin (1870–1953). American. *Woolworth Building (The Dance)*, 1913. Etching and drypoint. 33 x 27 cm. (13 x 10⅝ in.). Museum of Modern Art, New York, Edward M. M. Warburg Fund

99.
Lyonel Feininger (1871–1956). American. *Gelmeroda*, 1920. Woodcut. 49 x 43 cm. (19¼ x 17 in.). Private collection

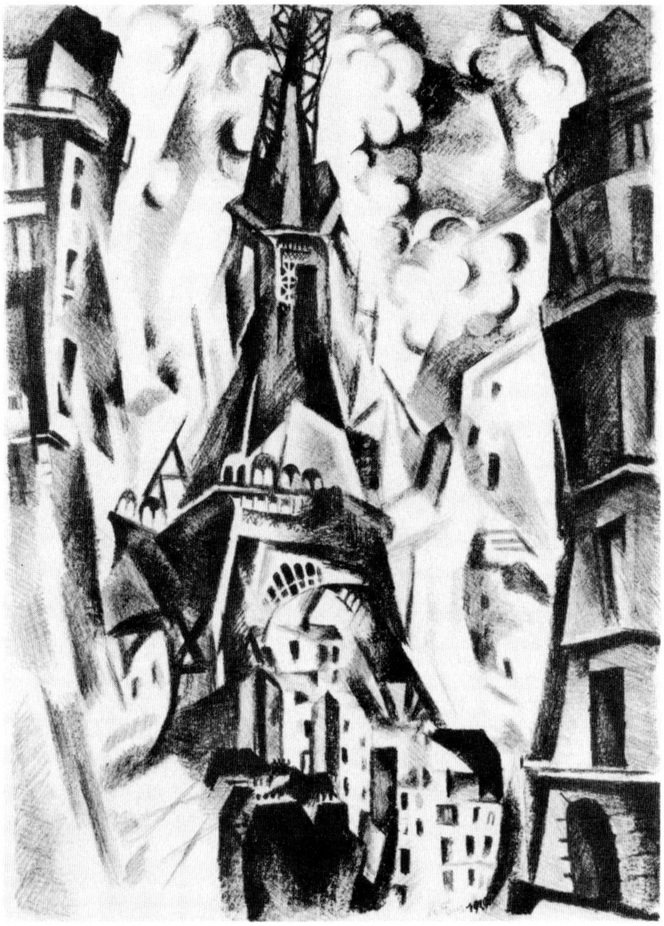

100

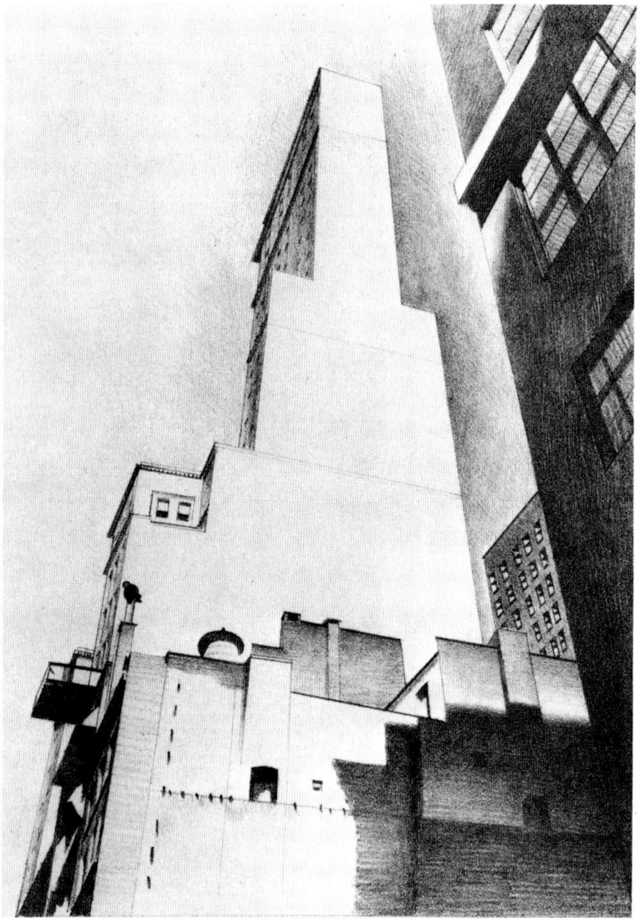

101

100.
Robert Delaunay (1885–1941). French. *The Tower*, 1926. Lithograph. 60.7 x 44.5 cm. (23⅞ x 17½ in.). Private collection

101.
Charles Sheeler (1883–1965). American. *Delmonico Building*, 1926. Lithograph. 24.8 x 17 cm. (9¾ x 6⅝ in.). Museum of Modern Art, New York, gift of Abby Aldrich Rockefeller

of us is a dynamic machine that makes the clouds churn around its summit and the dwarfed, antiquated buildings at its base tilt and sway. Indeed, recombined thus in precarious imbalance, the jumbled tower seems at the very epicenter of an earthquake. Boldly, Delaunay reincarnated the Eiffel Tower, the triumphant climax of nineteenth-century engineering feats, as a visionary futurist manifesto. In its lithographic version (a series of painted studies preceded the graphic work), printed in a deeply contrasted range of black and white, Delaunay's image reached its purest form.

Charles Sheeler's clean-lined vision of the blank sidewall of a tower is strictly postcubist. The Delmonico Building in New York City is seen from its windowless side, so that its rising white shaft soars off into space, pure and utopian (plate 101). The skyscraper is drawn with the subtlest of lithographic shading within ruled lines that follow exactly the sharply receding perspective of a preliminary photograph Sheeler himself made—a multimedia approach he often employed.

The New Figure Artists' visions of the human figure went through more radical change during a brief fifteen-year period at the beginning of this century than during the preceding four centuries combined. To be sure, over the long course of time the figure had been diversely modeled, foreshortened, twisted, stretched and flattened. But it was the advent of the cubist revolution, infused with Cézanne's reductionist dictum of the cylinder, sphere and cone, that would bring about the most profound alterations.

The first great graphic work that signaled the start of such a pivotal departure in ways of seeing was a lithograph of 1906–7 by Henri Matisse (plate 102), executed just as cubism was about to be heralded by Picasso's celebrated painting *Les Demoiselles d'Avignon.* Although Matisse's nude displays all curves rather than the typical sharp angles of cubism, the geometric common denominators of Cézanne are clearly dominant in a faceless, tubular figure that seems to store energy like a coiled spring about to be released. This automatonlike creature anticipates the romance of modern artists with the machine culture, which would emerge explicitly about six years later. An impressive sculptural depth was achieved here by Matisse with rich lithographic shadow. (It should be noted that the painter was also working in three dimensions at that time.)

The next stage in the figure's drastic modification can be seen in a Picasso drypoint of 1909 (plate 103), which, despite the classical

102.
Henri Matisse (1869–1954). French. *Nude,* 1906–7. Lithograph. 28.5 x 25.4 cm. (11¼ x 10 in.). Museum of Modern Art, New York, gift of Abby Aldrich Rockefeller

103.
Pablo Picasso (1881–1973). Spanish. *Two Nudes,* 1909. Drypoint. 13 x 11 cm. (5⅛ x 4¼ in.). Museum of Modern Art, New York, Purchase Fund

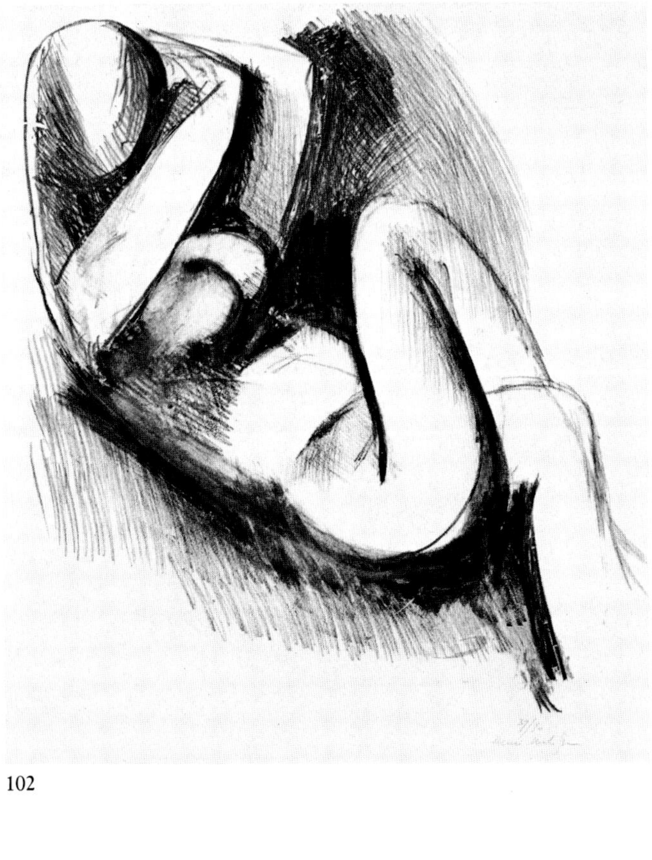

102

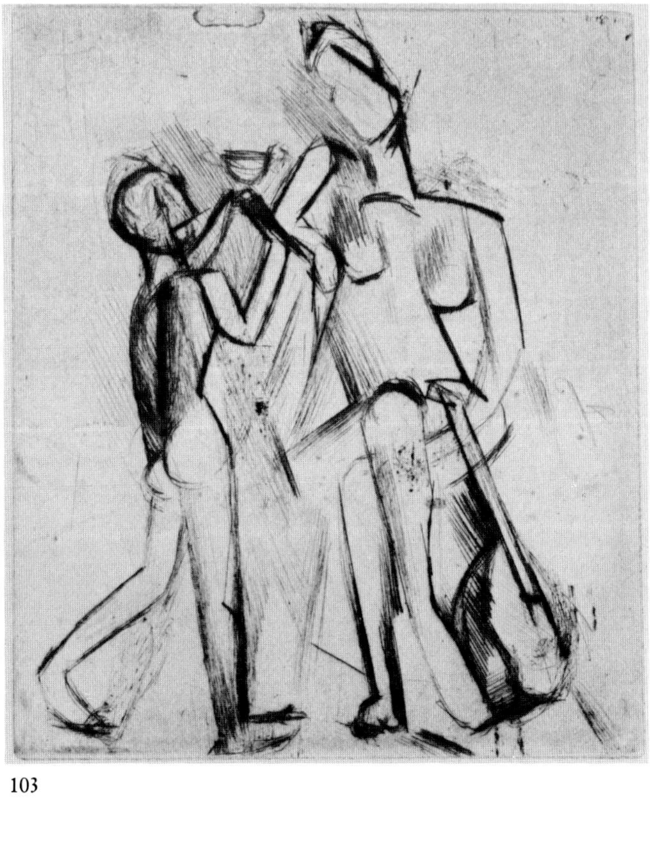

103

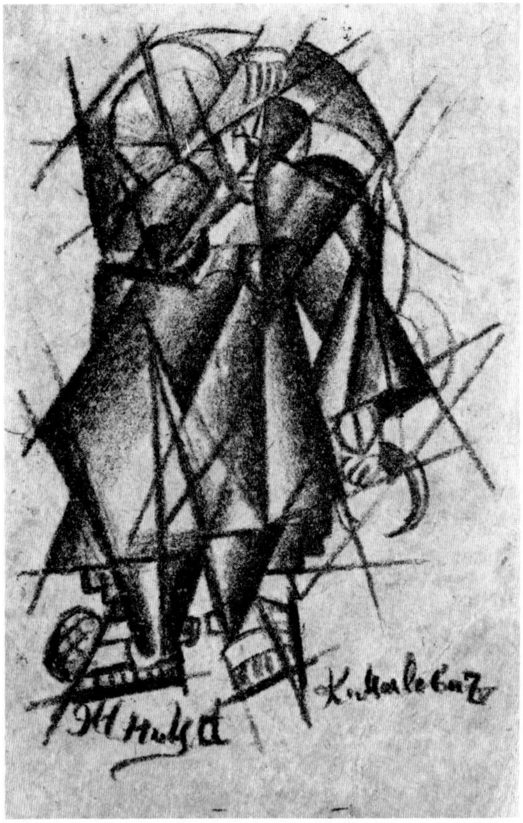

104

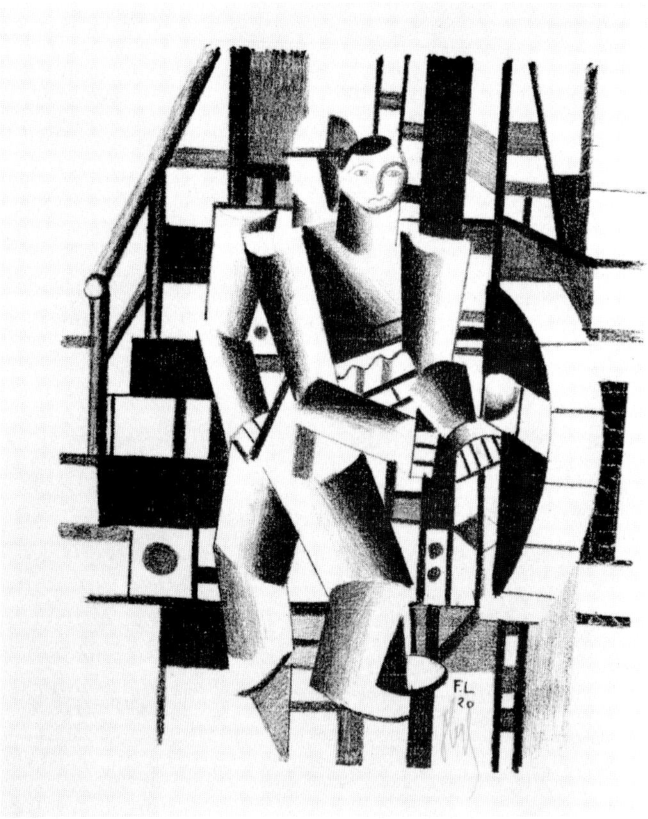

105

104.
Kazimir Malevich (1878–1935). Russian. *Woman Reaping*. Cover design for *Slovo kak Takovoe*, 1913. Lithograph. 14.7 x 9.8 cm. (5¾ x 3⅞ in.). Museum of Modern Art, New York

105.
Fernand Léger (1881–1955). French. *Construction Men*, 1920. Lithograph. 28.6 x 23.5 cm. (11¼ x 9¼ in.). Private collection

dialogue and overall triangulation of its composition, already discloses the schematic angles and deformations of cubism, especially in the seated right-hand nude. Her face is also without features, and her shoulders are stepped at different levels as if dislocated, with her right arm strangely abutted against the standing figure's arm. The powerful diagonal line of the woman's midsection is linked with the diagonal of the mandolin. These odd zigzag connections, together with apparent disregard for comparative scale, activate the image as well as agitate the white space between and around the figures, sometimes making their actual whereabouts highly ambiguous.

Cubism eventually traveled as far east as Moscow, where in 1913 Kazimir Malevich drew his many-faceted peasant woman at work (plate 104). This severely fragmented image reveals how the futurists combined cubism's simultaneity of views with the extension of many diagonals within a figure into the surrounding space. These intersecting "lines of force" and the many repetitions of the sickle's arc motif function like multiple-exposure photography that captures sequential motions in a single print. Here these devices effectively express the figure's energetic stride and cutting action. This blend of styles—a departure from the austere classic balances of Parisian cubism—was described as "cubo-futurism" by Malevich, who produced several such small, vigorous lithographs for now-rare publications of futurist poetry that have become collector's items.

The planar, firmly geometric female figure by Alexander Archipenko (colorplate 28) was published in Berlin in 1921 among a suite of lithographs based on or done as preliminary studies for sculpture. The elongated standing woman has been transformed into clearly delineated sculptural elements, such as the streamlined hourglass form punctured by two holes for the upper torso, the long planks and cone for the lower torso and limbs, and the crosscut cylinder for one arm. Graceful, even elegant, in spite of its robotlike form, this hieratic conception reveals Archipenko's Byzantine roots as much as his Parisian cubist experience. A monochromatic graphic work can become richly tonal when the artist prints the image in a vibrant colored ink rather than in the usual range of blacks or dark grays. Archipenko's lithograph, though published in only one color and thus requiring a single stone and printing cycle, is a superb example of such brilliant chromatic effect. The sculptor-printmaker controlled his color density range so sensitively that the background blue appears decidedly different from the blue of the less-worked areas within the figure.

A year earlier Archipenko's friend Fernand Léger had made his first and most powerful graphic statement, also published in Berlin (plate 105). Abstract geometric scaffolding, promoting a balanced composition that, paradoxically, is often spatially ambivalent, is one of the essential elements of cubism and its beneficiary constructivism. Léger's admiration for construction workers and his visual appreciation of the steel scaffolding on which they climbed allowed him to fit a forceful modern reality into the aesthetic vocabulary of his abstract design. The results are compositions such as this lithograph, where the limbs of the two intermingled figures are massive tubular shapes not unlike the architectural framework they are building around themselves. A fugal interplay of overlapping, juxtaposed and stepped black and white squares, rectangles, circles, beams and diagonal struts has been set up that is both powerful and extremely decorative.

What is so remarkable about the diversely abstract "new figures" created by these five modern masters is that they did not lose the humanist element. This element still breathes expressive life into what could have been merely a mechanistic, depersonalized image of contemporary reality.

Colorplate 28.
Alexander Archipenko (1887–1964). American. *Construction*, 1921. Lithograph. 46.3 x 29.2 cm. (18¼ x 11½ in.). Museum of Modern Art, New York, Purchase Fund

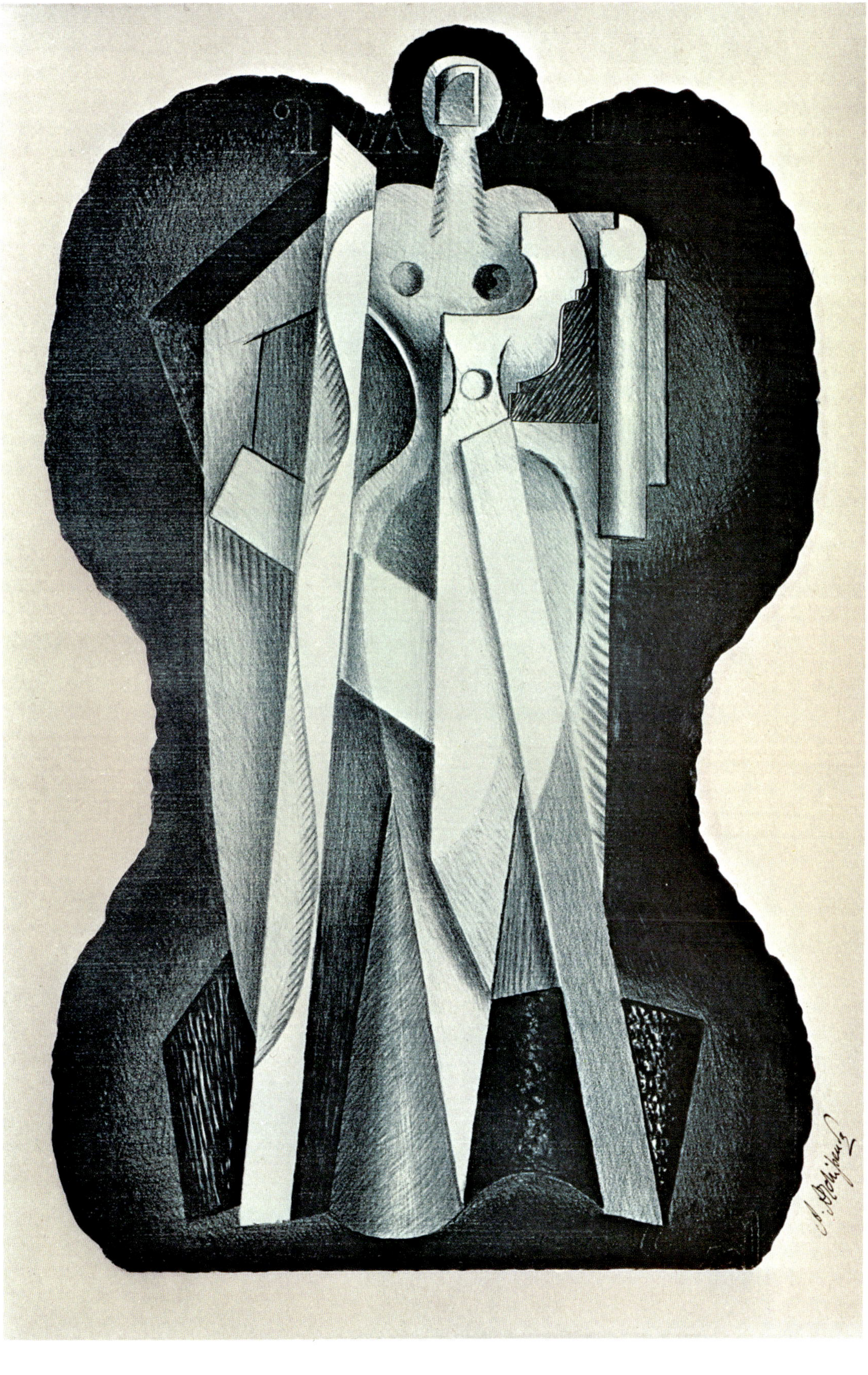

Images Without Objects It was inevitable that Cézanne's principle of geometric reduction would lead to abstract art, where the identifiable object or subject—be it figure, landscape or still life—would no longer compose the picture. Among those few artists who ventured that far during the inception of abstract art, even fewer left major statements in graphic art, and all such printmakers were Russian in origin: El Lissitzky, Malevich and Kandinsky. (Piet Mondrian, for example, made no abstract graphic works, and Frank Kupka only minor images.) That Lissitzky was trained as an architect is evident in his work as a painter and graphic artist, where his geometric abstract elements are often marked by architectonic solidity and structural cohesion, skillfully aided by suggestions of perspective and modeling (plate 106).

Lissitzky's teacher at Vitebsk was Malevich, who in Moscow in 1915 had ushered in the era of pure abstraction with his legendary black square. Even more powerful, in their uncompromising simplicity and concentrated focus, than the work of his gifted student are Malevich's abstract lithographs of 1920 (plates 107 and 108). Their spare components are flat beams and arcs, appearing to hover or glide in the limitless space of the white paper. While Lissitzky fills his space with

106.
El Lissitzky (1890–1941). Russian. *Proun 2c*, c. 1920. Lithograph. 45.5 x 34.5 cm. (17⅞ x 13⅝ in.). Private collection

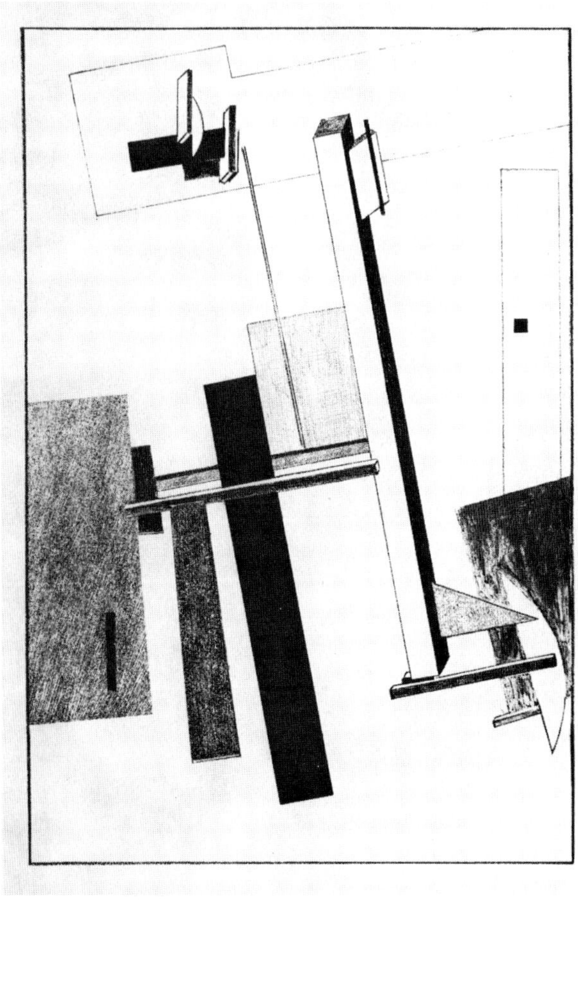

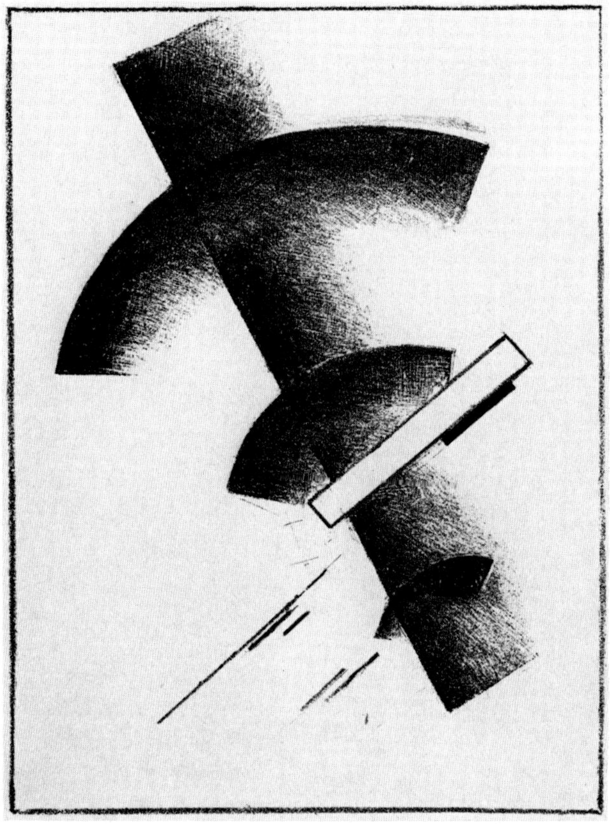

107

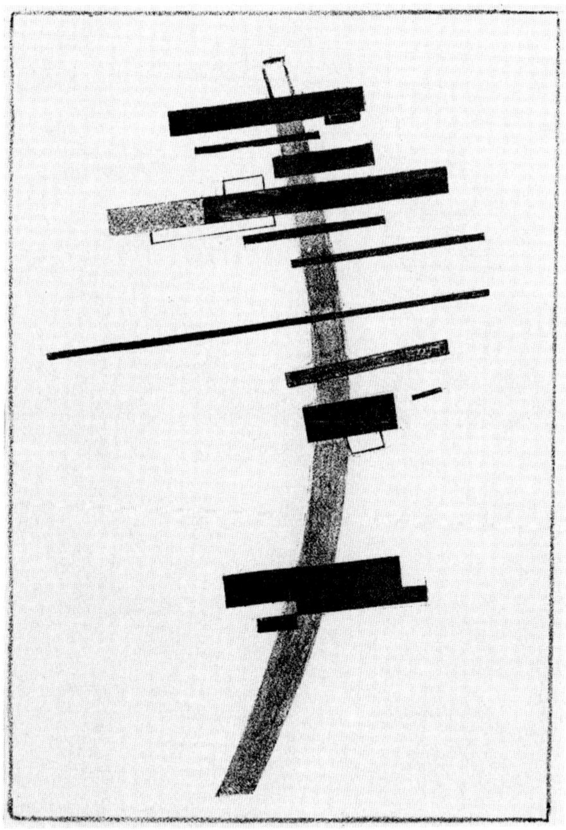

108

107.
Kazimir Malevich (1878–1935). Russian. *Suprematism. Splitting of Construction.* Lithograph in *Suprematizm. 34 risunka*, 1920. 27.6 x 20.2 cm. (10⅞ x 8 in.). Private collection

108.
Kazimir Malevich (1878–1935). Russian. *Sensation of the Motion and the Obstacle.* Lithograph in *Suprematizm. 34 risunka*, 1920. 26.8 x 18.3 cm. (10½ x 7⅛ in.). Private collection

an assortment of widely dispersed abstract elements, some of which continue beyond the picture's edges, Malevich rigorously clusters his limited components within the picture's ruled frame into a kind of monumental notation for a current, a formation that stimulates a sense of concentrated force.

Three years later, at the Bauhaus in Weimar, Kandinsky created his largest and most ambitious abstract graphic work (colorplate 29). Its elements and shapes are far greater in number and variety than those in Malevich's arrangements, and their vibrant color helps locate them at different depths for the eye. Although it is only a four-color lithograph, the grainy printing and overlapping color areas produce additional chromatic blends and luminosity in the forms. The checkerboard visible at the upper left, though it may be perceived as an abstract pattern, is nevertheless an identifiable object, and the three black squares floating off to the right seem like playful offspring set loose. The vaunted freedom from prior or conventional association, once an attribute of such "nonobjective" images, has gradually been diminishing as life catches up with art. Orbiting satellites, rocket launchers, space debris and other amazing phenomena of the contemporary world now seem to have been effectively prophesied in these visionary images created a half century earlier. Thus, their concepts are no longer as abstract as they once were.

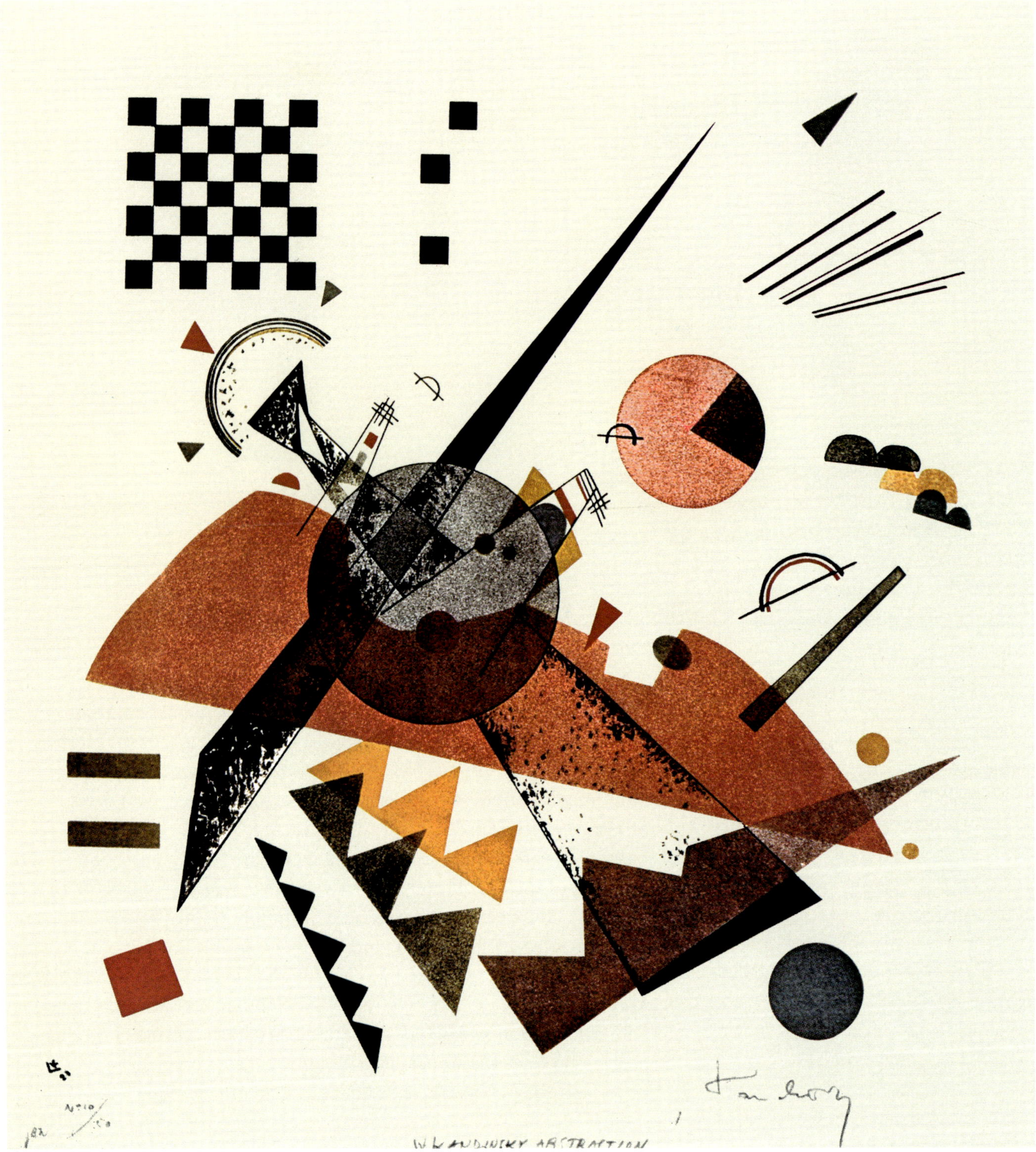
W KANDINSKY ABSTRACTION

4 Advice for Print Collectors

Since prints are usually far less expensive to acquire than paintings, print collectors may find their collections quickly mounting in size. It is easy to accumulate prints; a single gallery may have a large and varied inventory, and the range of images available for purchase can be bewildering. The process of acquisition, therefore, should be slow and cautious. The usual advice to collectors to "live only with art that you like"—the implication being that infatuation with a work will set in at first sight at the gallery (and it often does)—is not always useful. If one follows only instinctive responses and summarily rejects print after print because it does not immediately appeal, one can miss the enriching experience of learning to grow fond of a work of art through the gradual discovery of its qualities. This discovery can come about only by repeated exposure to the work.

To develop a keener sense for the print medium and all that it offers, the collector should become familiar with a wide variety of printmakers. Particular artists can be studied through a catalogue raisonné (reproductions and descriptions of all the artist's prints) or, if such a compilation cannot be located or does not exist, in a monograph on the artist and/or his epoch. Scholarly literature provides guidance for the collector as to the relative importance of a given work or period in an artist's development and the artist's role in art history. Such information enhances the collector's knowledge of art as well as arming him to make intelligent acquisitions.

Another way to become familiar with artists and their work is to study the originals in the great print collections of museums. In this way, as we have seen with respect to Dürer's *Melencolia I*, one learns to recognize an optimum impression and is thus better able to evaluate prints offered for sale. Established print dealers—and galleries are usually the most reliable sources—sometimes allow a collector to take a print on approval in order to compare it with an example of

Colorplate 29.
Wassily Kandinsky (1866–1944). Russian. *Orange*, 1923. Lithograph. 40.7 x 38.5 cm. (16 x 15⅛ in.). Museum of Modern Art, New York, Purchase Fund

the same print at a local museum. This comparison can become exciting, especially if it turns out that the impression for sale is even better than the one the museum has—a not uncommon occurrence.

Of course, the quality of the impression is not the only gauge of the value of a print. The paper should be scrutinized to see whether the original margins have been cut down or new margins have been added and whether tears have been mended or worn areas heightened by inking—to name just a few of the ways in which damaged prints can be repaired or reconstituted. Reputable dealers will disclose such "improvements," and museum specialists, if they are available, can also help in this aspect of investigation.

As noted in the first chapter, with modern prints the quality of the impression hardly varies from start to finish, for modern editions are usually limited to prevent wear of the plate, block or stone. But with prints made before the late nineteenth century such precautions were rarely taken, and worn, faded and imbalanced impressions of these prints abound. It is far better to own a single unworn (and thus faithful) impression of an antique print than to own seventy worn ones that do not reflect the original intentions of the artist. Resisting the temptation to accept less satisfactory prints and waiting patiently to acquire a fine impression can bring lasting rewards.

With the joys of collecting prints come responsibilities, the chief one being to protect them from deterioration. Prints, like all works on paper, are essentially fragile, and collectors should be alert to a number of serious threats to the life of their prints. The first is the ultraviolet rays emanating from artificial light and most especially from direct and indirect sunlight. Prints exposed to these rays over a period of time will yellow and fade. Consequently, prints must be hung in softly lighted areas or stored in solander boxes or print portfolios. For prints that are to be framed and hung, a special ultraviolet-filtering Plexiglas, ideal for covering, can be supplied by established framers.

Another enemy of prints is improper matting and mounting. It is said that more prints have been destroyed by careless or ignorant framers than by all the depredations of World War II. Special hinges are required for mounting (masking tape, transparent tape and the common variety of linen tape are dangerous), and acid-free, one hundred percent rag board must be used for mats and backings, since any contact with or even nearness to acid can be ruinous.

Still other threats to prints are improper humidity, extreme temperatures, and dust and pollution. A relative humidity of fifty to sixty-five percent is considered ideal. Unfavorable changes in temperature can be avoided by keeping prints away from heating and cooling vents. Proper framing or storage will protect against dust and pollution.

Glossary

abbreviations of Latin words are frequently encountered on antique prints. Following are some of the most common, with their meanings.

del. (*delineavit*, "he drew"): drawn by [name of artist].

exc., *excud.* (*excudit*, "he issued"): published by [name of publisher].

fec., *f.* (*fecit*, "he made"): made by [name of printmaker, usually the engraver or etcher].

imp. (*impressit*, "he printed"): printed by [name of printer].

inc., *incid.* (*incidit*, "he engraved"): engraved by [name of engraver].

inv. (*invenit*, "he designed"): designed by [name of designer].

lith. (coined word used ambiguously on lithographs, "he drew, or printed, on stone"): drawn or printed by [name of artist or printer].

pinx. (*pinxit*, "he painted"): painted by [name of painter].

sculp., *sc.* (*sculpsit*, "he engraved"): engraved by [name of engraver].

aquatint, an *intaglio* process developed in the mid-seventeenth century capable of producing tonal effects similar to those achieved in watercolor or wash drawings; almost always used in conjunction with etching, but rarely alone. Also, a print made by this process.

artist's proof, one of a certain number of *impressions* pulled for the artist's personal use at the time the impressions for the published *edition* are pulled; sometimes identified by the artist with a handwritten *A.P.*; in rare instances, numbered.

bite, the corrosive action of the acid that, in the *etching* process, eats away (virtually dissolves) portions of the metal plate. The depth of the bite is controlled by the strength of the acid solution and the length of time the plate is immersed in the acid bath.

bon à tirer ("good to print"), a French expression handwritten, usually by the artist, on the *impression* chosen to serve as the model for the printing of the entire *edition*.

burin or *graver*, a sharp, pointed metal tool used for incising lines on metal; made in a variety of sizes and shapes.

burnisher, a smooth, curved tool used for polishing, rubbing, smoothing and so on; made in a variety of materials and used in both *intaglio* and *relief prints*.

burr, the rough ridge of metal thrown up along each side of an incision made in a metal plate; traps the ink when the plate is prepared for printing and imparts a velvety, furry look to the printed line, as in a *drypoint*. Also, the roughened texture a *rocker* produces in a plate in the *mezzotint* process.

chiaroscuro woodcut, the earliest type of woodcut printed in colors in Europe; developed in the early sixteenth century to imitate the toned and highlighted drawings of the time.

drypoint (Fr. *pointe sèche*; Ger. *Kaltnadel*), the *intaglio* process developed in the mid-fifteenth century of drawing directly on a metal plate (usually of copper) by means of a steel needle; prized for the velvety tone of its printed line produced when *burr* is retained. Also, a print made by this process.

edition, the number of *impressions* from one design the artist elects to have printed and distributed.

engraving (Fr. *gravure au trait*; Ger. *Kupferstich*), the earliest of the *intaglio* processes, developed in the first half of the fifteenth century; in the process, the design is incised into a copperplate with a *burin* (*graver*). Also, a print made by this process.

etch, a solution of nitric acid and gum arabic used to "fix" the image drawn on a lithographic stone or plate and to make the stone or plate more receptive to water.

etching (Fr. *eau forte*; Ger. *Radierung*), an *intaglio* process developed in the early sixteenth century in which a design is inscribed onto a metal plate (usually copper) by means of acid instead of a cutting tool. Also, a print made by this process.

graver, see *burin*.

ground, acid-resistant material used to coat a plate before the image is drawn into it with an etching needle.

impression, any print; also, any *work proof*.

intaglio prints, any prints, such as *aquatints*, *drypoints*, *engravings*, *etchings* and *mezzotints*, that are printed from incised (recessed) lines and textures that have been cut, scratched or etched into the surface of a plate to hold ink for printing.

lithography (Fr. *lithographie*; Ger. *Steindruck*), a planographic process developed at the end of the eighteenth century, the key principle of which is the antipathy of grease and water. The image is drawn on a stone or a plate with a greasy ink (*tusche*) or a lithographic crayon; the entire surface is then treated with *etch* and dampened so that the greasy printer's ink will adhere only to the greasy image, not to the wet areas. The printing surface is planographic (flat), as opposed to the raised surface of *relief* and the incised surface of *intaglio*.

lithotint, a form of lithograph developed in the nineteenth century in which soft, liquidlike tones predominate.

mezzotint (Fr. *manière noire*; Ger. *Schabkunst*), an *intaglio* process developed in the mid-seventeenth century and primarily used to reproduce paintings; characterized in the printing by a lush, velvety tone and soft, almost fuzzy highlights. Also, a print made by this process.

monotype, a printmaking process, developed in the first half of the seventeenth century, often described as a halfway stage between painting and printmaking. The image is painted on a metal plate or a sheet of glass and quickly printed before the pigment dries. Since the printing lifts off much of the pigment, normally only one print can be made, as the name indicates.

ornament prints, detailed etchings or engravings of designs for ornamentation used as design guides in various crafts and professions, epecially during the eighteenth century.

photogravure, an intaglio process developed in the late nineteenth century involving the transfer of a photographic image to a copperplate, which is then etched in the aquatint manner. Also, a print made by this process.

planographic process, see *lithography*.

plate mark, indentations in the paper of *intaglio prints* made by the edges (usually beveled) of the metal plate during printing.

relief prints, any prints, such as *woodcuts* and *wood engravings*, that are printed from the inked raised portions of a woodblock or some other form of relief block. These portions stand out in relief after the areas not to be inked and printed have been cut away.

retroussage, the wiping of surplus ink off the plate in the *intaglio* process. Usually, however, the term is applied when some of the surplus is purposely left on the plate to achieve subtle tonal effects.

rocker, a mezzotint tool with many fine teeth on a curved blade.

roulette, a small spiked wheel set in a handle; used to roughen a metal plate.

state, a stage in the production of a print; also, the impression or impressions pulled at that stage—for example, first-state impressions are those pulled earliest from the plate or stone; second-state, those pulled after the first changes have been made in the image; and so on. (See also *work proof*.) Published impressions represent the final state (finished image). See plates 71 and 72.

stone mark, indentations in the paper of lithographs made by the irregular edges of the stone during printing when the paper on the press is larger than the stone.

tusche, a grease-based liquid compound used for drawing and painting on a lithographic stone or plate.

white-line engraving, see *wood engraving*.

woodcut (Fr. *gravure sur bois*; Ger. *Holzschnitt*), a relief print made by cutting into the long grain of a woodblock with gouges and a knife and printing from the raised areas thus created. The oldest of all the printmaking processes, woodcutting was practiced in China by the ninth century and in Europe by the early fifteenth. See also *relief prints*.

wood engraving (Fr. *gravure sur bois debout*; Ger. *Holzstich*), a relief process, also called *white-line engraving*, developed in the eighteenth century. In this process, a print is made by cutting into the end grain of a woodblock with engraving tools (*burins* and needles) and printing from the remaining raised surface. See also *relief prints*.

work proof, an impression pulled from a plate or stone for checking purposes at any stage during the creation of a print.

Reading and Reference

General

Adhémar, Jean. *Graphic Art of the 18th Century.* New York: McGraw-Hill Book Co., 1964.

———. *Twentieth-Century Graphics.* New York: Praeger Publishers, 1971.

Buchheim, Lothar-Günther. *The Graphic Art of German Expressionism.* New York: Universe Books, 1960.

Buchsbaum, Ann. *A Practical Guide to Print Collecting.* New York: Van Nostrand Reinhold Co., 1975.

Castleman, Riva. *Modern Art in Prints.* New York: Museum of Modern Art, 1973.

———. *Prints of the Twentieth Century: A History.* New York: Museum of Modern Art, 1976.

Eichenberg, Fritz. *The Art of the Print: Masterpieces, History, Techniques.* New York: Harry N. Abrams, 1976.

Getlein, Frank and Dorothy. *The Bite of the Print: Satire and Irony in Woodcuts, Engravings, Etchings, Lithographs and Serigraphs.* New York: Clarkson N. Potter, 1963.

Hayter, Stanley William. *About Prints.* London: Oxford University Press, 1962.

Hollstein, F. W. H., et al. *Dutch and Flemish Etchings, Engravings and Woodcuts ca. 1450–1700.* I–XVIII to date. Amsterdam: A. L. Van Gendt, 1949 ff.

———. *German Engravings, Etchings and Woodcuts ca. 1400–1700.* I–X, XVI and XVII to date. Amsterdam: A. L. Van Gendt, 1954 ff.

Ivins, William M., Jr. *How Prints Look: Photographs with a Commentary.* 1943. Reprint. Boston: Beacon Press, 1968.

———. *Notes on Prints.* 1930. Reprint. New York: Da Capo Press, 1967.

———. *Prints and Visual Communication.* 1953. Reprint. New York: Da Capo Press, 1969.

Karshan, Donald. "American Printmaking, 1670–1968." *Art in America,* July–August 1968, pp. 22–55.

———, and Richard V. West. *Language of the Print.* New York: Chanticleer Press, 1968.

Mayor, A. Hyatt. *Prints & People: A Social History of Printed Pictures.* New York: Metropolitan Museum of Art, 1971.

Roger-Marx, Claude. *Graphic Art of the 19th Century.* New York: McGraw-Hill Book Co., 1962.

Rosenwald, Lessing J. *Recollections of a Collector.* Jenkintown, Penna.: Alverthorpe Gallery, 1976.

Sachs, Paul J. *Modern Prints and Drawings: A Guide to Better Understanding of Modern Draughtsmanship.* New York: Alfred A. Knopf, 1954.

Shadwell, Wendy. *American Printmaking: The First 150 Years.* Preface by Donald Karshan. Washington, D.C.: Smithsonian Institution Press, 1972.

Stubbe, Wolf. *Graphic Arts in the Twentieth Century.* New York: Frederick A. Praeger, 1963.

Zigrosser, Carl. *The Book of Fine Prints: An Anthology of Printed Pictures and Introduction to the Study of Graphic Art in the West and the East.* 2d rev. ed. New York: Crown Publishers, 1974.

———. *The Expressionists: A Survey of Their Graphic Art.* New York: George Braziller, 1957.

———, and Christa M. Gaehde. *A Guide to the Collecting and Care of Original Prints.* New York: Crown Publishers, 1965.

Techniques

Brunner, Felix. *A Handbook of Graphic Reproductive Processes.* 3d ed. New York: Hastings House, 1968.

Peterdi, Gabor. *Printmaking: Methods Old and New.* Rev. ed. New York: Macmillan Co., 1971.

Russ, Stephen. *A Complete Guide to Printmaking.* New York: Viking Press, 1975.

Particular Kinds of Prints

Barnicoat, John. *A Concise History of Posters 1870–1970.* New York: Harry N. Abrams, 1972.

Field, Richard S. *Fifteenth-Century Woodcuts and Metalcuts from the National Gallery of Art.* Washington, D.C.: National Gallery of Art, 1965.

Hayter, Stanley William. *New Ways of Gravure.* Rev. ed. London: Oxford University Press, 1966.

Hillier, Bevis. *100 Years of Posters.* New York: Harper & Row, 1972.

———. *Posters.* New York: Stein and Day, 1969.

Hind, Arthur M. *Early Italian Engraving: A Critical Catalogue with Complete Reproduction of All the Prints Described.* 7 vols. 1938–48. Reprint. Nandeln, Liechtenstein: Kraus Reprint Co., 1970.

———. *A History of Engraving and Etching from the Fifteenth Century to the Year 1914.* 1923. Reprint. New York: Dover Publications, 1963.

———. *An Introduction to a History of Woodcut, with a Detailed Survey of Work Done in the Fifteenth Century.* 2 vols. 1935. Reprint. New York: Dover Publications, 1963.

Levenson, Jay A.; Konrad Oberhuber; and Jacquelyn L. Sheehan. *Early Italian Engravings from the National Gallery of Art.* Washington, D.C.: National Gallery of Art, 1973.

Margolin, Victor. *American Poster Renaissance.* New York: Watson-Guptill Publications, 1975.

Shestack, Alan. *Fifteenth-Century Engravings of Northern Europe from the National Gallery of Art.* Washington, D.C:. National Gallery of Art, 1967.

Strauss, Walter L. *Chiaroscuro: The Clair-Obscur Woodcuts by the German and Netherlandish Masters of the XVIth and XVIIth Centuries—A Complete Catalogue with Commentary.* Greenwich, Conn.: New York Graphic Society, 1973.

———, ed. *The German Single-Leaf Woodcut 1550–1600.* 3 vols. New York: Abaris Books, 1975.

Some Public Collections of Prints

UNITED STATES

Baltimore:	The Baltimore Museum of Art
Boston:	Museum of Fine Arts
Cambridge, Mass.:	Fogg Art Museum, Harvard University
Chicago:	The Art Institute of Chicago
Cincinnati:	Cincinnati Art Museum
Cleveland:	Cleveland Museum of Art
Detroit:	The Detroit Institute of Arts
Los Angeles:	Grunwald Center for the Graphic Arts, University of California
	Los Angeles County Museum of Art
New Haven, Conn.:	Yale University Art Gallery
New York City:	Cooper-Hewitt Museum, the Smithsonian Institution's National Museum of Design
	The Metropolitan Museum of Art
	The Museum of Modern Art
	The New York Public Library
Philadelphia:	Philadelphia Museum of Art
St. Louis:	The St. Louis Art Museum
San Francisco:	The Fine Arts Museums of San Francisco California Palace of the Legion of Honor
Washington, D.C.:	Smithsonian Institution
	National Collection of Fine Arts
	National Gallery of Art
	National Museum of History and Technology

OTHER

Amsterdam:	Rijksmuseum, Rijksprentenkabinet
	Staatliche Museen, Kupferstichkabinett
Bologna:	Pinacoteca Nazionale
Cologne:	Wallraf-Richartz-Museum
Dresden:	Staatliche Kunstsammlungen, Kupferstichkabinett
Florence:	Gabinetto Disegni e Stampe degli Uffizi
Frankfurt:	Städelsches Kunstinstitut und Stadtische Galerie
London:	British Museum
	Victoria and Albert Museum
Munich:	Staatliche Graphische Sammlung

Nuremberg: Germanisches Nationalmuseum
Ottawa: National Gallery of Canada
Oxford: Ashmolean Museum
Paris: Bibliothèque Nationale
Musée du Louvre
Collection de Gravures et Dessins E. de Rothschild
Rome: Gabinetto Nazionale delle Stampe
Rotterdam: Museum Boymans-van Beuningen
Stuttgart: Staatsgalerie Stuttgart, Graphische Sammlung
Toronto: Art Gallery of Ontario
Vienna: Graphische Sammlung Albertina

Index

Numbers in *italics* indicate pages on which black-and-white illustrations appear.
Numbers in **boldface** indicate pages on which colorplates appear.

Acknowledgments

Cooper-Hewitt staff members have been responsible for the following contributions to the series: concept, Lisa Taylor; administration, Christian Rohlfing, David McFadden and Kurt Struver; coordination, Peter Scherer. In addition, valuable help has been provided by S. Dillon Ripley, Joseph Bonsignore, Susan Hamilton and Robert W. Mason of the Smithsonian Institution, as well as by the late Warren Lynch, Gloria Norris and Edward E. Fitzgerald of Book-of-the-Month Club, Inc.

The author wishes to thank the following for their kind assistance: Riva Castleman, Elaine Dee, Otto Fried, Brenda Gilchrist, Joan Hoffman, John Kremitske, Lisa Little, Philip Nelson, Joyce O'Connor, Elizabeth Roth and Lisa Taylor.

Credits

The Brooklyn Museum: color 9, 14, 18. Cooper-Hewitt Museum: 13, 14, 36, 48, 49, 50–55, 65, 76 and color 13 (Scott Hyde); 34, 37, 38, 43, 58, 64, 70, 78, 83, 96 (George D. Cowdery). The Metropolitan Museum of Art, New York: 17, 46, 56; color *frontispiece*, 3, 5, 8, 10. The Museum of Modern Art, New York: 18, 39, 62, 63, 67, 69, 71–74, 80, 88–90, 95, 97, 98, 101–4; color 1, 4, 6, 11, 15, 17, 22, 25, 27, 28 (Kate Keller); color 21, 26, 29 (Malcolm Varon). Philadelphia Museum of Art: 12. Private collections, courtesy of the owners: 1–11, 15, 16, 19–33, 35, 40–42, 44, 45, 47, 57, 59–61, 66, 68, 75, 77, 79, 81, 82, 84–87, 91–94, 99, 100, 105–8; color 2, 7, 12, 16, 19, 20, 23, 24.

DESIGN ASSISTANT: Dolly Carr

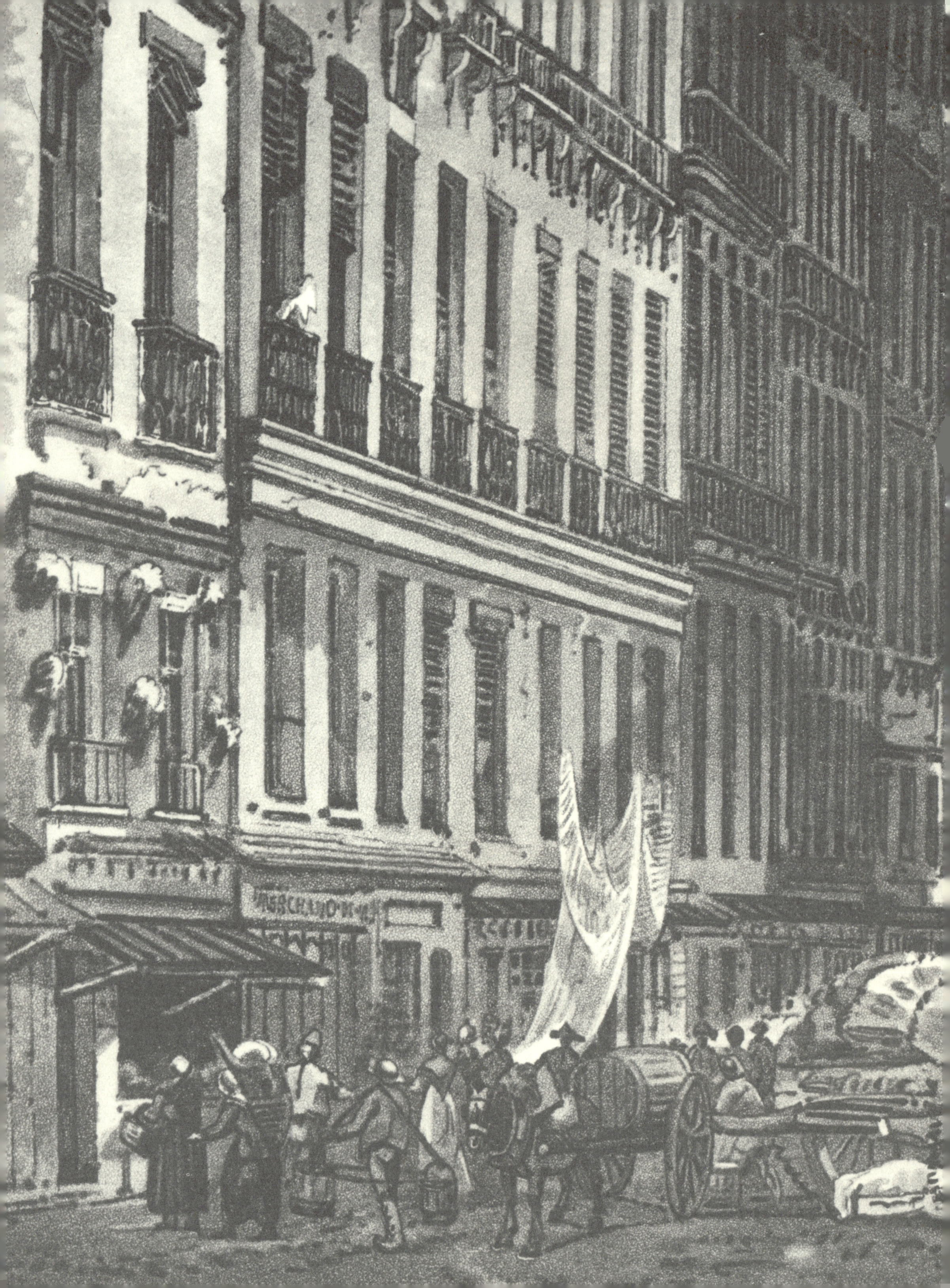